Building the Bridge

Building the Bridge

10 Big Ideas to Transform America

WILL MARSHALL, EDITOR

CHUCK ALSTON AND TOM MIRGA, ASSOCIATE EDITORS

FOREWORD BY VICE PRESIDENT AL GORE

ROWMAN & LITTLEFIELD PUBLISHERS, INC.
Lanham • New York • Boulder • Oxford

ROWMAN & LITTLEFIELD PUBLISHERS, INC.

Published in the United States of America
by Rowman & Littlefield Publishers, Inc.
4720 Boston Way, Lanham, Maryland 20706

12 Hid's Copse Road
Cummor Hill, Oxford OX2 9JJ, England

British Library Cataloguing in Publication Information Available

Library of Congress Cataloging-in-Publication Data

Building the bridge : 10 big ideas to transform America / William
   Marshall, editor ; Chuck Alston and Tom Mirga, associate editors.
     p. cm.
   Includes index.
   ISBN 0-8476-8455-5 (pbk.)
   1. United States—Politics and government—1993–   2. United
States—Social policy—1993–   3. United States—Economic
policy—1993–   I. Marshall, Will. II. Alston, Chuck. III. Mirga,
Tom.
JK271.B725   1997
306'.0973—dc21   96-51532
                                                    CIP

ISBN 0-8476-8455-5 (pbk. : alk. paper)

Printed in the United States of America

♾ ™ The paper used in this publication meets the minimum requirements of
American National Standard for Information Sciences—Permanence of Paper for
Printed Library Materials, ANSI Z39.48-1984.

Contents

Foreword

Vice President Al Gore

Four years ago when President Clinton and I were newly elected, the Progressive Policy Institute published a collection of essays called *Mandate for Change*. As we began the task of governing, many of the ideas in that book became the policy of the Clinton Administration and eventually the law of the land. Welfare reform and reinventing government were two of the best known Clinton initiatives whose general outlines were present in that first volume. Of course not everything in that volume became Administration policy but even those ideas that we rejected helped to stimulate our thinking and clarify our options.

Now, the American people have given us the great privilege to begin a second term in office, and I welcome the arrival of yet another PPI policy book. *Building the Bridge: 10 Big Ideas to Transform America* is a provocative set of essays dealing with the great challenges of our time; entitlement reform, education reform, creating a smaller, smarter government, new strategies for dealing with crime and with America's families, the environment, economic growth and our place in the world. Some of the ideas in this book are so much in line with the policies of the first term that it will not be surprising to see them adopted in a second term. Others are sharply at odds with our approach and with my own views. But taken as a whole, this book can serve as a useful starting point for what will certainly be long and difficult discussions on complicated issues.

Nevertheless, the eventual disposition of each recommendation is not nearly as important as the effort, present in every essay in the book, to break out of the old debates in order to find original solutions to problems. In this respect, the book has a remarkable intellectual consistency and the scholars of the

Progressive Policy Institute should be congratulated for making the effort to move the political debate beyond ideology to a discussion of real solutions to real problems.

President Clinton and I believe that good governance consists of just such efforts. Wherever possible we have sought to break out of the old debates and forge new solutions and new coalitions to old problems. As we move into a second term we welcome everyone who will take the time and effort to join with us as we build that bridge to the twenty-first century and I congratulate the Progressive Policy Institute on this engaging collection of ideas.

Acknowledgments

This book was a collaborative effort. I am grateful to the contributing authors, whose analyses and ideas are pioneering a new progressive politics. I also want to offer special thanks to my associate editors, Chuck Alston, who helped to oversee the project from start to finish, and Tom Mirga, whose extraordinary editorial skill and stamina helped us make our case more clearly and concisely.

DLC political director Ed Kilgore, Jeremy Rosner of the Carnegie Endowment for International Peace, and National Performance Review deputy director John Kamensky also made major intellectual and editing contributions.

I wish to further thank my co-authors on the New Progressive Declaration, Bill Galston, Doug Ross, and Al From, a true visionary with whom I've enjoyed a creative collaboration for more than a decade.

At PPI and DLC, Steven Nider, Debbie Boylan, Stephanie Soler, Doron Weiss, Eliza Culbertson, David Datelle, Navin Givishankar, and Jonathan Kaplan contributed research, fact-checking, and other invaluable assistance; my thanks also to hard-working interns Katherine Hendler, Allison Denny, Tamara Hubinsky, and Jennifer Merolla.

I want especially to acknowledge the extraordinary efforts of three people: Chris Soares and Abbe Milstein, who prepared graphics, researched chapters, and checked facts and endnotes with great care and diligence; and Anne Saunders, who coordinated virtually every facet of this project.

I am indebted as well to Senator Joseph I. Lieberman, who as chairman of the Democratic Leadership Council has led our cause with intelligence, conviction, and wit; and to the PPI Trustees, for their moral, intellectual, and financial support of our work. Finally, let me thank Ronald Goldfarb, our agent, and Jonathan Sisk and Rowman & Littlefield for their faith in this project.

Chapter 1

From Big Government to Big Ideas

Al From and Will Marshall

Conventional wisdom has it that by reelecting a Democratic president and a Republican Congress, the voters offered no mandate in 1996. The conventional wisdom couldn't be more wrong.

In fact, the voters reaffirmed the mandate for fundamental change in government that has become a dominant theme of American politics over the past sixteen years. They declined to return Congress to Democratic control, chastened a Republican majority still smarting over its failed "revolution," and strongly endorsed a "New Democrat" president who on key defining issues has distanced himself from liberal orthodoxy.

While Washington pundits were quick to interpret the 1996 results as a vote for the status quo, the electorate is sending a different message. In 1984 and 1988 (and again in 1994, when Democrats seemed to be backsliding), voters repudiated the old liberal faith in big government. In 1992, however, they embraced Bill Clinton's vision of a leaner, more disciplined, and yet active government. And the public's strong adverse reaction to the radical right's attempts in 1995–1996 to eviscerate federal programs set the stage for Clinton's thirty-one-state sweep last year.

The big losers in 1996 were the extreme partisans of the left and right, whose ideological holy war has made it virtually impossible for our political system to respond to the new challenges that confront America on the eve of the twenty-first century.

Yet 1996 was no mandate for moderation. The answers to our problems won't be found in the mushy middle of the tired, left-right debate. We now have an opportunity to create a new vision for governing that springs from the "vital center" of American politics—a fresh agenda of big ideas that adapts our public institutions to the new demands of the Information Age.

1

Building the Bridge: 10 Big Ideas to Transform America outlines a governing philosophy and agenda for a new progressive era in U.S. politics. It seeks to answer the central political question of our time: What comes after the era of big government?

Just as the Progressive Policy Institute's (PPI) *Mandate for Change* was the source of many New Democrat reforms that President Clinton and Vice President Gore pushed in their first term, we offer these ten break-the-mold ideas as the second wave of progressive innovations for the next four years.

Clinton's impressive victory—only the third time this century that a Democrat has twice won the White House—broke the GOP's so-called "lock" on presidential elections. It also vindicated Clinton's efforts to redefine the party along New Democrat lines. Since 1990, when he took over as chairman of the Democratic Leadership Council (DLC), Clinton has labored to realign his party with the economic interests and moral sentiments of what he termed "the forgotten middle class." His innovations have moved Democrats beyond liberal dogma and defense of the big government status quo.

Clinton's 1996 triumph holds important lessons for congressional Democrats and liberal activists:

- *Americans want a new approach to governing.* When it comes to the role of government, the public rejects both liberals' penchant for big government solutions and the radical right's drive for an emasculated government that leaves people to fend for themselves. A post-election survey by Mark Penn (see next chapter) showed that voters prefer the "third way" that they associate with Clinton and the New Democrats: a decentralized, nonbureaucratic government that empowers people to solve their own problems. But while the public thinks Clinton is committed to a new vision of governing, they aren't so sure about Democrats generally, which is a major reason why Democrats failed to regain Congress.

- *The old politics of class warfare doesn't work.* President Clinton won not by demonizing U.S. businesses or castigating the successful, but by offering a growth-oriented economic message that appealed to both low-income and middle class families. The President reassured fiscally conservative suburbanites by emphasizing his commitment to deficit reduction, which he linked to the strong economic expansion that has produced a record number of jobs as well as low inflation and interest rates.

- *Values matter.* Clinton also confounded left-right orthodoxy by competing and winning on the previously inhospitable terrain of values. As Penn notes on the following pages, Clinton redefined the pro-family agenda around such issues as family leave, expanded college aid, school uniforms, curfews, and the television "V-chip." Derided by Washington pundits as small-bore ideas, these cross-cutting initiatives resonated powerfully with Americans concerned about strains on the family and the breakdown of social order.

 • *Nothing succeeds like success.* Ultimately, Clinton won not because he cleverly repositioned himself as a "centrist," but because his New Democrat innovations worked. His insistence on fiscal restraint and trade expansion restored economic confidence and contributed to the surge in jobs. His "reinventing government" initiative produced a smaller, more responsive federal government. His social policies made work pay and helped reduce the welfare rolls. His crime prevention proposals put more cops on the beat even as serious crime rates fell across the nation.

Clinton's Historic Mission

President Clinton presides over a society in the throes of a rapid technological and economic transformation. Global markets, information technology, and new communications networks have increased the velocity of change. U.S. businesses have responded by reducing hierarchies, decentralizing many decisions, and downsizing. But as the rest of society hurtles into the Information Age, our highly centralized and bureaucratic government remains rooted in the Industrial Era.

At the beginning of this century, progressive leaders like Theodore Roosevelt and Woodrow Wilson worked to adapt America's nineteenth century political order to the new requirements of a rapidly industrializing society. Likewise, Bill Clinton's historic mission today is to renew our democracy by modernizing outdated political and governing arrangements.

From its stress on market-led growth and open trade to its attempts to redesign government and anchor social policy in the mainstream values of work, family, and mutual responsibility, the Clinton administration has made the first, tentative steps in the right direction. It has established important beachheads in the struggle to bring about structural changes in government and the nation's policy agenda. These include:

 • Cutting the federal deficit and growth in spending by one-half or more on the way to a promised balanced budget.

 • Injecting choice and competition in public education through charter schools.

- Helping communities defend themselves through community policing and more police on the streets.

- Replacing welfare dependency with work.

- Stimulating community initiative and economic development in the inner cities.

- Reinventing government, including a sharp reduction in the federal workforce.

- Linking increased college aid to national service.

- Expanding trade and assisting emerging democracies.

The task now is to steadily enlarge these beachheads—to move these policy innovations from the margins of a big, bureaucratic government to the center of a leaner, reinvented government that equips people and communities to tackle their own problems. This means, for example, moving from deficit reduction to a more fundamental reordering of the nation's spending priorities. This shift entails eliminating corporate welfare, structural reform in Medicare and Social Security, and new public investments in health care, education and training, and basic research. It also entails moving from welfare reform to a more comprehensive overhaul of U.S. social policy, replacing public subsidies that foster dependency with a new empowerment agenda based on work, saving, entrepreneurship, and home ownership.

The end of big government does not mean the end of big ideas. At this pivotal moment, what America needs is not a politics of modest ambitions, crimped vision, and incrementalism, but a contemporary version of the "bold, persistent experimentation" that was Franklin D. Roosevelt's greatest legacy.

This book offers ten big ideas for building President Clinton's oft-invoked "bridge to the twenty-first century." Taken together, these initatives would transform our understanding of how citizens, their communities, and their public institutions can work together to overcome our common problems.

We recognize, of course, that no president—least of all one facing a Congress controlled by the opposition party—could achieve all this in one term. But we believe that President Clinton can and must move his modernization project to the next stage by articulating a new vision of progressive governance and setting in motion the political and substantive dynamics that can lead eventually to its realization. *Building the Bridge* thus combines big ideas with pragmatic, attainable steps that a Democratic president and a Republican Congress can and must take together to carry out the mandate for change that both have been granted by voters.

Next Steps

Governing in the vital center does not mean split-the-difference moderation and compromise. It means grappling with the challenges that are central to renewing the promise of American life in the coming century. And it requires that the two parties not only compete over a new substantive agenda, but that they also adopt a style that makes bipartisan problem-solving possible.

Here are four steps our political leaders should take to begin rebuilding the vital center:

• First, they should move swiftly to restore the public's confidence in the basic integrity of our political system.

The post-Watergate system for financing campaigns collapsed in 1996. So-called "soft money," indirect spending on campaigns not limited by federal law, poured in from corporations and unions—and even from foreign countries. Interest groups spent millions trying to annihilate political enemies or protect friends from other political hit squads. The airwaves were clogged with attack ads, often false and always shrill. None of this engaged the public's interest as Americans stayed home in droves: Only 49 percent voted, a seventy-two-year low.

In addition to fueling an arms race in campaign advertising, special interest money is often aimed at blocking systemic government reform. To enhance prospects of real substantive change, and to restore trust in the political process, the President and Congress must take swift action on campaign finance reform. It is time to consider radical options, such as adopting a "can't vote, can't give rule" to bar contributions from outside a candidates' district or state, and a constitutional amendment ending protection for self-financed campaigns and so-called "independent" advertising campaigns by interest groups often closely linked to candidates.

• Second, the President should work with congressional leaders in both parties to construct "center-out" coalitions to pass major legislation.

For too long, militant liberals and conservatives have indulged in a style of political combat based on sharpening partisan differences in order to energize and dun contributions from key constituencies and interest groups. The politics of polarization fails the most basic test of public accountability: It doesn't get the public's business done and it makes meaningful change all but impossible.

Our leaders must work to restore the tradition of bipartisan collaboration that undergirded most of our major legislative accomplishments, from Social Security to civil rights to the landmark environmental bills. They should start with two issues that already have attracted bipartisan support: a systematic assault on "corporate welfare" and the proposed G.I. Bill for American workers that languished in the last Congress.

In addition to tapping prominent Republicans for key posts in his administration, the President should work closely with centrists on both sides of the aisle and be prepared to appeal directly to the American people for support when necessary. In short, Clinton must reassert the tradition of presidential leadership in a party whose power base over the last generation has been Congress.

• Third, President Clinton should seek to institutionalize New Democrat innovations within his own party.

In the first Clinton administration, too many key posts went to liberal activists who often didn't understand and sometimes were even hostile to many of the New Democrat ideas that helped elect Clinton in 1992. This time around, the administration should make innovation and reform, rather than the single-minded quest for diversity, the touchstone of its staffing decisions.

The administration should also look beyond Washington to the growing ranks of civic entrepreneurs who are busy across America inventing new responses to our common problems. Leaders in the charter school movement, for example, should be brought into the Education Department. Likewise, people with real economic development experience and leaders of community-based groups that build housing and spur retail development in the cities should join the Department of Housing and Urban Development. Because these innovators will fail without the explicit and sustained political backing of the White House, it is also crucial that New Democrats on the White House staff, often marginalized in the first term, be placed in key strategic and substantive posts.

• Finally, President Clinton should use his tremendous prestige as the Democrat who broke the Republican lock on the presidency to leverage major changes within the institutional Democratic Party. The Democratic National Committee needs new leaders who can reassert the primacy of the party's basic principles and collective needs over the demands of powerful constituency and interest groups that now exercise disproportionate control over the party machinery. And because the same groups are often the most resistant to changes in government, it is essential that the President challenge them to update their own thinking as many emerging Democratic leaders have done.

A Window of Opportunity

If these steps are taken, then the public's search for a new political configuration that produces solutions to real problems may finally bear fruit.

Today's sterile left-right debate can be replaced with a new debate that is centered on the challenges of the Information Age.

Voters can once again participate in elections that offer the opportunity to choose between positive alternative agendas for change instead of an obligation to curb the power of narrow interests and factions.

The progressive tradition in American politics can find new life serving its old function of reforming and revitalizing public institutions.

And most of all, the country can become well equipped to make the next century another American Century.

The 1996 elections created a window of opportunity to initiate these critical changes, and endorsed the leadership of a President who is acutely aware of his responsibility for America's future.

Building the Bridge is our contribution to the hard but exciting work just ahead.

Chapter 2

Seizing the Center: Clinton's Keys to Victory

Mark Penn

President Clinton's decisive victory in last year's presidential race was grounded in a strategy that began taking shape a year and a half before Election Day. By adopting strong, defensible, centrist positions on the federal budget, welfare, crime, immigration, and taxes, the President won more support in 1996 than in 1992 among critical voting blocs—women, suburbanites, Catholics, independents, the middle class, and married people. Although Republicans carried the small percentage of voters who said these were their most important issues, the GOP did not win the broad electorate's approval on them. If congressional Democrats had followed Clinton's lead on most of these issues, the party would have retaken the House.

Voters sent a clear message last November: They want the President and the Republican Congress to forge centrist solutions to our most vital problems—finishing the job of welfare reform, reforming entitlements, and protecting our children from gangs and drugs, to name a few. Furthermore, they want to see action within the context of smaller but more efficient government.

These conclusions are drawn both from my observations as President Clinton's poll-taker, and from a nationally representative, post-election telephone survey of 1,200 voters I was asked to conduct for this book. Taken on November 9–11, 1996, the poll has a sampling error of plus/minus 3 percent.

Outflanking the GOP on Issue After Issue

In the campaign just ended, the President outmaneuvered the Republicans on each of the following crucial issues:

9

Balancing the budget

Like the GOP, President Clinton came out for a balanced budget. But unlike them, he insisted on a budget that would protect fundamental American values as embodied by Medicare, Medicaid, education, and the environment. This step deprived the Republicans of the mantle of fiscal conservatism. By showing that he, too, cared about the deficit, the President distinguished himself from the more liberal congressional Democrats. This position proved pivotal in winning greater support among senior citizens and the middle class. Most voters support the objectives of entitlement programs and do not want to see them gutted. However, they recognize that those programs' costs must be contained, and they believe the President's balanced budget approach is the right one.

Welfare

This issue posed perhaps the greatest threat to the President's reelection chances. Although the public sympathizes with people caught in the cycle of welfare dependency, they believe the system is rife with abuse. By signing the welfare reform bill, Clinton closed off the Republicans' potentially most profitable means of exploiting votes. His action sealed his reelection by serving as proof of his fiscal conservatism and of his status as a "different kind of Democrat."

Crime

President Clinton neutralized this traditional Republican advantage early in his first term. The decline in violent crime rates during his first four years in office, combined with the crime bill he signed—with its expanded death penalty, "three strikes and you're out" provision, 100,000 new cops, handgun restrictions, and the ban on assault rifles—created a wall the GOP could not breach. Republican attempts to portray the bill as a weak, liberal solution to crime and to even repeal some of its provisions backfired. Conservative gun owners agreed with the GOP, but the majority of people concerned about crime—including a high proportion of women—agreed with the President.

Immigration

Republicans tried to exploit this issue against the President in California and Florida, among other states. They were frustrated, however, by Clinton's strong record on immigration—he had hired more border guards, increased deportations, and insisted on strict enforcement of immigration rules and procedures. With these moves, the President moved close to even on immigration among white voters. Republicans, meanwhile, increased Clinton's share of the Hispanic vote with their anti-immigration efforts, in particular by adding provisions to last year's immigration bill (stripped before final passage) that would have allowed states to bar illegal immigrant children from public schools.

Taxes

The President neutralized Republican presidential candidate Bob Dole's 15 percent tax cut with his own targeted tax cuts for education, child rearing, home sales, and health care. Voters favored Clinton's plan over Dole's by two to one. The public, which had spent much of the prior year listening to talk about the benefits of a balanced budget, did not think Dole's plan was credible. Many Americans also questioned the wisdom of a large cut: Deficit reduction, which would have been threatened by such a cut, appeared to be fueling the country's recent economic success. Finally, President Clinton had little to gain politically by matching Dole's cut. Early in the campaign, our polling showed that 20 percent of the electorate would base its vote mainly on anticipation of getting a tax cut; 75 percent of these voters were already firmly in the Republican camp. In the end, Dole got the votes of the tax cutters. But he failed to raise tax cuts to a central campaign issue—only 6 percent of voters said it was the most important issue to them, far too small a base on which to win an election.

Clinton and the Congressional Democrats

The approval gap on these issues casts the difference between the President and congressional Democrats in sharp relief. As table 2.1 shows, the President stood 10 percentage points higher in approval than Democrats in Congress on the budget, and 9 points higher on crime and welfare. As I observed earlier, had the Democrats stood more closely with the President on these issues, they would have won the House.

Having failed to break through on any of the issues they needed to win, Republicans turned in desperation to a negative campaign based on wedge issues and character attacks. This was a formula for recovering their base, but not for winning a majority of Americans. The President countered with his belief that the public did not want division, but instead wanted the two parties to find common ground.

Table 2.1
Approval Ratings on Key Issues

Issue	President Clinton		Congressional Democrats		Margin for Clinton[†]
	Approve	Disapprove	Approve	Disapprove	
Balancing Budget	69	28	59	28	10
Welfare	64	31	56	32	9
Crime	71	24	64	26	9
Education	72	35	66	24	-5
Taxes	56	39	50	33	0
Medicare	65	30	62	27	0

[†]The difference between the approval and disapproval ratings for President Clinton minus the difference between the approval and disapproval ratings for congressional Democrats.

Source: Poll by Penn & Schoen Associates, Inc., taken 9–11 November 1996.

Reaching Out To Protect Our Children

The President's family values initiative was really about helping parents assert control over their children amid competing commercial and peer influences. He appropriated this traditional Republican issue and remade it on his own terms, as evidenced in a series of initiatives beginning with education and extending to tobacco, family and medical leave, violent TV, children's health, curfews, school uniforms, keeping teenage mothers in school, and drug testing of teens seeking drivers' licenses.

During the campaign, Republicans took the position that where conflict existed between government power and family life, government should stay out. What they failed to understand was that while parents want government out of their own private lives, they welcome government help in their fight against outside influences corrupting their children. Toward the end of the campaign, Dole reiterated his opposition to the family and medical leave measure Clinton signed early in his first term—a law supported by a staggering 88 percent of the electorate. More than two-thirds of voters supported the President on every one of his new family values issues. The results of his initiative were dramatic: Clinton closed a 15–point gap during the course of the campaign among married voters and married voters with children. While evangelical Protestants still voted heavily against the President, Catholics—

particularly Catholic women—were attracted to the values implicit in the President's program. By the end of the campaign, when voters were asked who would implement programs that would be better for children, they said Clinton over Dole by 60 percent to 30 percent—one of the widest issue gaps of the race.

An Activist Presidency

President Clinton's philosophy that government should empower and equip people to take advantage of opportunities was favored by 53 percent of voters when pitted against either the old politics of large-scale government programs (13 percent) or the Republican ideal of taking government out of our lives completely (30 percent). As an example of the Republicans having gone too far, 71 percent of voters said they opposed eliminating the U.S. Education Department—which was Dole's single most damaging admission in his first debate against Clinton.

In contrast to Dole's vision of a minimalist government, the President used his executive authority to advance his empowerment philosophy. For example, his revamping of meat inspection rules, which echoed the types of measures that the Progressives took early this century, was favored by 80 percent of voters.

With Congress in gridlock from the fall of 1995 to the spring of 1996, Clinton employed a combination of volunteerism (such as his challenge to business to help move people from welfare to work), cooperative action (such as the new television ratings system), and executive orders (such as state welfare reform waivers) to advance his priorities. Job approval of President Clinton hit 64 percent; job disapproval of Congress, meanwhile, rose to 58 percent.

Making the Most of the Economy and Bipartisanship

During the campaign, President Clinton appealed to the nation's optimism about the economy, and sought to break through the partisan gridlock on the balanced budget, welfare, and other issues as voters have long desired. In contrast, congressional Democrats typically played to voters' worst economic fears, and showed limited interest in working across the aisle. By taking this tack, these Democrats obliterated two of their potentially most important advantages.

The President's successful economic program clearly helped him capture new voters and win the election. Congressional Democrats, however, invested heavily in wooing the so-called "downscale" voters whom they believed were the key constituency in the 1994 election. Even as unemployment kept dropping to record lows in 1996, most Democrats, egged on by the labor unions, focused relentlessly on wage stagnation and the perceived lack of good jobs. They systematically deprived themselves of the greatest edge the party controlling the White House can have—a successful economy.

In his 1996 State of the Union address, the President broke with his party's economic doomsayers and declared this to be the healthiest economy in 30 years. By Election Day, 56 percent of voters were saying the economy was on the right track, and 70 percent were reporting that their personal economic situation had improved. Twenty-three percent of voters said the economy and jobs were the most important factors influencing their vote in 1996—more than double the share of voters for the next highest category, which was balancing the budget.

Taking credit for economic growth was only part of the success story. For Democrats, the key to reelection in 1996 lay in passing legislation, and not simply in blocking unpopular bills. President Clinton fought for a balanced budget deal in late 1995–early 1996 because he wanted to prove to a despairing electorate that Washington really could get things done. Though Clinton worked hard throughout the campaign to reach a deal, Dole concluded in the spring that a breakthrough would not work to his advantage. Americans, however, did see bipartisan progress in 1996 on health insurance portability, an increase in the minimum wage, welfare reform, and eventually an immigration bill. These breakthroughs helped persuade a majority of Americans to conclude that the country as a whole was back on the right track. Among those who said we were on the right track, 70 percent voted for Clinton and 58 percent voted for Democratic candidates for Congress.

Changing Voters' Perceptions

Exit polls and our post-election survey show that Clinton's strategy of adopting strong centrist positions was the key to his success. His share of support among women rose from 48 percent in 1992 to 54 percent in 1996. Among independents, his support rose from 38 percent to 43 percent in 1996. In every income category between $15,000 and $75,000, Clinton's share of support rose: in 1992, only 45 percent of voters making $15,000–30,000 voted for him, but in 1996, 53 percent did; of voters making $30,000–50,000, Clinton's share increased from 41 percent to 48 percent; and among voters making $50,000–$75,000, Clinton's support rose from 40 percent to 47 percent. Married voters with children, only 40 percent of whom had supported Clinton in 1992, voted for him at a rate of 48 percent.

These increases in support reflect voters' changing perception of Clinton. Indeed, voters expressly recognize Clinton's New Democrat credentials and note that the rest of the Democratic Party lags behind. By 57 percent to 37 percent, voters think Clinton is a different kind of Democrat from those who have run for president before him. But by 54 percent to 41 percent, voters think the Democratic Party remains pretty much the same as it was. On the role of government in general, by 50 percent to 42 percent, voters think that Clinton is a new type of Democrat who thinks government's role is to empower people to make the most of their lives; by 40 percent to 36 percent, they think that Democrats running for Congress are liberals who favor big government solutions. On the economy, by 50 percent to 39 percent, voters think Clinton is the type of Democrat who favors policies like a balanced budget to stimulate growth; by 39 percent to 37 percent, they think the party's congressional candidates are the type of Democrats who favor higher taxes and more programs.

Where Do We Go From Here?

The message of the 1996 election was clear: Voters want the President and Congress to continue forging solutions in the vital center that deal with our most significant problems in ways that are compatible with a smaller government. When we asked the 1,200 voters in our post-election survey for their top priorities, they replied in this order:

- Move 1 million more people from welfare to work.

- Reform Social Security and Medicare.

- Strengthen our efforts to fight drugs and teach our kids they are wrong.

- Pass a juvenile justice bill to fight teen gangs.

- Continue to fight race and sex discrimination.

- Balance the budget to keep interest rates low.

- Expand educational opportunities with higher school standards and tax cuts for college tuition.

- Increase resources for research on AIDS and breast cancer.

- Expand health care reform to cover the unemployed and 1 million more children.

- Continue to fund 100,000 cops on the street.

After that top ten list, the next highest priorities were training more workers for twenty-first century jobs; stepping up enforcement of immigration laws; dealing with the problems of the inner cities by empowering people in disadvantaged communities to help themselves; and encouraging business development.

Clearly, this list is neither traditionally Democratic nor Republican. To the contrary, its basic theme is that the President should stick with the "third way" he has charted during the last four years. The President's success in 1996 should encourage all Democrats to embrace the types of bold innovations outlined in the following chapters.

Chapter 3

The New Progressive Declaration: A Political Philosophy for the Information Age

A Pivotal Moment

At the dawn of the 21st century, Americans face a turning point in our history—a pivotal moment in which our old civic virtues must find fresh expression in new democratic institutions and in a new covenant between citizens and their commonwealth.

Our country is being transformed from top to bottom. The industrial order of the twentieth century, with its great concentrations of economic and political power, is giving way to a new society shaped by the centrifugal forces of the Information Age: microchip technologies, global markets, and new communications networks. This historic shift has released tremendous energy and creativity while, at the same time, rocking the economic and social foundations on which our leading public and private institutions rest.

While we cannot hold back the forces impelling us into the Information Age, neither can we ignore the insecurity that these revolutionary changes breed or the reactionary impulses they threaten to unleash. We must, instead, manage the transition to enable all Americans to adapt to new conditions and take advantage of new opportunities. Above all, we must have the courage to break free of the past, to sweep aside old political ideas and governing structures that no longer serve the greater public good.

We know we can do this because we have done it before—during the Progressive era early in this century when Americans reinvented their democracy to cope with the dislocations and demands of rapid industrialism and urbanization.

As it evolved over the course of this century, industrial democracy was built on an unwritten social compact whereby large, hierarchical institutions—big business, big labor, big government—offered Americans security in return for their allegiance. People looked to these large-scale organizations to assure their economic and personal well-being by fine-tuning the economy, raising living standards, protecting the health and dignity of workers, regulating corporations in the public interest, aiding the poor, providing educational opportunity and social insurance, defending civil rights, and more.

Since the early 1970s, however, a slowdown in economic growth, technological change, and globalization have combined to erode the big institutions' ability to hold up their end of the bargain. Many wage earners nowadays cannot depend on their company to stay put, let alone guarantee them a job. Organized labor's clout follows its dwindling membership. Global markets undercut the ability of national governments to referee economic competition, manage business cycles, or provide an ever-expanding array of social benefits. In short, the social compact of industrial society is breaking down, leaving many average working families to fend for themselves amid the turmoil of transition.

As these changes have intensified economic insecurity, America's historic sources of social and cultural stability have also come under severe stress. The dissolution of families, the erosion of traditional moral norms, the decline of social trust and civic engagement, and the growth of intergenerational poverty and welfare dependency have combined to deplete America's reserves of social capital. Yet as the old economic structures collapse, we need the support of strong social and civic networks more than ever.

Our chief political and governing institutions, meanwhile, have failed to cope effectively with these disruptive changes. Instead, special interests, ossified bureaucracies, and outdated ideologies have stalemated our democracy. Most Americans have ceased believing that the solutions to today's problems are to be found in a larger, stronger central government. This course—still supported by traditional liberals—serves more to defend the past than to build the future.

Many conservatives argue that the federal government is the source of our problems and that dismantling it will solve them. This strategy may help clear away outdated programs, but shrinking government does not automatically expand liberty or strengthen democracy. The market is the best means ever devised for creating wealth. Yet the market's "invisible hand" cannot create equal opportunity, or defend civil rights, or renew our civic culture.

America needs a third choice that replaces the left's reflexive defense of the bureaucratic status quo and counters the right's destructive bid to simply dismantle government. New Progressive's offer such a choice—a new public philosophy that sees government as society's servant, not its master—and as a catalyst for a broader civic enterprise controlled by and responsive to the needs of citizens and the communities where they live and work.

This Declaration offers our vision for a New Progressive Politics. New Progressives seek to replace the old politics of top-down paternalism with a new politics of individual and civic empowerment. Because we can no longer rely on big institutions to take care of us, it is time to craft new policies and institutions that enable us to take care of ourselves and each other. Ultimately, our challenge is to create a new way of governing that fosters the skills and habits of civic enterprise that have atrophied over the past century of centralization.

The political innovations and governing institutions introduced by the original Progressives and later by Franklin Roosevelt's New Deal served industrial America well. But they cannot help Americans answer a new and very different set of challenges facing our democracy as we look to a new century.

- *Economic anxiety.* The transition to global markets and knowledge-based enterprises threatens to put the American Dream out of reach for many working families, and it erodes stability and security for many others.

- *Social disintegration.* The breakdown of social order—of families, neighborhoods, and communities, and of the essentials of public safety—erodes the mutual trust and responsibility on which self-government depends.

- *Political dysfunction.* The rise of centralized bureaucracies, special-interest lobbyists, and big money politics has left most Americans feeling that we've lost control of our own government.

- *Cultural fragmentation.* The growing diversity of our population, rising racial tensions, and the fashionable ideology of group entitlement threaten to erode the shared beliefs that hold us together and splinter us into warring groups locked in a struggle for power.

- *Global confusion.* The end of the Cold War has weakened the domestic consensus behind vigorous U.S. global leadership, leaving us uncertain of our role in the world, torn between the impulse to lead and the temptation to turn inward.

These challenges demand more than new policies; they demand sweeping changes in the basic structure of government. Politicians routinely raise expectations that new policies will "cure" some public problem only to deepen public skepticism toward government when broken public systems again fail to deliver.

To restore public confidence in government we must first restore the problem-solving capacities of government. We advocate a new model for progressive governance that does not merely hand down programmatic "solutions" from Washington but instead creates an enabling environment where citizens and communities can fashion their own responses to local problems.

New Progressives are under no illusions that moving from a government that controls to one that enables will happen without a fight. The old structures of power will not dismantle themselves. We must take them on directly, mobilizing citizens to wrest power from entrenched defenders of the old order: left-right ideologues, lobbyists, technocrats, and the innumerable interests that have colonized Washington, from self-styled tribunes of the poor and elderly to favor-seeking corporations. Ultimately, we will have to confront our own demands for public benefits that we are increasingly reluctant to pay for.

As the era of big government comes to a close, we must reconstruct the progressive agenda in keeping with the organizational, political, and social imperatives of the Information Age.

Large centralized bureaucracies are yielding to flexible, self-adapting systems that can adjust rapidly to today's environment of faster economic change, wide dispersals of information, and instantaneous global communication. The new organization is exemplified by the Internet, a decentralized communications network controlled by its users.

People who have direct access to valuable information, who face exploding choices in the marketplace, and who are encouraged to participate in decisions at work will not be satisfied with bureaucratic, one-size-fits-all solutions imposed by government. Indeed, the self-managing skills Americans are mastering and the more entrepreneurial organizations where many of us work suggest the need for parallel efforts to restore effective self-governance to our society and our politics.

As big institutions lose their power to deliver security and stability, Americans need to fall back on the support of strong families and networks of mutual aid. To renew our civic life, we must reaffirm the shared values which enable us to transcend our differences and work together toward common purposes: work, family, personal responsibility, tolerance, and a sense of obligation to one another.

The challenges we face defy conventional left-right prescriptions. We are confident nonetheless that Americans will devise new and ingenious ways to tackle common problems. And we are fortunate in that the information revolution's tendency to diffuse power from large, hierarchical institutions to decentralized, self-adapting systems plays directly to our historic strengths. After all, no nation has more experience than ours with two prime examples of such self-organizing systems: democracy and markets. Our task now is to rediscover the special genius of American democracy—to revive our lost traditions of citizenship, economic self-reliance, and voluntary civic action within self-governing communities.

A Governing Philosophy for the Information Age

The New Progressive philosophy rests on three cornerstones—three ideals rooted in the progressive tradition of American democracy: equality of opportunity, mutual responsibility, and self-government. They suggest a very different political purpose, social ethic, and approach to governing than those that prevail today.

A Different Political Purpose: Equal Opportunity for All, Special Privilege for None

The first cornerstone of the New Progressive politics has animated generations of American leaders and has attracted millions of immigrants to our shores. It is, simply, the promise of equal opportunity for all to get ahead and special privilege for none. It is the ideal of a society in which individuals earn their rewards through their own talents and efforts within a system of fair and open rules.

From the earliest struggles to extend the franchise to today's unfinished fight against racial discrimination, Americans have progressively enlarged the sphere of individual liberty at the expense of unearned and unjustified privilege. We have discovered that simply banning formal legal privileges, though vitally necessary, is not enough.

There is no invisible hand that creates equal opportunity; it is a conscious social achievement that requires affirmative acts.

Equal opportunity means a fair chance for every individual to succeed based on talent and effort. It requires removing discriminatory barriers and providing meaningful arenas for self-development and self-improvement. It means a commitment to public investment in the elements common to all economic activity, and the rejection of special-interest subsidies that give the influential a public leg-up in the marketplace.

For decades, government has sought to redistribute opportunities and wealth within the framework of a relatively mature and stable industrial economy. The result has been growing layers of public subsidies, entitlements, and preferences to an ever-expanding universe of beneficiaries. The politics of entitlement is foundering today on unsustainable costs and a culture of dependence that has permeated citizens and businesses alike. For many Americans, the quest for distributive justice through an expanding welfare state now threatens to foreclose avenues to individual opportunity based on hard work and merit.

The answer is not, as many conservatives assert, to simply disable government or abandon key public responsibilities. Rather, it is to refocus government on enforcing fair rules of competition, cultivating an educated, public-spirited citizenry, and enabling individuals to succeed by dint of their own efforts. This principle is not a guarantee of individual success, and it is not a formula for top-down distribution of social goods. The promise of America is the promise of equal opportunity, not equal results.

A Different Social Ethic: A New Compact of Mutual Responsibility

The second cornerstone of the New Progressive politics is the principle of mutual responsibility. The core idea is simple: As a moral matter, we cannot rightly benefit from any association to which we are not prepared to contribute our fair share or fulfill the duties of our role.

The ethic of mutual responsibility rejects libertarianism—the idea that we have no obligations other than the ones we choose. Because we are social beings, we live in a dense network of interdependence that we are not free to deny or reject.

The ethic of mutual responsibility is equally at odds with the philosophy of entitlement—the belief that we can make demands on others, or on the community, without giving something back. The reason is simple: Just about everything of value, whether material resources or social capital, is produced and sustained through human action, usually in cooperation with others. To demand something of value without contributing anything in return is to assert as a matter of right that some should work for others without compensation. That is wrong as a matter of morality. And in a free society, those who do the work will soon respond to shirkers by withdrawing their support from common enterprises.

Mutual responsibility rests on a foundation of personal responsibility. We are not helpless victims of external forces—whether they be poverty, prejudice, faceless bureaucracies, or heartless corporations. We are capable of understanding what is required of us, and of acting on that understanding. That is the faith of a free society, and of democracy itself.

We are born with the capacity for personal responsibility. But as every parent knows, we are not born responsible. The capacity must be developed over an extended period, starting with the family. While our society must hold all adults responsible for their acts, we must also work to ensure that every child has a decent chance to develop responsibility.

For adults, personal responsibility begins at home. We have an obligation to take care of ourselves and our families—and to avoid unnecessary dependence on others. Regardless of economic or social status, we have an obligation to obey the law and to convey to our children the importance of law-abidingness.

Finally, our public discourse and institutions must cultivate the civic virtues and character required to preserve our liberties. Many liberals and conservatives today embrace an impoverished view of citizens as passive consumers of benefits, whether from government or the market. To sustain democracy, however, citizens must participate in decisions and contribute to the commonwealth, not merely demand rights and entitlements. We envision a new politics in which public benefits are closely linked to public work: Whenever possible, policies should be structured so that citizens who contribute to the community are rewarded, and those who benefit from the community give something back.

Policies conceived in this spirit of reciprocity are far more likely to work and to enjoy sustained public support. The G.I. Bill was one of the most popular and effective measures in our history because it expressed the nation's gratitude for our veterans' extraordinary service. And John F. Kennedy's Peace Corps was electrifying because it challenged the most fortunate Americans to give something back through service to their country.

A Different Means to Public Ends: Empowering Citizens and Communities

The third cornerstone of the New Progressive politics is a new principle of genuine self-government for the Information Age: Public institutions that empower our citizens to act for themselves.

Early in this century, the concentration of economic power in large corporations fueled public demands to centralize political power in national institutions. Bureaucracy and a strong national government were modernizing forces that spurred enormous material and social progress in industrial society. But they also diminished many Americans' independence as workers and citizens and weakened or displaced civic institutions.

The new economic arrangements make it possible—indeed, often necessary—for many Americans to direct their own work and careers and so regain a measure of freedom and autonomy lost during the Machine Age. Likewise, today's dispersals of economic power suggest a corresponding diffusion of political power, away from central institutions to people and local institutions.

The scale of our economic and political life is changing. The opportunity is at hand to revitalize economic self-reliance and self-governance by returning power from large institutions to people, from remote managers to front line workers, from social service agencies to parents, and from the national government to more accessible and accountable institutions, whether they be local government agencies or community organizations. While many U.S. businesses have reorganized themselves, flattening hierarchies and developing more participatory forms of decision making, our political system remains mired in the past. Efforts to improve government's performance by shrinking bureaucracy have met with entrenched resistance, exacerbating the loss of public confidence and sparking demands for the wholesale elimination of public agencies and functions.

Simply dismantling old bureaucracies, however, won't help Americans cope with new problems. The real challenge lies in replacing top-down bureaucratic government with a new model for bottom-up self-governance.

The new model decentralizes power, expands individual choice, and injects competition into the delivery of public goods and services. From charter schools to tradeable pollution allowances, it uses the flexibility and ingenuity of private markets to serve public purposes.

Where bureaucracy seeks to control people, the new model seeks to empower them. Reversing a century-long trend, it stresses local initiative before looking to Washington for solutions. And instead of creating government programs for every problem, it uses information, market incentives, civic networks, and performance standards to equip individuals and communities to solve their own problems.

The new approach fundamentally redefines the relationship between citizens and the government. It requires that they be active participants in producing public goods such as a clean environment and safe streets, not simply passive recipients of government largess. It defines "public" as the domain of citizens, not just government and it trusts in the broad, common sense judgments of citizens rather than the narrow expertise of technocratic elites. It is not simply a formula for less government, but for more effective and democratic governance. As Washington steps back from the impossible task of micro managing our incredibly complex and diverse society, local governments, individual citizens, and community institutions must assume more responsibility for tackling public problems.

In the new division of responsibility, government remains indispensable but its role changes. Government must be a catalyst of public action rather than a creator of programs. It must collect and spread information that is essential to informed debate and public deliberation. It must invest in promising public enterprises without trying to manage or control them. It must sustain institutions, especially public education, that promote equal opportunity and it must referee economic competition. It must continue to set and enforce public health and safety standards. And the national government must continue to concern itself with national matters: conducting defense and foreign policy, advancing our global economic and environmental interests, regulating interstate commerce, and protecting civil rights and liberties. But wherever possible, government at all levels must now empower people and communities to do things for themselves rather than delegating that responsibility to central bureaucracies.

This new philosophy of civic empowerment expands individual choice and strengthens community institutions, not to make government irrelevant, but to make it a more effective instrument of our common life. Indeed, the more we rely on political decentralization and individual choice, the more we need shared goals, clearly articulated, to guide our endeavors and to unite our country. Unity of ends, diversity of means: that is *e pluribus unum* for the twenty-first century.

Five Strategies for Renewing Our Democracy

Equality of opportunity, mutual responsibility, self-governing citizens and communities—these are the organizing principles of the New Progressive politics. They point toward radically different governing strategies that confront five overriding challenges facing our nation as we approach the twenty-first century:

- We must restore the American Dream by accelerating economic growth, expanding opportunity, and enhancing security.

- We must reconstruct our social order by strengthening families, attacking crime, and empowering the urban poor.

- We must renew our democracy by challenging the special interests and returning power to citizens and local institutions.

- We must defend the common civic ideals and the spirit of tolerance that enables America to draw strength and unity from its amazing diversity.

- And we must confront global confusion by building enduring new international structures of economic and political freedom. Unfortunately, the major parties today avoid these urgent tasks, either because the most likely solutions challenge current arrangements and interests, or because they believe there is no political constituency for actually solving problems. Yet the large and growing body of independent voters who have abandoned both parties suggests the emergence of a constituency for radical change.

If we are serious about restoring opportunity for average working families, rebuilding the social order on a new balance of rights and responsibilities, and reinvigorating our civic life, we must confront our real problems as well as powerful and entrenched interests that fear change and retard America's progress. New Progressives are willing to wage that struggle. We challenge liberals and conservatives, Democrats and Republicans, to replace today's politics of evasion with a new politics of public remedy. Such a politics requires liberals to reform and even dismantle bureaucratic systems they have long defended, and it requires conservatives to support new public initiatives that tackle problems, such as urban poverty, they have long ignored.

The following strategies move America beyond today's stultified left-right debate toward a new era of public activism and innovation.

Restoring Opportunity—From Institutional Dependency to Individual Empowerment

After World War II, public policies and informal understandings between business, labor, and government worked together to help promote upward mobility, stabilize business cycles, and cushion families during economic downturns. Most Americans looked to the national government to keep the economy stable, and to their companies and unions to provide a secure livelihood in return for hard work and loyalty. Since the early 1970s, however, slow growth, technological change, and global markets have combined to undermine these arrangements. The economic tide isn't rising fast enough, nor is it lifting all boats.

America urgently needs a new strategy for stimulating stronger economic growth within a global marketplace and enabling everyone to share in it.

First, the primary focus of public policy must shift from redistributing existing wealth to fostering conditions that enable people to create new wealth. This means substantially expanding public and private investment. It also means reducing subsidies to business, both to curb wasteful public spending and to spur the forces of market competition that impel firms and workers to innovate and become more efficient. Above all, government should use its budgetary, tax, regulatory, trade, and monetary policies to help promote the conditions firms and workers need to make greater technological progress. This is because the only way an economy can permanently raise its growth rate is to create more new economic knowledge—including not only new products and processes, but also new ways of managing and organizing every aspect of work.

Second, we must create policies and institutions that enable everyone to assume more responsibility for managing their economic careers and security in the dispersed settings of a global economy. No matter how enlightened a corporation, militant a union, or caring a government, they can no longer guarantee anyone a particular job for life in today's volatile global market-place. Our new economic strategy therefore must lessen worker dependence on big institutions and provide new opportunities to take charge of their own bottom line.

When wage earners change jobs, for example, they should have the same control as top executives over the principal sources of family security such as health insurance and retirement income. Along with a universal system of private health insurance that moves with the worker, we must make private pensions portable and gradually convert social security from a transfer program to a new system of individual private savings supplemented by modest public pensions for the needy. The unemployment system, designed for cyclical shifts rather than for a structural change in our economy, should likewise be revamped to give workers control over the public resources they need to move to new jobs and careers.

If the new economic bargain compels U.S. workers to accept more of the risks of competing in volatile world markets, it must also empower them to reap a fair share of the rewards. We must replace today's ruthless "winner take all" outlook with a new vision of democratic capitalism based on sharing gains as well as risks. Workers will have stronger incentives to become more productive and innovative if a substantial part of their compensation is tied to their firm's performance as well as their own. They also should be able to secure an equity stake in their company, and take it with them when they are laid off or otherwise decide to leave.

Third, because knowledge is the new wealth of nations, empowering workers above all means assuring them access to learning. Today, almost all workers—not just top managers and professionals—must become proficient learners. We must dramatically lift the quality of public schools by setting and enforcing world-class performance standards and by using parental choice and competition to spur innovative ways of preparing young Americans for productive work and citizenship. Since earnings increasingly track learning, we must organize new, life-long learning systems that enable workers to constantly update their skills or acquire new ones. As it has done at key points in U.S. history, from the creation of universal public education to the G.I. Bill, government must once again be a catalyst for a new public educational system that will be the foundation of equal economic opportunity in today's world as well as a necessary condition for our nation's continued economic and political leadership in the twenty-first century.

Fourth, businesses also must take on new responsibilities. One is to invest in developing their human capital—the knowledge and problem-solving skills of all their employees. Another is to replace the adversarial view of labor-management relations with a more flexible and collaborative organization of work. This means empowering workers to participate in decisions affecting productivity, quality, work assignments, and other matters that can determine a firm's success or failure in today's fast changing global markets. And when corporations shed employees or move overseas, public policy should ensure that these companies share the responsibility for helping displaced workers and assisting in the recovery of devastated communities. Finally, as many companies jack up executive compensation while "downsizing" their work-forces, it is time for a serious national debate about corporate accountability and governance in the new economy.

Fifth, workers, their families, and communities must organize to promote their own economic interests as big institutions no longer shelter them from a dynamic global marketplace. Faced with the upheavals of industrialism, Americans did not wait for government to step in: Workers formed unions to protect their interests and communities created settlement houses and other social institutions to cope with the dislocations caused by the new organiza-tion of work, urbanization, and an influx of immigrants. Likewise, working Americans today need to adapt existing institutions such as unions to the knowledge economy and create new associations that enhance their economic power and promote community self-help.

Reconstructing the Social Order on a Foundation of Strong Families

In industrial America, it was widely assumed that public institutions could and should fill the breach created by failing families and communities. Gov-ernment professionalized and bureaucratized social work, replacing local vol-unteers with university-trained "experts" and displacing many traditional community-based efforts to provide needy people with spiritual as well as material aid. In time, however, the government's social safety net became a snare for many poor citizens, a final destination rather than a way station back to family, work, and self-reliant citizenship.

The shift to a post-industrial economy has dealt an especially cruel blow to America's poor families and communities. The loss of well-paying manufac-turing jobs has stimulated a violent trade in illicit drugs and created a dearth of "marriageable males" who can support a family on their earnings. Yet instead of being a buttress for struggling families, welfare paternalism too often has aided and abetted the break-up of families, the spread of teenage pregnancy, and the disintegration of healthy communities.

Middle class families also have come under great economic and cultural stress. Stagnant incomes have forced more families to send a second earner to work to maintain middle class living standards. Inflation has severely eroded the value of tax deductions for children, leaving working parents with less money as well as less time to raise their children. And nearly half of all U.S. marriages end in divorce, often causing grave psychological harm to children as well as lowering their standard of living.

Instead of spending more to mitigate the social damage done by family dissolution, a new strategy for rebuilding the social and moral order in America should begin by strengthening the family. As Americans struggle to master new, knowledge-based work and attain and maintain middle class living standards while getting less support from big institutions, they must turn to a strong, functioning family as the primary source of the security, socialization, and investment necessary to prepare the next generation and sustain the present one.

Society can no longer profess neutrality about family structure in the face of overwhelming evidence that most children do best when they grow up in intact, two-parent families; that family breakdown is at the root of exponential increases in violent crime, especially by juveniles; and that welfare dependency is endemic among unmarried mothers. Since bureaucratic compassion has proved a poor substitute for the nurturing and moral guidance that parents traditionally have supplied, we must pursue new public and private strategies intended to support parents' efforts to fulfill their responsibilities.

For example, we need new public initiatives that reduce taxes on working parents, assist community efforts to discourage teen pregnancy, and ensure that in cases of divorce, childrens' interests are put first. But fortifying the family is everyone's responsibility, not just government's: Unless employers, government, communities, and the media aggressively combine to fortify the faltering institutions of marriage and family, social order, economic prosperity, and renewed self-governance will all move beyond our reach.

Returning Power to Self-Governing Citizens and Communities

The centralized institutions of the Industrial Era offered Americans security in exchange for power to make decisions for them. But as big government became the arbiter of most public questions, its reach and costs expanded. Special interests organized to defend programs, immortalizing initiatives intended as temporary remedies to pressing problems. And as the costs of government rose, its ability to solve problems declined as rule-bound bureaucracies focused on process rather than outcomes.

These developments have sparked unprecedented public disillusionment with government. Yet in any democracy worthy of the name, bashing government is ultimately an exercise in passing the buck. The time has come for

Americans to stop complaining about the government and to start reclaiming our government from special interests and imperious bureaucracies.

To govern ourselves in a society that has become too complex and fast changing to manage from the top and at a distance, citizens must take back responsibility and political power for the decisions that affect both themselves and their communities. The key to renewing our democracy is not just less government, or greater reliance on markets, but a new model of governance that empowers citizens to do more as central bureaucracies do less.

To be sure, central governments still have a role to play in setting broad rules and standards, assuring fairness and justice, and tackling those issues that transcend regional, state, and national boundaries. But the presumption for democratic action must be reversed. Citizens and local institutions, rather than distant government agencies, should be the public problem-solvers of first recourse.

For example, there is no way that new programs from Washington can "solve" the problem of teen pregnancy. But the federal government could encourage the spread of "second-chance homes"—community-based maternity homes run by local civic or religious organizations—by letting young mothers use their welfare payments to pay for bed and board.

Environmental protection offers another example. While the federal government should continue to focus on cross-boundary and international issues, set broad standards, provide technical information, and measure outcomes, community-led action is critical for localized problems such as indoor air pollution, drinking water quality, care of waste sites, and habitat conservation. Likewise, we should move from centralized regulation to market-based incentives, such as tradeable allowances, that can curb pollution in more cost-effective and flexible ways by focusing reductions on those who can make them most efficiently.

Finally, returning power to the people also entails changing the way we finance politics and elections. We must create a more open and competitive political system in which the influence of special interest money is sharply reduced, incumbency advantages are lessened, and campaign costs are lowered by making free television time available to viable candidates.

Defending Common Ground

Industrial America was a mighty engine of cultural assimilation: Successive waves of immigrants were rapidly melded into the dominant, Anglo-American culture. But changing patterns of immigration and growing ethnic diversity, along with a new ideology of group rights and entitlements, have called into question the old model of "Americanization." Because we can no longer take our cultural cohesion for granted, we must all work harder to identify and affirm the common beliefs and values that form the core of our national identity and allow us to transcend our differences. We must defend America's common ground—the values and institutions we share in common as well as our mutual rights and responsibilities as citizens—against those on both ends of the political spectrum who would divide us along lines of race, ethnicity, gender, religion, or other group identity.

Growing racial animosity constitutes a grave threat to our civic culture. It is fueled by persistent white racism, the deepening poverty and social chaos in many urban communities, preferential policies, a cynical "wedge politics" that exploits racial fears, and a new ideology of group difference that fosters a cult of victimization and challenges the very idea that transcendent ideals can unite us. Unfortunately, the left-right debate feeds this polarization, with many conservatives cynically pandering to white fears and grievances and many liberals condescendingly excusing bigotry and self-defeating behavior among blacks.

America urgently needs a new agenda for racial equality grounded in the traditional liberal principles of individual rights and equal opportunities. Such an approach would energetically enforce laws barring discrimination against members of ethnic and racial minorities. But it would also shift the focus of public debate from race preferences that violate these principles and exacerbate racial discord to a new national commitment to create economic opportunities for the urban poor. A major national effort to promote work, savings, entrepreneurship, and small business creation in the inner city is both a moral and economic imperative for our racially troubled society.

Reaffirming the American credo that we should each be judged as individuals with equal rights and responsibilities—not as members of separate groups—is critical if we are to avoid the ethnic, cultural, and racial fragmentation that is ravaging societies from Bosnia to Turkey to the former Soviet Union. America can offer the world no greater gift today than to provide a successful example of multiethnic democracy at work. We have an obligation to reject linguistic, racial, and ethnic programs that have separation as their motive, and to engage in a relentless quest for new policies and institutions that strengthen the framework of individual freedom, civic equality, and tolerance that make a common polity and culture possible.

Confronting Global Confusion

After World War II, U.S. leaders created an extraordinary system of military, political, and economic alliances that held communism in check, sped the recovery of war-torn nations, fostered open trade and unprecedented economic cooperation, and firmly anchored Germany and Japan in the democratic camp.

Today, as the bipolar, East vs. West order of the Cold War yields to global confusion and disorder, America once again must design strategies and institutions that promote our interests and values in a new era of international politics.

We begin with a fundamental fact: The United States is the world's strongest nation by an even wider margin than before. If we were to disengage from our global commitments, as some have argued, the resulting vacuum of power and leadership would be enormous and profoundly dangerous. Nonetheless, we cannot simply continue to bounce from crisis to crisis without some overarching sense of national strategy. A formless ad hoc policy of reactions to events abroad will not long command public confidence or support. What's needed is a clear definition of America's purposes in the post–Cold War era.

Some missions remain unchanged. Our security interests dictate active U.S. diplomacy aimed at preserving the peace among the world's great powers. We must also continue to ensure the military balance of power in regions that remain vital to our security, especially Europe, the Pacific Rim, and the Middle East. Our alliances in these regions are critical strategic assets that enhance our security as well as our global reach and influence.

At the same time, we must adapt our Cold War assumptions and institutions to new global realities, such as the demise of the Soviet threat and the rise of new dangers, especially the spread of weapons of mass destruction. For example, to back up our diplomacy, reassure our friends, and deter potential foes, we must maintain a strong defense—but the reduced threat of war in Europe permits us to trade some of the massive force structure built up during the Cold War for new investments in advanced weaponry and the emergent technologies of "information warfare." Likewise, the end of East-West conflict enables us to press for more equitable and reciprocal trade relations with our trading partners, whereas in the past we often allowed the imperative of Western unity to override our economic interests. U.S. intelligence agencies, foreign aid, the diplomatic establishment—our entire foreign policy apparatus—should be thoroughly reexamined and reconfigured for new missions.

As America's post-war leaders understood, we can best safeguard our interests by building enduring structures of economic and political freedom. We might start, for example, by convening a second "Bretton Woods" conference to grapple with new tensions caused by the integration of global markets and capital flows across borders. In the burgeoning Asia Pacific, there is a need for economic and political organizations that parallel those that have fostered democracy and economic cooperation in Europe. And, to supplement strong U.S. leadership, we need more effective multilateral institutions to confront such global issues as terrorism, environmental protection, immigration and refugees, epidemics of disease, and drug trafficking.

The collapse of the Cold War order presents America with an opportunity to construct a new international system upon a foundation of democracy, free markets, and human rights. Although the "Third Wave" of democratization that swept the world in the last fifteen years may have crested, there is as yet no coherent ideological challenger to liberal democracy on the horizon. We believe a new strategy of democratic realism, of using our resources and alliances to enlarge the zone of market democracies and leverage progress toward political and economic freedom in strategically vital countries and regions, best unites America's interests and ideals.

The Progressive Precedent

In this age of sound-bite politics, a movement of transformative ideas may seem beside the point. Nothing could be further from the truth. The challenges of today resemble those of a century ago. And the response we offer mirrors—in new circumstances—the Progressive movement that reshaped our politics and renewed our country.

Recall what we faced: America was experiencing a great economic transition from agriculture to the new Industrial Age. As our population moved from rural small towns to rapidly expanding big cities, there was a pervasive sense of social dislocation and disorder. Cultural conflicts erupted, triggered by unsettled issues of race and waves of immigration unprecedented in size and diversity. Public institutions were condemned as ineffective, corrupt, and exclusionary; citizen confidence in government plummeted. Party politics was dominated by the conflict between representatives of unchecked corporate greed and the tribunes of a dying agrarian order.

In response to these challenges, innovative thinkers and civic activists stepped forward with a set of bold ideas for renewing the promise of American life in the radically new conditions of the Industrial Age.

The Progressive movement began, not as a party, but rather as a powerful new vision that influenced both parties as well as citizens and leaders who sought to act outside established party structures. While it scored important early successes (both Theodore Roosevelt and Woodrow Wilson implemented portions of the Progressive agenda), the movement's key contribution was long term: It created the intellectual and policy predicate for the New Deal and for the rise of a strong centralized government using the tools of legislation, regulation, bureaucracy, and executive leadership to address our national problems.

The ideas the Progressives launched shaped our politics for most of the past century. Those ideas were right for their time. They faced facts and solved problems. Through much of the twentieth century, the expansion of central government power helped address the challenges of opportunity, security, equality, and social unity.

But now, as we leave the Industrial Era and enter the Information Age, this approach can no longer move us forward.

Like the Progressives a century ago, we seek to initiate a new politics based on ideas, not just the clash of organized interests. Like them, we hope to craft an agenda that seizes the opportunities of the future rather than clinging to a vanishing past. Like them, we hope to build new common ground, not new partisan divisions; not just to transform one political party, but to renew the American Dream.

A Call to Action

We have outlined a New Progressive politics for the Information Age. At its heart is a new compact that calls for replacing old policies and institutions that take care of people with new ones that enable them to take care of themselves. We have offered a new governing philosophy: of equal opportunity for all and special privilege for none; of mutual responsibility; of civic empowerment. And we have sketched a vision of this philosophy in action: new strategies to restore the American Dream, reconstruct our social order, renew our democracy, defend our common civic ground, and confront global confusion.

We are realistic about the difficult challenges that lie ahead. Yet we are optimistic about our country's ability to conquer them.

We are optimistic because U.S. entrepreneurs already are pioneering the new knowledge industries; because many of our workers already are exchanging the mind-numbing drudgery of manual labor for jobs that allow them to think, create, and share in decisions; because our children increasingly are able to trade the boredom and mediocrity of factory-style mass education for innovative schools that prepare them for a lifetime of active self-education; because women and minorities are creating businesses and entering professions at a rapid clip while immigrants continue to pursue their dreams on our shores; and, because liberal democracy has prevailed against the various "isms" that have violently challenged it in this century.

And, finally, we are optimistic because we share Thomas Jefferson's confidence in the wisdom and capacities of free people, armed with knowledge, to meet the demands of transforming change without losing their way or their liberties.

The ideas we offer here are proposals, not pronouncements; rough drafts, not finished products. We hope they will serve as a catalyst and framework for a long overdue national discussion to move us beyond the sterile left-right debate. The New Progressives constitute not a party or faction but a broad civic movement dedicated to radical reform. We welcome progressive-minded citizens of all stripes to this discussion: Democrats, Republicans, independents, liberals, conservatives, and moderates.

Our goal is nothing less than to create the politics and policies to preserve basic American values of equal opportunity and self-government in the Information Age.

We can at most begin this task; it will take many to complete it. Like Progressivism a century ago, the New Progressive politics must be the work of many hands.

(The drafters of this declaration are Will Marshall, president of the Progressive Foundation and the Progressive Policy Institute; Al From, chairman of the Foundation and president of the Democratic Leadership Council; William A. Galston, professor at the University of Maryland School of Public Affairs and a former deputy assistant for domestic policy to President Clinton; and Doug Ross, director of the Foundation's scholars' network and former assistant secretary for employment and training at the U.S. Department of Labor.)

10 Big Ideas to Transform America

Chapter 4

A New Deal on Social Security

Robert J. Shapiro

Social Security is, at once, the most popular of all government's programs and the grand monument to New Deal liberalism. In the last decade of partisan conflict over almost everything about government, it alone has been immune from criticism and cuts. But a half-century of economic and social changes have left the old program fiscally precarious and, in certain respects, surprisingly flawed as social and economic policy. If Franklin D. Roosevelt's moral vision is to endure, progressives must modernize his enterprise. We must stop channeling public monies into windfall cash retirement benefits for virtually everyone, and create a new, two-tier system of both mandatory private saving and public provision for people's retirement security.

Change won't come easily. For most Americans, Social Security embodies an inviolate commitment in which every generation helps support those preceding it, and the benefits people receive represent their just returns on investments they make every month of their working lives. Nor *should* reform come easily: Social Security checks are the most important source of income for most elderly Americans, and still the government's most effective policy for reducing poverty.

But without genuine change, Social Security annual revenues will fall behind annual payments by 2013. Through the years of the baby boom's retirement, from 2015 to 2050, the current system's revenues could fall some $4 trillion short of its obligations, in today's dollars.[1] But if we do it right, reform could produce a better retirement security system, with more self-reliance and greater personal responsibility, smaller windfalls for the most well-to-do, and a more reasonable tax burden on working families. The system can even contribute to economic growth along with reducing poverty.

39

Ultimately, a sound Social Security system must rest on our own habits and attitudes. As the New Progressive Declaration makes clear, a welfare state mentality that promises open-ended support for everyone is a false benevolence that cannot be sustained indefinitely. But a Darwinian alternative that leaves everyone on his or her own is equally unacceptable. To rebuild Social Security and be proud of the result, we must combine the nation's spirit of compassion with new provisions for personal self-reliance.

This will be no magic or painless solution, and retirement security for everyone cannot be sustained without contributions from all of us. And this result can come only from a national debate that involves all Americans and from reforms that can win vast support. We do not yet have all the answers, but do we have the basic elements of a sound, progressive strategy. They are:

- *Control mounting costs.* Social Security's obligations are growing at an unsustainable rate. We have to reform the benefits of everyone except elderly people on limited incomes. Everyone should agree to put off retirement a little longer to support the system, and well-to-do retirees should accept smaller cost-of-living adjustments (COLAs).

- *Ensure fairness for workers.* Social Security today transfers income from working people to retirees, whether they need it or not. Families with modest incomes should not be forced to get by on even less, so that retirees with income to spare can collect large windfalls. At a minimum, President Clinton and the Congress should rule out another hike in the payroll tax rate, which was raised seven times in the 1980s. To promote further intergenerational equity, we should also consider exempting some portion of people's income from the payroll tax, which could be paid for by repealing some tax subsidies for influential industries and affluent individuals.

- *Expand personal saving for retirement.* Genuine Social Security reform means replacing its current pay-as-you-go financing system with one that supplements public pensions with private saving. We should start by no longer financing the budget deficit with payroll tax revenues, and by saving more for ourselves. It could work like this: The roughly one to two percentage points of the payroll tax which the government does not need to finance current retirement benefits—the so-called Social Security surplus—would be returned to Americans for their personal retirement saving.

This reform, a third way between preserving the status quo and embracing a radical privatization of the program, would create a two-tier system that combines public provision and private saving. By doing so, we can begin to test both the market's ability to generate secure and healthy returns on a universal basis and the American people's acceptance of mandatory private saving. The results can provide a sound basis for deciding as a nation whether mandatory private saving can play a larger role in providing universal retirement security.

• *Engage all Americans in the decision.* We should create a truly nonpartisan, blue-ribbon National Commission to document the problem's dimensions and examine the range of possible solutions. Former Presidents Bush, Carter, and Ford should help President Clinton initiate the national discussion, and could serve as Commission co-chairs. The panel's deliberations should be open to the public and accompanied by public education to ensure that everyone is fully informed about the problem and the effects of all proposed solutions.

What's Right with Social Security

Social Security is one of America's most successful social policies. More than 90 percent of older Americans today receive the monthly checks, which comprise nearly 40 percent of all elderly income.[2] These checks reduce poverty among the elderly by nearly 75 percent; without them and Medicare, more than half of all seniors would fall beneath the poverty line.[3] Thanks to Social Security, less than 13 percent of elderly people today are poor (a *smaller* share than for the rest of America).

Without a mandatory, public system, tens of millions of seniors would find themselves financially unprepared for retirement. Nearly half of all benefits go to people whose other sources of cash income fall below the poverty line. Only 70 percent of the elderly derive any income at all from private savings and investments, and such income accounts for only one-quarter of the total cash resources of all the elderly.[4] Far behind comes income collected from private pensions or earned by seniors who continue to work.[5]

Low administrative costs are another benefit of a universal public system. The actual cost of running the Social Security system is equal to only 1 percent of the value of the benefits paid out, compared to 6 percent to 11 percent for private pension plans.

Social Security also provides what private pensions generally cannot: Absolute security in the value of the benefits. While the value of private pension funds may rise or fall with the movements of inflation and the stock and bond markets, only a government with taxing power can guarantee the purchasing power of its coverage. Investing in the stock market has produced healthy returns over a period of decades. But a new analysis by Yale University economist Robert Shiller has found that in fifteen years in this century, the real value of the Standard & Poor's index was at least 40 percent lower than a decade previous, including seven years in the mid–1970s and early 1980s.[6] Wealthy people with market savvy can minimize these risks for themselves, but everyone else needs protection.

What's Wrong with Social Security

But the Social Security system has its limits. It rests on a delicate balance between its capacity to generate benefits and our appetite to consume them. And this balance is always threatened by the political temptation to provide more benefits today and pay the costs later. When the numbers and incomes of the workers who pay for the benefits finally fall behind the numbers and demands of the retirees who receive them, the system can break down.

Social Security faces this prospect. It arises not merely from the demographics of the baby boom and the subsequent baby bust (the generation born between 1965 and 1985), but also from some of the system's basic features.

In one sense, the impending crisis was built into Social Security at its conception. When Roosevelt created the program during the Depression, thousands of private financial institutions had failed and millions of people had lost their savings. The need to relieve their desperation could not wait for a generation of new private saving to accumulate. The prudent course at the time was to create a purely public, pay-as-you-go system. It started with a small group of people receiving small cash benefits financed by a 1 percent tax, and its pay-as-you-go financing was secure as long as the number of workers and the economy's payroll tax base grew faster than the number of retirees and the size of their benefits.

This approach works as long as the economy delivers rising growth rates, or as long as the labor force grows at a faster rate than the size of Social Security benefits and the numbers of beneficiaries. Before the system was ten years old in 1950, the country entered a period of strong growth and a fast-growing labor force. When growth and wages began to slow sharply in the early 1970s, the baby boom and the women's rights movement came to the rescue, bringing large numbers of baby boomers and women into the work force.

Social Security also rode the wave of rising expectations and incomes enveloping the country in the 1950s and 1960s. With little protest, benefits and the payroll tax rate that financed them both increased sharply. In 1940, the average Social Security benefit had equaled about 20 percent of the average wage; by 1970, 36 percent of the average wage. Since then, it has stabilized at about 41 percent, not counting the addition of other benefits, notably Medicare.[7] Meanwhile, the payroll tax rate (*not* counting Medicare) rose from 3 percent in 1950, to 6 percent in 1960, to 8.2 percent in 1970, to 10.2 percent in 1980, and to 12.4 percent today.

This system has a fundamental weakness. To fulfill its initial mission, Social Security had to provide the first retirees with more than they had paid in. This feature proved too attractive to reverse. Over the next half century, the system has continued to deliver to virtually everyone cash benefits that far exceed what they have paid in. In this sense, Social Security has come to embody the basic economic defect of the modern welfare state: the proposition that everyone should be able to consume more than he or she produces.

This flaw runs through the structure of the basic benefit schedule. When a person retires, his original monthly benefit is determined, first, by taking the history of the monthly earnings on which he paid payroll taxes, and then adjusting them for inflation. Next, his average monthly earnings are adjusted upward again, for the real wage growth throughout the economy over the course of his working life. After that, a progressive factor is introduced: Each person's initial monthly benefit is then determined by replacing 90 percent of roughly the first $400 of earned income, 32 percent of roughly the next $2,000 or so, and 15 percent of roughly the next $3,000. Finally, in each subsequent year, the retiree's cash payment is adjusted upward to offset inflation.

This formula means that Social Security's total costs do not simply increase with inflation and the number of retirees. Rather, every year, each new crop of retirees receives *larger* real cash benefits than those preceding them with the same real lifetime earnings.

Economists C. Eugene Steuerle and Jon M. Bakija have analyzed the lifetime cash retirement benefits going to an average two-earner working couple—a husband who earned average wages and a wife who earned half the average. (All figures are given in 1993 dollars.)[8] If the couple retired in 1960, they should collect $102,000 in Social Security over the course of their retirements. If the same couple retired in 1980, they should receive more than $208,400. And if they retired in 1995, they should collect $226,600. By 2030, when the last baby boomer retires, our couple should receive more than $316,000.

Since benefits rise every year while the payroll tax has been adjusted only periodically, the system delivers large windfalls to almost everyone. For our hypothetical two-earner couple that retired in 1960, the value of their previous payroll taxes—adjusted for both inflation and a 2 percent average rate of return on the payments—totals $13,300 (once again, in 1993 dollars). But they would collect $102,000, for a net real windfall of $88,700. If they retired in 1980, they would have paid in $75,200 and collected $208,400, for a $133,300 net gain. After 1980, years of rising payroll taxes begin to eat away at the net windfall benefits, but they still are substantial: $78,600 if our couple had retired in 1995, and $29,400 in 2030.

With rising payroll taxes, not everyone can expect a windfall. Already, affluent single men who retired in 1995 can expect to collect benefits worth less than the value of the taxes they paid. On average, women live longer and so receive more benefits than men; but by 2010, highly paid single women will face a similar shortfall, as will affluent couples.[9] However, the current system—if it survives—will continue to provide substantial windfalls to most people.

These examples reveal that Social Security is *not* genuine insurance. An insurance system sustains itself by providing people a cash benefit roughly equal to their previous cash payments, adjusted for inflation and a market rate of return, and less a market rate of profit. By contrast, Social Security is a perpetual income transfer system that promises that almost everyone can receive far more than he or she ever paid in, sustained by regularly raising taxes on workers not yet eligible for its benefits.

Those Darned Demographics

The rising payroll tax revenues from the flood of baby boomers, women, and new immigrants entering the work force have kept the system afloat, despite slower economic growth. Unfortunately, the baby boom ended, and birth rates returned to much lower levels. When this demographic roller coaster collides with a benefits structure that still promises most people large windfalls, resting on pay-as-you-go financing, it could shake Social Security at its foundations— unless we reform it.

The demographic problem lies as much in the baby bust as in the baby boom. The number of retirees will actually grow more slowly over the next thirty-five years (an average of 1.8 percent a year) than it grew over the previous twenty-five years (on average, 2.2 percent a year).[10] But the number of workers paying payroll taxes will decelerate much faster: The work force paying for the benefits grew by an average of 1.6 percent a year from 1970 to 1995; but from now to 2030, the number of workers is expected to grow by less than 0.5 percent a year.

The era of rising benefits was launched on sound foundations in 1950, when there were 100 workers to support every six retirees.[11] Today, the system's costs continue to rise although the ratio has fallen to almost twenty-seven retirees for every 100 workers. By 2030, when the last of the boomers retires, every 100 workers will have to help support nearly 43 retirees.

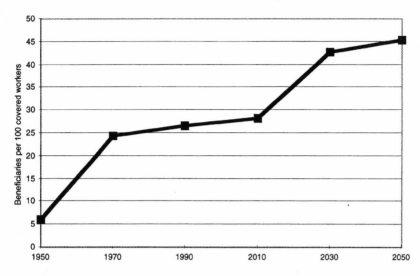

Fig. 4.1. Growth in OASI beneficiaries, 1950–2050. Board of Trustees, OASDI, *Annual Report*, 1993.

Thanks to science and good living, more of us live long enough to retire, and on average we collect our benefits for more years. In 1935 when Social Security was enacted, only 60 percent of those born sixty-five years earlier were still alive; today, that share is 77 percent. If the projections are right, it will reach 85 percent by 2030. Furthermore, in 1935, those reaching age sixty-five lived on average for another thirteen years. A sixty-five-year-old today can expect to live another seventeen years, and by 2030, a sixty-five-year-old should expect to live twenty more years.

Preserving Social Security on Sound Foundations

These numbers do not lie, and neither can our political leaders. President Clinton and the leaders of Congress should help educate Americans about what will happen to Social Security if we do not reform it. Instead of promising to never touch the system, both political parties should pledge to preserve its mission under new and more sound arrangements.

The President, his White House predecessors, and congressional leaders should jointly pledge to build a new national consensus to reinvent Social Security. The first step is to create a blue-ribbon, nonpartisan National Commission on Retirement Security to lay out the dimensions of the problem and the range of responsible solutions.

The first principle of reform is that Social Security should continue to ensure that low income retirees have the resources to lead dignified lives. This is Social Security's great achievement, and it cannot be sacrificed. The second principle of reform is that every generation should contribute to solving this national problem, because retirement security is everybody's concern.

Three specific steps follow from these principles:

- *The burden of reform should not fall on families struggling to raise their children.* Social Security reform should be on the table, but higher payroll taxes should not.

- *Baby boomers can make the largest contribution by working a little longer.* This is only appropriate, since they and their parents will pass on to future generations not only the burden of their retirement security, but also a mountain of additional federal debt. The Commission should evaluate the effects of gradually raising the age of eligibility for Social Security in two-month increments beginning in 2004, to reach age sixty-six by 2010, sixty-seven by 2016, sixty-eight by 2022, and sixty-nine by 2028. This would not only ease the economic burden on the busters, it will also give boomers more time to save income before they retire.

- *Retirees in comfortable circumstances should also help sustain the system.* Means-testing the Social Security system has many pitfalls, but the annual cost-of-living adjustments for well-to-do retirees could be reduced without significant distortions.

Financing Social Security: The Myth of the Trust Fund

The crisis in Social Security will arrive sooner than many believe, because the last attempt to "save Social Security" has failed. In 1983, President Ronald Reagan created a national commission that urged the government to immediately begin saving for the baby boomers' retirement. Congress responded by raising payroll tax rates (and cutting benefits modestly), to generate more than $1 trillion in excess revenues and income over the next thirty years.

In theory, these surplus revenues could be "saved" to finance later benefits: The Social Security Administration would lend its annual surplus to the Treasury, which would use it to reduce the national debt. In this way, every year the surplus would go back into the economy to support higher business investment, which in turn would generate higher growth, just as if the surplus had been saved. By the time the retiring boomers began to claim benefits exceeding the payroll taxes paid by their children, the Treasury could pay back the loans from Social Security from the revenues generated by the larger economy produced by the decades of additional capital investment underwritten by surplus Social Security revenues.

It hasn't worked out that way. Workers today pay the higher payroll taxes without generating any additional saving to help finance their own retirement benefits. Instead of using the surplus payroll tax revenues to provide the capital for higher growth, the government has absorbed the surplus by running huge budget deficits. In effect, we "save" tens of billions of dollars a year by paying higher payroll taxes, and then immediately consume them in other government services.

The result is history's greatest example of double-account bookkeeping. The Social Security Trust Fund holds a growing mountain of Treasury debt securities —nearly $550 billion in 1996—accumulated from the surplus payroll tax revenues and the interest earned from loaning them to the Treasury. Every year and for the next two decades, these balances will grow by $70 billion to $100 billion a year. According to the official story, Social Security's books look flush and secure until 2029, when the system hits the wall.

But Social Security's assets are also the government's liabilities. By 2015, for example, payroll tax revenues are expected to fall $56 billion short of Social Security payments. The Social Security Administration will redeem $56 billion of its trust fund, but the Treasury will have to raise the $56 billion from an economy that has not gained a single dollar in additional saving and investment from the surplus revenues collected by the high payroll tax. By 2020, the annual shortfall will exceed $200 billion; by 2030, $700 billion; and by 2040, $1.2 trillion. Under the current system, the government can bridge these gaps and redeem Social Security's claims only by raising other taxes, cutting other programs, or borrowing more from the public, since the trillions of dollars earmarked to help pay the tab will have been spent decades before.

The 1983 reforms were based on a sound principle: move from a pure pay-as-you-go system to one with partial prefunding by saving resources today for the future. But the government did not abide by this principle. While the new National Commission examines permanent solutions, we can at least begin to save the current surplus payroll tax revenues. The government has proved incapable of saving these funds, so workers should be permitted to save them for themselves. For example, we can implement the proposal by the co-chairmen of a recent commission on entitlement reform, Senators Bob Kerrey, Democrat of Nebraska, and Alan Simpson, Republican of Wyoming, to return these surplus revenues to the taxpayers as deposits in individual, private retirement accounts, invested like today's Individual Retirement Accounts (IRAs). To ensure that this step does not simply increase the budget deficit and federal debt, Congress can offset the revenues lost to the Treasury by closing uneconomic industry tax subsidies, as outlined in previous PPI reports.[12]

This approach would introduce a measure of prefunding for retirement security in the form of direct personal saving. And by returning part of the payroll tax to workers, this step would lessen the regressive burden of that tax on moderate income working families. However, these positive effects would still be modest and would not be permanent, because the annual payroll tax surplus will decline over the next 15 years and hit zero in 2013. As this chapter will discuss below, the Commission should also evaluate strategies to make mandatory private saving a permanent feature of Social Security reform.

Saving for Retirement

Social Security's problems come not only from flawed policies and inescapable demographics, but also from changes in our own habits and behavior. The future would look less daunting if Americans saved for themselves at higher rates. Higher saving by everybody would not only lessen future pressures on Social Security, but also expand the tax base to support the system and raise people's incomes by increasing private investment and economic growth.

Opportunity and need are the two facts of economic life that drive people to save. Opportunity comes first: People generally save more, and at higher rates, when their incomes rise rapidly. The main reason that private saving has declined is that the opportunity has diminished: Most people's incomes have stopped rising appreciably.

But Social Security itself also plays a role in the low-savings story. As slow income gains have reduced opportunities to save, expectations of large windfalls from Social Security reduce many people's perceived need to save. Economists disagree about the power of this effect, but few doubt its existence. By one estimate (not the largest, by far), each dollar of expected Social Security wealth reduces annual private savings by two to three cents.[13] If that's anywhere near accurate, the current program may have cut our private saving rate by as much as one-half. And if that's true, the increases in Social Security lifetime cash benefits, especially for the more affluent, also have played a role in the slower economic growth of the last generation.

Inadvertently, Social Security also reduces national savings by increasing consumption. By design, it transfers cash from young working people, who are more likely to save, to retirees, who consume virtually all their income—and the system has been doing so at rising rates. Because this system provides retirement support in the form of monthly annuity payments, these resources are likely to be entirely consumed. This helps explain why an average seventy-year-old today consumes about 25 percent more than the average thirty-year-old, as compared to 1960, when seventy-year-olds consumed 35 percent less than those aged thirty.[14]

Even people facing retirement within ten years, those aged fifty-five to sixty-four, do not save at healthy rates. On one level, this group appears to be saving enough, combined with Social Security, to maintain a modest lifestyle in retirement: In 1989, they had median wealth of about $97,200, or three times their median income.[15] But more than two-thirds of their wealth is tied up in their homes, while their financial assets average less than $30,000. Even those with a college education report average financial holdings for retirement of only $60,000. The risk for many is that they will outlive their assets.[16]

We face a classic vicious cycle. Slow income growth and the promise of substantial Social Security benefits discourage people from saving, which heightens their dependence on Social Security. But their low saving dampens economic growth, reducing the potential wage base supporting the benefits that their low saving has made more important. And maintaining those benefits under the current arrangements contributes to continued low saving and economic growth, both by reducing the need to save and increasing national consumption.

The Flawed Saving Schemes of the Right and the Left

Lately, both conservatives and liberals have offered proposals to help break this cycle. Thus far, their approaches are deeply flawed. Some conservatives now advocate radical privatization of Social Security, by either allowing people to voluntarily opt out of the current system and save for themselves, or by shifting everyone's payroll tax payments to personal savings accounts. These schemes have more to do with a free market ideology and a political goal of reducing government than with providing genuine retirement security. For example, making Social Security voluntary would lead to an exodus by higher income taxpayers, worsening Social Security's future financing crisis for everyone else.

Reformers on the right with more modest ambitions argue for replacing Social Security with complete mandatory private saving, on the model of Chile. They promise that everyone could build huge nest eggs by investing their payroll tax payments in the stock market. They have not explained, however, how we would get from here to there. The problem is a multitrillion dollar transition during which baby boomers and busters would have to pay twice, once into their own saving accounts and again to maintain benefits for the tens of millions of Americans already retired or preparing to do so— benefits which today run about $350 billion a year. Chile, which started with a much less generous and broad public system than ours, financed its transition by running a decade of annual budget surpluses equal to roughly 4 percent of their gross domestic product. In the United States, such a plan would require either budget surpluses even more vast, or new taxes of comparable size, or several trillion dollars in additional federal borrowing and debt.

The privatizers' promise of huge future nest eggs for everyone is also unfounded. They typically cite the soaring stock market of the last decade as evidence that their approach can make everyone a millionaire. The market does provide higher returns than government securities, but it does not produce miracles. In particular, this reform would not repeal the economic law of diminishing returns: The flood of new funds into the stock market would bring down the average return on all investment in the economy. The plan would also jeopardize the retirement security of the baby busters when it collided with the law of supply and demand, since the value of their holdings would decline as the wave of boomers sold theirs to live on. Nor could such a system protect low and moderate income seniors during a steep stock market decline or periods of inflation when stocks lose real value. For example, in the years 1975, 1976, and every year from 1978 to 1983, the stock market's real value was 40 percent or more lower than it had been ten years before.

Finally, the claim that a flood of new business capital would spur enough additional growth to finance both the transition and everyone's retirements is a pipe dream. As noted in Chapter 12, higher traditional business investment has only a modest impact on growth. And even if the baby bust generation somehow increased its productivity enough to keep the system solvent (additional annual gains of 1.5 percent to 2.0 percent a year might do it), they would have to both realize a 40 percent increase in their standard of living and be willing to turn it all over to the elderly boomers.[17]

Some Social Security reformers on the left have their own version of this approach, in which the federal government invests surplus payroll tax revenues in the stock market. In effect, this approach would create a two-tier system with the government controlling both tiers. In this way, they believe, Social Security would collect high returns which could keep it afloat without substantial additional changes. In fact, this approach is both too modest and too radical.

First, the numbers don't add up. The annual payroll tax surplus will decline and finally disappear over the next fifteen to twenty years, so that maintaining our current arrangements through the boomers' retirement from 2020 to 2050 would still involve substantial benefit cuts or payroll tax increases.[18]

Even more troubling, neither government nor business would be safe if Washington became the single largest owner of the stock market and a major shareholder in every large corporation in the country. On the one hand, a government stake in the fate of particular companies could well intensify its often cozy relationships with influential industries, affecting policy decisions from trade to environmental protection. On the other, the government could not insulate itself from the pressures of powerful constituencies to vote its shares to serve their purposes, from affirmative action to right-to-life, or simply to reflect the views of the president or Congress.

This problem cannot be solved by creating an ostensibly independent body to manage the government's stock portfolio. This body would be subject to the same public pressures, if one step removed, in voting the shares. Nor can we evade the problem by simply barring government from voting the shares at all, since this fix would allow corporate executives to be even less accountable to their stockholders than today. The dilemma lies in the basic proposition of major government holdings in private companies, however it may be disguised.

Nonetheless, higher personal saving has to be an important part of any long-term Social Security reform. Demographics alone dictate that some of the baby boomers' claims will have to be funded by previous saving, because the baby busters will not be able to maintain real retirement security for the baby boomers simply from their wages. It's time to recover the attitudes and habits of self-reliance and thrift, and retire the proposition that everyone should consume more than they produce.

To these ends, the Commission should evaluate proposals for gradually shifting some part of the current payroll tax to mandatory personal savings accounts. The goal is to create a safe and progressive two-tier system that would include a public benefit to ensure the basic retirement security of all low and middle income retired Americans, as well as mandatory private savings that can generate returns at current interest rates.

We can test the security and public acceptability of this strategy by returning the current payroll tax surpluses to those paying them, as deposits in individual private retirement accounts. Over recent decades, U.S. equities have generated returns that are healthy over the long run but unstable over shorter periods. A crucial question is whether the markets can develop ways to guarantee the truly stable and sound returns that most retirees need. If the market passes this test and Americans like the results, mandatory private saving could be extended. Still, the transition to such a system would be neither free nor painless. It would probably have to be financed in part through additional benefit reforms or revenue increases from some other source.

Since most people know little about investing and do little of it, we would have to carefully examine how best to balance the potential risks and rewards of a greater element of mandatory private saving. For example, investment in these accounts could be restricted to the new inflation-indexed Treasury bonds and very broadly based stock indexes. And for the foreseeable future, Social Security would continue to play the primary and dominant role in most Americans' retirements.

Who's Protecting Whom?

Social Security's great achievement in sharply reducing poverty among seniors sometimes obscures the system's less progressive aspects. Perhaps inadvertently, Social Security today transfers resources not only from middle-class suburban taxpayers to poor inner-city widows, but also from struggling garment workers in North Carolina to wealthy retirees in Boca Raton.

The most regressive part of these arrangements is the current payroll tax. While income taxes favor low income families by exempting everyone's initial income and applying higher tax rates as people's incomes rise, the payroll tax takes almost an opposite approach: Wages and salaries are taxed only up to $65,000; they are taxed at a flat rate; and income from interest, dividends, and capital gains is exempt. As a result, moderate and average income Americans find themselves paying a 12.4 percent retirement tax on virtually all they earn, while affluent people pay no retirement tax on the portion of their salaries exceeding the cap nor on any of their capital income. Only at the very bottom do these taxes turn progressive, since the Earned Income Tax Credit refunds the payroll taxes paid by working-poor families.

On the benefit side, the current Social Security formulas contain some elements that favor the well-to-do and others that favor everyone else. But in the end, higher-earning people receive larger monthly checks than those who earned less, and the gap can amount to *hundreds of thousands* of dollars over the course of a person's retirement. For example, a low income, one-earner couple who retired in 1995 will collect Social Security totaling a little less than $135,000 (measured in 1993 dollars), while a high-earning, one-earner couple will receive more than $305,000.[19] And when the last baby boomers retire in 2030, the current system will pay a low earner a little more than $187,000 while his high-earning counterpart will collect $493,000.

The combination of high payroll tax burdens on average working families and larger benefits for well-to-do retirees raises serious questions about the current program's intergenerational transfers. Young critics of the system have a valid point: The average retiree aged sixty-five to sixty-nine today has a higher income, counting Social Security, than a typical person in their twenties paying the payroll taxes.[20] Older Americans also bear lower overall tax burdens than everyone else with comparable incomes. For example, a person over age sixty-five with an average income pays less than 8 percent of that income in federal taxes, while a working person with the same income pays more than 22 percent. Retirees also receive more in-kind benefits from government than other groups, and their incomes often go further because they support smaller households.

In 1979 for example, the average retiree, had only 90 percent as much cash income as the average working person. But taking other factors into account—taxes, living expenses, and in-kind benefits—the typical senior had 14 percent more disposable income than the typical worker.[21]

Still, most elderly people are far from affluent. Many shoulder or face the burden of financing their own long-term care. Moreover, most very old people continue to live in very strained circumstances, in part because older retirees receive much smaller Social Security benefits than more recent retirees. The typical American in her late seventies lives today on less than $15,000—including Social Security—and those in their eighties have to get by on an average of less than $13,000 a year. The current Social Security system has some serious distributional flaws, but its defects do *not* include overly generous payments to millions of very elderly widows and widowers.

Accordingly, the Commission should evaluate the range of issues and approaches for reducing the regressive aspects of the current intergenerational transfers. As noted earlier, shifting part of the payroll tax to mandatory private saving accounts would ease some of the tax's regressive effects. On the benefit side, this chapter suggested earlier that we should limit cost-of-living adjustments for affluent retirees. We should also consider additional means-testing measures. Some analysts believe that sharp benefit reductions for affluent people would erode the broad public support the program enjoys today, and so ultimately harm lower income retirees. While there is no hard evidence to back up these concerns, there are good economic reasons to be cautious about strictly means-testing Social Security benefits. In particular, if people know that a higher private income when they retire will mean much smaller benefits, it may discourage the saving that produces the income. This effect could probably be minimized by a modest adjustment in the upper end of the benefit formula.

A different approach would involve a more basic reform: Exempt from payroll taxes the first few thousands of dollars that all people earn in wages, and replace the revenues through other tax reforms affecting higher income people. For example, exempting the first $2,000 of wages from the retirement tax, on both the employee and employer's side, would cost about $28 billion a year. These funds could be replaced by closing industry tax loopholes and reducing income tax deductions for the very well-to-do. This approach would not only lessen the regressive income transfers under the current system, it also should spur job creation by reducing a company's cost of hiring new workers.

Conclusion

Social Security presents President Clinton with a challenge worthy of his second term: lead a national dialogue and help build a consensus to preserve Social Security's achievements and purpose on new foundations that are more fiscally sustainable, economically sound, and socially progressive.

Americans must accept that the most popular program of the postwar era must change to survive. Only the President can lead this effort, and only a truly nonpartisan, blue-ribbon National Commission can fairly evaluate the alternatives and assure Americans that change can serve everyone's interests.

Two simple principles can guide these reforms. First, we cannot and should not perpetuate the outdated and unsustainable tenet that everyone, regardless of their resources, should consume much more than they produce over their lifetimes. Second, we can and should guarantee that everyone will have the resources required to live in dignity when they retire.

Certain directions for these reforms are evident. The current charade of Trust Fund financing should end. Large windfall payments to affluent people should be reduced. Baby boomers and busters should agree to work longer before retiring. The payroll tax system can be made more progressive. And perhaps most important of all, some provision for mandatory private saving should be introduced to restore a two-pronged, public-private approach to retirement security.

But none of this will be possible, unless and until we agree to end our long collective silence about the problems of Social Security.

Notes

1. Social Security Administration, *Source Material for Alternative II, 1996 Annual Report of the Board of Trustees of the Federal Old Age and Survivors and Disability Insurance Trust Funds* (Government Printing Office, 5 June 1996).

2. David Cutler, "Reexamining the Three-Legged Stool," in *Social Security: What Role for the Future?* ed. Peter Diamond, David Lindeman, and Howard Young (Washington, DC: National Academy of Social Insurance, 1996), 127.

3. Gary Burtless, "Social Security Income and Taxation: Four Views on the Role of Means Testing," *Social Security: What Role for the Future?* 177.

4. Cutler, "Reexamining the Three-Legged Stool," *Social Security*, 126–127.

5. Some 43 percent of elderly Americans collect private pension payments, which total 17 percent of all income received by elderly people; 22 percent of seniors continue to work, and these earnings also account for 17 percent of the elderly's cash resources. See David Cutler, "Reexamining the Three-Legged Stool," *Social Security: What Role for the Future?* 127.

6. The fifteen years in this century in which the real value of the Standard & Poors composite index fell by 40 percent or more in the succeeding ten years were 1908, 1909, 1910, 1911, 1912, 1937, 1938, 1939, 1965, 1966, 1968, 1969, 1970, 1971, 1972 and 1973. Unpublished analysis by Robert Shiller, Yale University.

7. Henry J. Aaron, Barry P. Bosworth, and Gary T. Burtless, *Can America Afford to Grow Old? Paying for Social Security* (Washington, DC: The Brookings Institution, 1989).

8. C. Eugene Steuerle and Jon M. Bakija, *Retooling Social Security for the 21st Century, Right and Wrong Approaches to Reform*, (Washington, DC: The Urban Institute Press, 1994), 107.

9. A single man retiring in 1995 after earning an average of $60,000 a year, in current dollars, can expect to collect benefits totaling $37,100 less than the value of the payroll taxes he paid. Single women with comparable earnings retiring in 2010 will absorb a shortfall of $84,100 over the course of their retirements. Finally, an affluent baby boomer couple that earned an average of $100,000 a year in today's dollars while working, and retiring in 2010, also will collect considerably less than they paid in: The value of their contributions should come to $476,300, and they would expect to collect $394,200, for a net cost of $73,100. Ibid.

10. Barry Bosworth, "Fund Accumulation: How Much? How Managed?" in *Social Security: What Role for the Future?* 94.

11. Steuerle and Bajika, *Retooling Social Security*, Table 3.4, 49.

12. See Robert J. Shapiro, "Cut-and-Invest: A Budget Strategy for the New Economy" (Washington, DC: Progressive Policy Institute, Policy Report No. 23, March 1995).

13. See discussion in Lawrence H. Thompson, "The Social Security Debate," *Journal of Economic Literature* 21 (December 1983): 1425–1467.

14. Alan J. Auerbach et al., "The Annuitization of Americans' Resources: A Cohort Analysis," NBER Working Paper #5089 (Cambridge, MA: National Bureau for Economic Research, October 1994).

15. Cutler, "Reexamining the Three-Legged Stool," *Social Security: What Role for the Future?* 145.

16. Of everyone who reaches age sixty-five, roughly one-third can expect to die before reaching age seventy-five; another one-third will die before age eighty-five, and the last one-third will live beyond that. Ibid., 132.

17. Robert Brown, "Social Security and Retirees: Two Views of the Projections: An Actuary's Perspective," *Social Security: What Role for the Future?* 30.

18. In addition, government investments in the stock market would profit the government less than expected, since the government's investment would replace some private investment and so reduce income tax revenues from the dividends and capital gains on the displaced private investments.

19. Steuerle and Bakija, *Retooling Social Security*, 134–137.

20. In 1993, people aged sixty-four to sixty-nine had median incomes of $20,500, supported in part by the payroll taxes of twenty- to twenty-four-year-olds with average incomes of $12,500, and by twenty-five- to twenty-nine-year-olds with average incomes of $19,500.

21. Steuerle and Bakija, *Retooling Social Security,* 138.

Chapter 5

Modernizing Medicare and Medicaid: The First Step Toward Universal Health Care

David B. Kendall

The last two national elections amply demonstrated the political volatility of the health care issue. Without question, the historic setback Democrats suffered in 1994 was due in part to public apprehension about the Clinton health care plan—an effort to secure universal access to health insurance through a new federal entitlement. By the same token, public alarm about Republican plans to contain Medicare and Medicaid costs clearly contributed both to the President's reelection and to Democratic gains in the House this past November.

But even as these two flawed initiatives to expand access to care and to rein in costs were drawing fire, a third issue surfaced—health care quality. This stemmed from the massive shift to managed care strategies in employer-sponsored health insurance plans. From 1988 to 1996, the portion of workers and their families using managed care health plans more than doubled, from 29 percent to 74 percent as shown in Figure 5.1, a trend that shows no signs of slowing.[1]

So, where do matters stand as 1997 begins?

- Managed care, while having succeeded in dramatically holding down health care costs, is under attack as a brutal clampdown on consumers, and a perceived threat to life itself. Despite the baleful media reports on how sick patients are suffering, even dying, due to heartless cost-containment pressures, voters deciding ballot initiatives in the man-

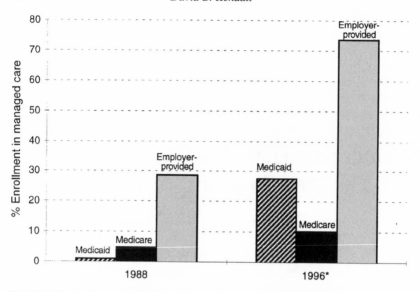

Fig. 5.1. Managed care penetration rates for Medicare and Medicaid versus employer-provided coverage. Medicaid data from Office of Managed Care, Health Care Financing Administration (HCFA). (*Medicaid data is for 1995, the latest year available.*) Medicare data from *Health Care Financing Review, 1996 Statistical Supplement,* HCFA. Data for employer-provided coverage from *Health Benefits in 1996, Executive Summary,* KPMG Peat Marwick.

aged care-dominant markets of California and Oregon firmly rejected so-called patient protection measures that would have imposed costly, government micro-management of managed care.

• We are no closer to universal access to health care than we were in 1994. While last year's Kassebaum-Kennedy legislation did ease the "job lock" problem caused by preexisting condition clauses in employer-sponsored plans, it will not appreciably reduce the number of uninsured Americans, who typically are either temporarily unemployed or have jobs that offer no insurance.

• We have made virtually no progress toward reining in the short-term costs of Medicare and Medicaid. Even worse, we have yet to address the massive, long-term cost crisis that will begin in eight years when the number of working people who support each retiree receiving Medicare acute care and Medicaid long-term care begins to decline. Moreover, this demographic trend will accelerate as baby boomers reach age sixty-five during the period from 2011 to 2027.

Rather than confront these realities, however, America's political leaders have used Medicare to advance narrow partisan agendas. Republicans proposed huge cuts in Medicare's spending growth to make good on their pledge to balance the budget while also offering big tax cuts. Democrats and labor unions spent millions on political ads assailing Republicans for attempting to gut the program. Unfortunately, the apparent success of "medigoguery" in the recent election diminishes prospects that the two parties will stop using Medicare as a partisan club and join forces to fix its urgent problems. The danger is that too many Democrats will see reflexive defense of Medicare as a political trump card, and too many Republicans will shy from any serious effort to reform the program.

But progressives cannot ignore the need for fundamental reform of Medicare and Medicaid. The programs must be changed if we are to remove the fiscal, political, and structural obstacles they pose to the goal of covering the forty million uninsured Americans; and if we are to prevent their exploding costs from crowding out other vital public investments. For example, in the President's most recent budget, nondefense discretionary spending—which encompasses education and training, housing and urban aid, highways, criminal justice, and research and development—was essentially frozen at $275 billion, while Social Security, Medicare, and other entitlement programs were allowed to rise from $875 billion to $1.2 trillion in 2002.[2] As Figure 5.2 shows, the future of progressive government hinges on our willingness to restrain the growth of entitlements.

During the presidential debates, both Bob Dole and President Clinton endorsed the idea of a blue-ribbon commission on Medicare reform, similar to the 1983 commission which staved off bankruptcy in Social Security. Such a commission, however, must avoid short-term fixes, such as payroll tax increases and modest benefit reductions, intended to postpone the basic structural changes that Medicare needs. Moreover, Medicare's future should not be decided in isolation, but must be linked to the larger project of building a universal system of private health insurance. That requires changing government's role from entitling people to receive medical benefits to empowering consumers to make cost-conscious choices within a robust health care marketplace.

President Clinton can leave no greater legacy than a "new deal" on Medicare, Medicaid, and other entitlements—a bargain that preserves the great social achievements they represent by restraining their costs and adapting their structure to reflect the new technologies and organizations of the Information Age. As the first president from the baby boom generation, Clinton has a special responsibility to ensure that the burden of caring for the boomers in their retirement doesn't fall solely on their children.

David B. Kendall

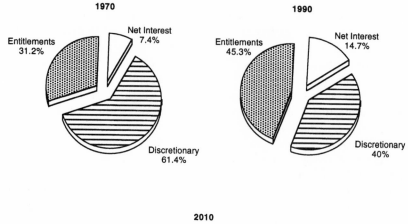

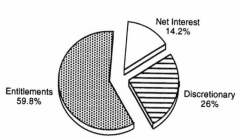

Fig. 5.2. Entitlement versus discretionary spending, 1970, 1990, 2010. Data for 1970 and 1990 from *Budget of the United States Government, Fiscal Year 1997*. Estimates for 2010 from *Bipartisan Commission on Entitlement and Tax Reform, Final Report*, 1995.

What the Market Tells Us

Even as politicians argue over how to restrain Medicare and Medicaid costs and whether it is possible to modify the old-fashioned fee-for-service delivery system, health care in the private sector is moving in a dramatically new direction. In a trend that is entirely independent from any changes in government health care policy, the traditional system of physicians practicing independently is rapidly yielding to a new system, in which networks of doctors, hospitals, and insurers compete for the business of patients.

In the emerging media stereotype, "managed care" means an insurer-owned health maintenance organization (HMO) in which accountants, with no knowledge of or interest in medicine, consistently overrule the clinical judgment of doctors to save money. In fact, managed care is a widely varied and constantly evolving array of organizations, many of which put teams of health care professionals fully in charge of both clinical and budgetary decisions. Indeed, Minnesota employers are experimenting with a brand of managed care in which they deal directly with doctors and hospitals, eliminating the insurer's role altogether. But no single type of organization is the "perfect" model, and consumers today face an alphabet soup of choices which range from PPOs (preferred provider organizations) to PSNs (provider-sponsored networks) to IPAs (independent practice associations).

In theory, these organizations reduce health care costs by eliminating inappropriate or unnecessary care. Managed care's quality improvement efforts, thus far, have been largely limited to greater use of primary and preventive care for which the benefits are well known. What's missing is reliable information about the quality of specialized services, such as treatment for breast cancer or heart disease. Without it, horror stories about the quality of care will fuel demands for costly regulations that have no assurance of solving the problem.

Managed care opponents are fighting against one of the most powerful market-driven trends in the history of medicine. Apart from managed care's impressive growth rate—which some researchers estimate will reach 80 percent of the total insured population by the year 2000[3]—competition among managed care plans has begun to break the back of medical inflation. In fact, the gap between medical inflation (4.5 percent in 1995) and nonmedical inflation (2.7 percent) is at its narrowest point since 1981.[4]

The glaring exceptions to this rapid change are the public programs, Medicare and Medicaid, in which recipients are typically guaranteed a fee-for-service delivery system if they choose it, regardless of the cost to taxpayers. Not surprisingly, 89 percent of Medicare beneficiaries and 72 percent of Medicaid beneficiaries remain in fee-for-service systems. Medicare and Medicaid's isolation from the rest of the marketplace keeps their costs high. It also prevents the federal government from using the two programs to address problems in the broader health care marketplace.

The Liberal and Conservative Approaches

The traditional liberal and conservative approaches to health care erect insurmountable obstacles to improvements in access, cost, and quality.

For traditional liberals, preserving Medicare (and to a lesser extent, Medicaid) as a government-run, fee-for-service health insurance entitlement is an unshakable article of faith. Many cling fiercely to the dream of extending the Medicare model universally—to transform the entire U.S. health system into a Canadian-style, single-payer system. Others have no larger health care agenda apart from "saving" Medicare from reform, even though unrestrained Medicare spending creates fiscal, political, and structural obstacles to the progressive goal of universal access to health insurance.

To the extent conservatives have any coherent approach to health care other than the protection of the status quo as "the best health care system in the world," they are increasingly attracted to the cure-all known as the Medical Savings Account (MSA), a new tax subsidy aimed at diverting public and private insurance premiums into personal accounts for the purchase of routine health care services from individual providers. The basic thrust of MSAs is to use the power and resources of government to limit health insurance to coverage of catastrophic illnesses.

Single-payer and MSA advocates share a hostility to collectively purchased private health insurance, and an unwillingness to come to grips with the fact that patients' demands for and the supply of catastrophic care are the main sources of medical inflation. Under a single-payer system, these costs would have to be accommodated by either steady increases in public funding, tight restrictions on care, or the kind of provider regulation that has universally resulted in reduced access. For example, recent budget-cutting measures in Ontario, Canada, have forced obstetricians to refuse new patients, leading one expectant mother to wonder: "Do I simply sit in emergency and scream until someone delivers my baby?"[5] Under MSAs, insurance premiums would resume their steady upward spiral unless integrated with the cost-reducing pressures of managed care. Both would hold improvements in access and quality hostage to expanded public expenditures, a singularly unrealistic, long-term task in view of the looming demands of aging baby boomers.

While the public generally, and Congress specifically, are not about to embrace either a single-payer system or a full-fledged commitment to MSAs, the domination of public policy by these two eccentric views is potentially disastrous. Given rising public concerns about the quality implications of managed care, the left and right might well converge on a policy of disabling managed care without addressing cost and access issues—an outcome that would virtually guarantee the United States meeting the baby boom retirement crisis hobbled by the devastating medical inflation rates of the 1980s, and with the ranks of the uninsured rising.

A New Paradigm for Health Care

Health care is a textbook example of a public policy area in need of a new paradigm, one which transcends the entitlement mentality of the left and the "I got mine" mentality of the right. Two key principles of the New Progressive

Declaration are especially relevant for health care policy: creating public institutions that empower citizens to act for themselves, and pursuing public goals through market means.

Today, government operates as a provider of health insurance in Medicare and Medicaid, as a subsidizer of private health insurance through the tax deduction for employer contributions to health care plans, and as a regulator of both public and private health insurance.

For all their undoubted value in guaranteeing health insurance to the elderly and the indigent, Medicare and Medicaid are bureaucratic dinosaurs. They restrict choice of health plans for their beneficiaries, and rely on regulatory fiat rather than market forces to address cost and quality of care. Any Information Age reform of these entitlements must inject choice and competition into their operations, and must replace paternalistic decision making with informed empowerment.

Employer-sponsored health care benefits are exempt from federal income and payroll taxes. This powerful tax subsidy is the main reason why employers offer benefits to most of their workers and not just executives. But its control by employers discriminates decisively against the unemployed, those who work in small- and medium-sized enterprises without health benefits, and those who would prefer an insurance option other than what the employer offers.

The current regulatory practices of government in health care rely almost exclusively on command-and-control strategies such as mandated benefits rather than market forces and consumer information. Thus, consumers are at the mercy of struggles between the regulators and the regulated.

In all its roles, government is constantly and inevitably choosing among the goals of expanding access, controlling costs, and ensuring quality.

True reform of the health care system should address the issues of cost, access, and quality simultaneously—and in a manner tailored not only to immediate needs, but to the period just over the horizon, when baby boom retirees threaten to make costs unsustainable, greater access unaffordable, and quality care unachievable.

Beginning with Medicare and Medicaid, government must become a catalyst for a decentralized, market-based, information-driven health care system. The three goals of reform should be:

• Introducing market discipline into Medicare and Medicaid, restraining costs, increasing choice, and improving quality.

• Blazing a path to universal access to private health insurance by linking all government health insurance subsidies to market prices and individual need.

- Using government policy to set the ground rules for competition in the marketplace, ensuring choice and information for consumers, and encouraging private-sector, health-care purchasing cooperatives to maximize the benefits of this new system to all consumers—be they Medicare or Medicaid beneficiaries, employees, or individual purchasers.

The Threat to Medicare and Medicaid: Soaring Costs

Clearly, Medicare and Medicaid have been a success: They have provided health care for millions of the elderly, the poor, and the disabled, and long-term care for many others as well. Before their enactment in 1965, one half of the elderly and most of the poor were uninsured. Today, none of the elderly and only one-third of the poor are uninsured.

But their key shortcoming is equally clear: soaring costs. In the short run, high per capita costs are the problem. In the long run, the baby boom generation will greatly increase the number of beneficiaries. The numbers on past and future spending dramatize the cost spiral:

- Since their inception, Medicare and Medicaid's share of the economy has grown sixfold. It doubled from 1967 to 1973, doubled again from 1973 to 1987, and will double a third time from 1987 to 2000, at which point it will represent 6 percent of gross domestic product, reflecting both higher medical costs and more beneficiaries.[6]

- The Medicare Part A trust fund, which covers hospital costs, is already operating in the red and will be bankrupt in 2001, unable to pay the health bills for all of its beneficiaries.[7]

- Medicare payroll taxes would have to be more than doubled to sustain current spending levels and keep the program operating in the black past 2030.

- In 2030, the share of national resources required to care for Medicare and Medicaid beneficiaries alone will be about the same as what we spend today caring for *all* Americans.[8]

Medicare and Medicaid's basic structure inherently drives up costs. Both were created as open-ended entitlements to government-sponsored, fee-for-service coverage. For the disabled and retirees sixty-five and older, patients choose their hospitals and doctors and Medicare pays their bills directly. Most beneficiaries also have private, supplemental insurance (which costs roughly $800 a year on average) or use an employer-provided retirement benefit to pay for the "gaps" in Medicare coverage: deductibles, copayments, and limits on lengthy hospital stays. All beneficiaries also pay a $45 monthly fee to help pay doctors' bills (known as the Medicare Part B premium). These premiums cover only 25 percent of the total Part B costs; taxpayers foot the remaining 75 percent.

Unlike Medicare, Medicaid eligibility is based on income and family status. Under the first of its two parts—acute care—children and pregnant women living under or near the poverty level are guaranteed medical coverage. Welfare recipients with children also qualify. One-third of the nonelderly poor lack coverage, however, primarily because Medicaid does not guarantee coverage to poor individuals without children. (Medicaid also pays for the supplemental Medicare coverage of the elderly poor). State governments, which operate Medicaid, can use managed care plans only if they obtain federal waivers, which have become increasingly common under the Clinton administration.

The second part of Medicaid—long-term care—guarantees nursing home coverage to low income Americans with few assets. Many middle-class households, however, have come to rely on Medicaid for long-term care. The reason in some cases is that they have exhausted their resources during an initial nursing home stay; in other cases, individuals transfer their assets to relatives in order to qualify for Medicaid.

In their current form, Medicare and Medicaid cannot rely on market forces to govern the price for services. In effect, beneficiaries can demand unlimited services for covered benefits at whatever reimbursement rate the government is willing to pay. Not surprisingly, seven years after they were created, the actual cost of Medicare and Medicaid exceeded projections by 400 percent.

To be sure, Medicare and Medicaid costs are being driven up by the same forces inflating costs in the private sphere: new technology, trends in medical education and specialization, and medical malpractice insurance, to name a few. But Medicare and Medicaid have five features that clearly make matters worse:

Outmoded delivery system

Under Medicare and Medicaid's fee-for-service medicine, doctors have an incentive to overtreat patients because they are paid a fee for every service they perform. In contrast, managed care health plans receive a fixed sum regardless of the number of services they provide, and thus have an incentive to economize.

Lack of preventive and primary care

Fee-for-service medicine tends to put a specialist in charge of every disease, and no one in charge of the patient. As a result, preventive and primary care take a back seat to specialty care. One study looked at the utilization under Medicare of three preventive measures that are universally conceded as beneficial: biennial mammograms for older women, annual eye exams for diabetics, and electrocardiograms within three months of a diagnosis of congestive heart failure. Sixty percent of Medicare recipients who would benefit from these procedures did not receive them.[9] In Medicaid, the lack of access to primary care has prompted many beneficiaries to turn to hospital emergency rooms for routine care. Without appropriate primary and preventive care, costs increase and patient health declines.

Regulatory price controls

Medicare and Medicaid control spending not through market forces but government price-setting. Specifically, Congress and state legislatures have made provider payment rates a matter of law, which means that elected officials determine the amount that health care professionals can earn from Medicare and Medicaid. During the annual political struggle over setting these rates, the senior citizens' lobby and health care provider groups invariably predict disastrous consequences from lower payments. While no one doubts there is a level of provider payments below which access and quality will suffer, the politicians making these decisions have no objective way to separate exaggerated claims from honest assessments of the impact of cost restraint.

Expanding ranks of beneficiaries

Eligibility for Medicare has remained constant despite great changes in the average lifespan and financial status of seniors. Medicare enrollment has expanded gradually to 14 percent of the population as the average life expectancy of sixty-five-year-olds has increased (by two-and-one-half years, to age eighty-two) since Medicare's inception. During that same time period, the average income of Americans aged sixty-five and older has also increased by 70 percent more than the income of nonelderly Americans whose tax payments support the entitlements. Moreover, older Americans' poverty rate is half the nonelderly's poverty rate. But the really alarming change in enrollment will occur early in the next century. Projections show the number of workers supporting each beneficiary will decline by nearly half, from 3.9 in

1995 to 2.2 in 2030 when all the baby boomers will have retired. These demographic changes will increase Medicare's acute care and Medicaid's long-term care costs and decrease our ability to pay for them.

Consumption at the expense of investment

Higher Medicare and Medicaid spending is crowding out funding for other vital functions of government. In just over ten years, Medicare and Medicaid have doubled their share of both federal and state budgets, and now consume about one-fifth of these budgets. This trend means fewer funds for basic research, education, the environment, and public infrastructure such as highways. The entitlement cost spiral has also contributed massively to the continuing federal budget deficit, which in turn reduces private investment.

A New Deal for Medicare and Medicaid

Aligning the interests of beneficiaries and taxpayers is the top priority of Medicare and Medicaid reform: Beneficiaries should receive the highest quality medical care, at the lowest possible cost to taxpayers. To achieve this goal, we need a new deal for the health care entitlements. Rather than entitle people to coverage regardless of the cost or quality of care, Medicare and Medicaid should give them a subsidy large enough to pay for a private health plan offering high-quality care. Budgeting would be performance-based, not politically determined. High-quality, low-cost health plans—regardless of type (fee-for-service or managed care)—would set the benchmark for Medicare and Medicaid spending.

Reducing costs and improving quality through consumer choice

While it may sound counterintuitive, the highest quality medical care can have the lowest cost. The world-famous Mayo Clinic in Rochester, Minnesota, practices cost-effective medicine by following the precept, "do it right the first time." Mayo clinicians commit substantial resources "up front" to diagnose a patient's symptoms correctly. They do not waste time and money fixing the wrong problem. The cost of patient care in Rochester, which is served almost exclusively by the Mayo Clinic, is 22 percent below the national average.[10]

The rough framework for a system that promotes high-quality, low-cost health care is already in place among the nation's large employers, such as the IBM Corporation and the federal government. Instead of a single, employer-pays-all benefit plan, these employers provide a contribution for basic coverage and a menu of choices for each employee, which usually includes both managed care and fee-for-service plans. Once a year, after the employers have negotiated prices with a variety of provider groups for the next twelve months, workers select a plan based on their own budget and priorities.

Liberals often argue that consumers cannot effectively shop for health care because no one chooses when to become sick or injured. While this may be true in an emergency, the experience of millions of workers at large companies proves that consumers can make responsible choices about their coverage.

The main obstacle to effective consumer choice in health care is clear and reliable information about quality of care. Two leading experts, Doctors Paul Ellwood, leader of the Jackson Hole Group, and George Lundberg, editor of *The Journal of the American Medical Association*, have proposed quality measures, or health plan "report cards," as "the central tool for health care reform and redesign."[11]

Health plan report cards may soon become a familiar feature of insurance purchasing. The Foundation for Accountability, a coalition of the nation's largest private and public purchasers of care (representing more than eighty million Americans, including Medicare and Medicaid beneficiaries), recently created a common checklist of quality indicators. Beginning in 1998, these reports will provide consumers with the information they need to choose among health plans based on the plans' actual track records in handling such diseases as breast cancer, diabetes, and severe depression.

Medicare and Medicaid beneficiaries, who suffer more chronic conditions than the general population, would benefit most from the widespread adoption of these report cards. One recent study showed that in the early 1990s, managed care health plans produced the same health outcomes for the average patient as did fee-for-service arrangements, but had worse outcomes for patients with chronic conditions.[12] Clearly, timely and reliable report cards would help government set appropriate standards of care, if necessary.

Making more efficient use of services

By injecting competition into Medicare and Medicaid, health care delivery will become more efficient. Consider open-heart surgery, which has the best results and lowest costs when the same teams of doctors and nurses perform the operation regularly and frequently. The American College of Cardiology recommends a minimum of 200 to 300 open-heart surgeries per facility per year to achieve high quality care. Yet less than half of the hospitals in the highly competitive California marketplace perform the 200 minimum surgeries, and fewer than one-fourth perform 300.[13] Overall, California has four-and-one-half times more hospital beds than it needs, based on existing benchmarks for high-quality care. Closing these low-volume facilities and redirecting patients to centers of excellence would both cut costs and improve patient outcomes.

By 2001, the cumulative effect of such efficiency gains would reduce the need for physicians, specialists in particular, by one-third overall.[14] A competitive marketplace would drive down physicians' salaries and increase savings to consumers. The signs of change are already unmistakable: In 1995, the average physician's income declined to $187,000, reversing a decades-old upward trend.[15]

Consumers will need to be well organized in the marketplace to overcome predictable resistance to change from stakeholders in the current system. The creation of large purchasing groups that actively negotiate on behalf of consumers are critical to an efficient marketplace. In effect, these large groups would "manage the competition," creating a buyer's market for health care.

State governments have begun to purchase services actively on behalf of Medicaid patients. But Medicare, in spite of its potentially tremendous group purchasing power, is simply too big to act nimbly on behalf of consumers. To assert their marketing clout to its fullest, older Americans themselves and their leaders will have to create and voluntarily join such purchasing groups.

Equitable financing for coverage

Intended as a "safety net" for the elderly and the poor, Medicare and Medicaid in fact contribute enormously to inequities in health care coverage, and to the persistently high level of the uninsured.

Medicare provides full benefits to wealthy, readily employable older Americans who need no assistance. Moreover, these benefits are being paid for in no small measure by low-wage workers—many of whom lack health insurance themselves.

Medicaid, the insurer of "last resort," is in fact riddled with gaps in coverage. Despite the passage of welfare reform, Medicaid continues to be linked to welfare eligibility rules, rather than a simple income test. Thus, when welfare recipients find jobs, they will lose Medicaid coverage within a year regardless of whether their jobs pay little. In addition, Medicaid does not guarantee coverage to low income adults without children.

The route to fair and universal coverage is crystal clear: Medicare benefits should be reduced at higher income levels, the retirement age should be increased, and Medicaid should be extended to all the poor.

Step-by-Step Reform

Reform must proceed, step-by-step, to galvanize broad support, permit beneficiaries to adjust, and avoid unnecessary mistakes.

Step One: Preserve Medicare through consumer choice and responsibility

All Medicare beneficiaries should be given a health purchasing account that enables them to buy coverage every year. The amount would be based on the premiums of the highest quality, lowest cost health plans. Unlike MSAs, these health purchasing accounts would be used to pay for all health expenses—both ordinary and catastrophic.

Every year, the federal government would send consumers a statement of their account, a menu of their options, and information about the quality of care. Consumers could supplement their accounts with their own money to purchase more expensive plans. If a consumer enrolled in a less expensive health plan, he or she could use the savings however he or she saw fit.

In addition, older Americans could join Medicare Consumer Cooperatives, which would be established by senior citizens' groups, employers on behalf of their retirees, unions, or other voluntary organizations. The cooperatives would negotiate a menu of options on their members' behalf, producing better value for their money.

Medicare's benefit package—designed in the 1960s and changed little since—would be updated for the current marketplace. It would cover the system's current gaps in coverage by placing an annual limit on total out-of-pocket costs. This step would eliminate the need for supplemental coverage, which creates a duplicative insurance system.

The full range of plan types (e.g., HMOs, IPAs, PPOs, PSNs, and fee-for-service) would post bids for the cost of delivering the new package of benefits annually. The lowest-cost plans with the highest-quality ratings would set the benchmark. This benchmark premium amount would guarantee that all older Americans could afford to purchase high quality care.

Health plans would offer varying benefits within limits set by the government. Such regulations would achieve two purposes: They would prevent plans from shirking patients with high health costs (such as the severely mentally ill); and they would prevent consumers who know they will be needing health care in the near future from switching plans to take advantage of lower out-of-pocket costs.

Medicare's traditional fee-for-service plan would be treated the same as any other health plan, competing with all others on equal terms. If it offered the highest quality plan at the lowest cost, it would set the benchmark premium. It would have an annual budget set by the insurance premiums from older Americans and would be free to manage its costs effectively without congressional micromanagement.

A leading research firm, Lewin-VHI, estimates that this approach would save the government between $80 billion and $100 billion over seven years.[16]

If combined with other budgetary proposals common to both the Clinton administration and GOP 1996 budgets, the total amount would be well within the range of necessary savings for the short-term goals of balancing the budget and averting backruptcy.

Step Two: Add flexibility and accountability to Medicaid

Although Medicaid is subject to federal rules, it is wholly administered by the states. Thus, it makes no sense to dictate the details of a system of consumer choice and responsibility from Washington. Instead, states should be given flexibility to set up such systems on their own, but be held accountable for results. Congress should remove existing restrictions on the use of private health plans and competition in Medicaid, and cap the funding on a per-person basis, as President Clinton has proposed. This per-person cap would reflect the variations in state populations (and poverty levels) and would be adjusted using data from the Medicare system to account for regional cost differences. Many states such as Arizona, Ohio, Minnesota, and Wisconsin have pioneered systems that would readily fit this new federal framework.[17]

States would have a strong incentive to set up a consumer choice system because they would be driven by two outcomes: the cost and quality of the care. The inefficiency (and resulting inequity) of Medicaid's open-ended subsidy has produced extraordinary disparity in state spending on medical care. The variation was fourfold in 1993, from a high of $9,700 per beneficiary in New Hampshire to a low of $2,381 in Mississippi. Focused quite naturally on their own expenditures, some states have sought to hold down Medicaid costs even at the expense of patient's access to quality care, while others have adopted the strategy of maximizing federal payments. Federal Medicaid policy encourages the latter approach as much as the former.

The GOP's proposed block grants for Medicaid would give states flexibility, but would not hold them accountable. Specifically, states could simply cut beneficiaries from Medicaid to meet their budget, rather than let competition make the health care system more efficient. Funding should follow the patient, not a state bureaucracy.

During the 1995–96 congressional debate on the balanced budget bill, the National Governors' Association (NGA) tried to bridge the policy gap between President Clinton and Republicans with a proposal for block grants with per capita funding. Unfortunately, it was doomed both by its own flaws and unrelenting partisanship.

In the next debate, President Clinton, whose personal commitment to Medicaid is well known, should reach out to Republicans to revive the NGA proposal while fixing the problems. He should press for expansion of Medicaid coverage to all the poor by using the savings of a per capita cap on Medicaid.

**Step Three: Expand access and choice in the private sector
through tax credits**

America has a moral duty to cover its uninsured: Lack of health care coverage is clearly detrimental to one's health. One study estimates that the uninsured, who receive inadequate primary and preventive care, are 25 percent
more likely to die prematurely.[18] By comparison, the lack of health insurance
is eight times more life threatening than driving without a safety belt.

Moreover, changes in the marketplace are forcing the need for action: Just
as automobile manufacturers do not give away cars for free, a competitive
health care market will not give away care for free. In the past, providers
"shifted" the costs of caring for indigent patients to paying patients in the
form of higher charges. Today's competitive marketplace discourages charity
care and emergency care for the uninsured, to the extent that providers can
avoid admitting or treating the uninsured.

Tax policy is the place to begin rectifying this problem. Health care benefits,
unlike wages, are not taxed. This tax subsidy costs the federal treasury $84
billion a year, making it Washington's third largest health program after Medicare ($200 billion) and Medicaid ($135 billion). The tax break is inequitable:
People who work for companies that provide health benefits receive it, but
unemployed workers and those with less generous employers do not. Moreover, it is regressive: Like all tax deductions, it is worth more to high income
workers. The health care tax break for households with incomes above
$100,000 is *ten times greater* than it is for households with incomes below
$10,000.

Current tax policy also contributes to higher costs. The tax break is unlimited. Thus, the more your employer spends on health insurance, the bigger
your tax break. Moreover, the subsidy creates the false impression that health
benefits are a cost borne only by employers, and are not a part of overall
compensation. When employers appear to be paying the whole bill and Washington subsidizes the choices, workers have little incentive to demand the best-
value health plan they can get. In effect, the federal government picks up a
large chunk of the bill when employees pick more costly options.

A refundable income tax credit would be a more equitable, efficient alternative to current tax policy. The new credit would exist side by side with existing
employer-provided coverage; workers could elect to take their employers'
health care without losing the job-based tax break, or claim the credit on their
income taxes and use the money to buy coverage on their own or through
purchasing groups. The credit would be worth the same to all workers, regardless of their income and regardless of how much insurance coverage they buy.
It would also expand choices for workers with job-based coverage by creating
options outside the workplace.

The value of the tax credit would depend on the revenue available to pay for it. Setting aside one-fifth of the tax break for job-based coverage would fund a $900 tax credit for workers between jobs or without coverage, assuming that one-half of the uninsured used the credit. Alternatively, the tax credit could be phased in first for workers temporarily laid off or for children who lack coverage today.

A Time for Bold Action

Taken together, the steps outlined above would:

- rein in the Medicare/Medicaid cost spiral without sacrificing benefits or quality;

- extend coverage to millions of the uninsured;

- empower all Americans with more choice and control over their health care options, and;

- make access, cost, and quality mutually reinforcing factors in health care purchasing and delivery; not competing priorities.

The first step on the road to health care reform—modernizing Medicare and Medicaid—will be resisted fiercely, both by those who are invested in the current system at the expense of the public interest, and by those who are committed to the reactionary panaceas of a single-payer system or MSAs.

Modest as it was, the Kassebaum-Kennedy legislation of 1996 showed that bipartisan action on health care reform is still possible, even at a time when potential common ground is still contaminated by the poisonous partisan rhetoric of the 1994 Clinton health care fight and the 1995 Medicare furor.

A political system that lurches from one health care issue to another—access to care one year, cost the next year, quality still another year—cannot possibly make progress toward a system that promotes all three values, and may well create a nightmare scenario in which access declines, costs spiral out of control, and quality is sacrificed.

Bold bipartisan action on the health care system as a whole is the overriding challenge in health care policy for 1997.

Notes

1. "Health Benefits in 1996" (New York: KPMG Peat Marwick, 1996), 5.
2. Alan Murray, "Any Clinton Mandate Will Be Short on Cash," *Wall Street Journal*, 18 Oct. 1996, 1.

3. Arleen Leibowitz and Robert Brook, oral presentation on Managed Care to Senator William H. Frist (R-Tenn.), 25 July 1996.

4. Stephen K. Heffler et al., "Health Care Indicators: Hospital, Employment, and Price Indicators for the Health Care Industry: Fourth Quarter, 1995, and Annual Data for 1987–95," *Health Care Financing and Review* (Summer 1996): 220.

5. Brian Bergman and Mary Nemeth, "Pregnant Moms and a Medicare War," *Maclean's*, 20 Aug. 1996.

6. David B. Kendall, "A New Deal for Medicare and Medicaid: Building a Buyer's Market for Health Care" (Washington, DC: Progressive Policy Institute, October 1995), 5.

7. The Board of Trustees, Federal Hospital Insurance Trust Fund, "1996 Annual Report" (Washington, DC: U.S. Government), 2.

8. Calculated from data in the Bipartisan Commission on Entitlement and Tax Reform, *Interim Report to the President*, August 1994.

9. Physician Payment Review Commission, "1996 Annual Report to Congress" (Washington, DC: Physician Payment Review Commission), 350–352.

10. Mark Alan Chesner, "Survey of Health Insurance Premiums in 1050 U.S. Cities" (New York: Milliman and Robertson, 16 Nov. 1992).

11. Paul M. Ellwood, Jr. and George D. Lundberg, "Managed Care: A Work in Progress," *The Journal of the American Medical Association* (2 Oct. 1996): 1086.

12. John E. Ware, Jr., et al., "Differences in Four-Year Health Outcomes for Elderly and Poor, Chronically Ill Patients Treated in HMO and Fee-for-Service Systems," *The Journal of the American Medical Association* (2 Oct. 1996): 1039–1047.

13. Alain C. Enthoven and Sara J. Singer, "Managed Competition and California's Health Care Economy," *Health Affairs* (Spring 1996): 51.

14. Steven A. Schroeder, "The Latest Forecast: Managed Care Collides with Physician Supply," *The Journal of the American Medical Association* (20 July 1994): 239.

15. Carol J. Simon and Patricia H. Born, "Physician Earnings in a Changing Managed Care Environment," *Health Affairs* (Fall 1996): 124.

16. John F. Sheils et al., "Medicare Reform Options: An Analysis of Private Coverage, Beneficiary Spending, and the Budget" (Fairfax, VA: The Lewin Group, April 1996).

17. See Kala Ladenheim, "State Medicaid Managed Care for Aid to Families with Dependent Children Populations: Four States' Experience," *The Intergovernmental Health Policy Project, The George Washington University* (Washington, DC: The George Washington University, March 1996).

18. Peter Franks et al., "Health Insurance and Mortality," *The Journal of the American Medical Association* (11 Aug. 1993): 737–741.

Chapter 6

Common Standards, Diverse Schools: Renewing the Promise of Public Education

Kathleen Sylvester

When Thomas Jefferson described the promise of public schooling for the new American nation, he envisioned a system that would "provide an education adapted to the years, to the capacity, and the condition of everyone, and directed to their freedom and happiness."

Today, public schooling falls woefully short of delivering on Jefferson's promise. The public's long-held allegiance to public education is giving way to an urgent sense of duty to do what is best for children. Why should a parent whose child is a first grader in a bad school wait five years for that school to improve?

Only 1 percent of Americans surveyed by the Gallup Organization in 1996 would give the nation's schools an A, while 23 percent would give them a D or an F. Discontent extends well beyond issues of educational achievement. Parents rightly worry that schools are no longer safe places for their children. Some 135,000 guns are brought into schools each day, and metal detectors have become standard equipment in many. Illegal drugs are available in 70 percent of schools; 15 percent of schools report violence-prone gangs among their student bodies.[1]

The erosion of support for public schools is matched by growing support for privatization and vouchers. In the same Gallup poll, 36 percent of the public favored allowing students and parents to choose a private school to attend at public expense, up from 24 percent in 1993. Many parents are dissatisfied with their children's assigned public schools; 45 percent would choose

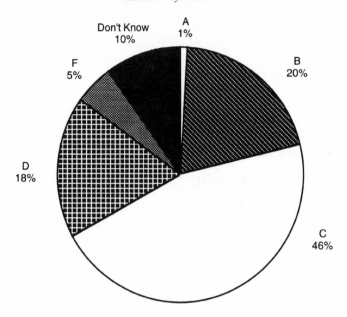

Fig. 6.1. Responses to the question, "What grade would you give the public schools nation-ally?" Data from "The 28th Annual Phi Delta Kappa/Gallup Poll of the Public's Attitudes toward the Public Schools," *Phi Delta Kappan* 78, no. 1.

another school if they could.[2] Increasingly, families that can afford to are abandoning the public system for private education.

Corporations, nonprofit groups, and even some government agencies are changing to meet the imperatives of the Information Age. Yet public schools remain a vestige of the Industrial Age "Taylor model" of organization. Centralized bureaucracies break down the process of education into discrete tasks, then prescribe the means by which each task must be carried out. Multiple layers of administrators concentrate on enforcing the *means* of the educational process while ignoring its *outcomes*.

The business world's abandonment of this outdated organizational model has profound implications for public education. As the report of the National Commission on Teaching and America's Future so clearly states: "There has been no previous time in history when the success, indeed the survival, of nations and people has been so tightly tied to their ability to learn. Today's society has little room for those who cannot read, write, and compute proficiently; find and use resources; frame and solve problems; and continually learn new technologies, skills, and occupations."[3] As the New Progressive Declaration notes, "Education, more than any other institution, is the key to empowering our citizens to act for themselves."

Yet the overall competence of American students has not improved in twenty-five years. Grade inflation and social promotion are accepted as common practice; for many students, a high school diploma is little more than a certificate of attendance. Average scores on the Scholastic Assessment Test (SAT) remain lower today than in the early 1970s;[4] the latest National Assessment of Educational Progress (NAEP) rated only 36 percent of high school seniors as "proficient" readers, and only 16 percent as proficient in math.[5]

For the 38 percent of high school graduates who never go on to college, and for the 78 percent who don't complete college,[6] a high school diploma is worth far less in the marketplace than a generation ago. The era of high-wage jobs for low-skilled workers is fast disappearing. Yet public education continues to prepare most high school graduates for low-skill, low-wage, service-sector jobs. These students have little chance of finding jobs that can support and sustain strong families. And societies that fail to produce strong families have little chance of success in the new global economy.

The need for change is critical. School enrollment is at a record high with projections rising for the next decade and by 1998, American schools will enroll fifty-three million children.[7] New immigrants and increasing numbers of children from disadvantaged families will need public schools that offer them opportunities to do well. If our schools fail these children, all of society will bear the costs of increased poverty and social unrest.

Why the Old Solutions Won't Work

As the new century approaches, Americans face a fundamental choice. We can commit ourselves to rebuilding public education by setting high standards and allowing schools to use diverse means for achieving them. Or we can allow public education to atrophy by continuing to tolerate low standards and making more rules about how teachers should teach to achieve those low standards.

The opportunity to rebuild public education is at hand; the need for reform is urgent, and the public is ready for radical change. But the answer to this enormous challenge does not lie in the old solutions.

For two decades, the left has argued that education reform is fundamentally a question of more resources and better management. The result? Twenty years of top-down prescriptions for change from those who hold the monopoly on public education, and twenty years of tinkering with the methods by which education is delivered. Schools have tried restructuring and reorganizing; experiments with school-based management; new and improved curricula;

smaller classes; longer class periods; and new computers. But even generous doses of shiny new technology cannot fix a fundamentally flawed system.

For too long, professional "educrats" have held the exclusive franchise on public education. They make most of the rules, and they decide what children need and how schools will meet those needs. Unlike other professionals, classroom teachers have little discretion over how they do their jobs, and they are seldom held accountable for their performance. Bad teachers are rarely fired; excellent teachers are rarely rewarded. School boards fire superintendents and school board members lose elections, but the core of adults responsible for public education remains immutable—and largely immune from public pressure.

On the other end of the political spectrum, the right's simplistic insistence on vouchers for private schools diminishes pressure for public school reform precisely at the time such pressure is needed most. Full-scale voucher systems would let both politicians and communities avoid making hard choices. Politicians could declare victory and proclaim themselves reformers. Communities would be lured into complacency, waiting for the market effect—waiting for public schools to react to the exodus of students and dollars. Vouchers have another fatal flaw: They would send public dollars to schools with no public accountability and no obligation to meet public objectives.

It's time to hold the public education system accountable for what the public rightly and sensibly demands—safe and orderly schools in which children master basic knowledge and gain lifelong learning skills. We must renew our national commitment to the fundamental premise that strong public education is essential to a strong democracy. For two hundred years, public education has been the foundation of equal opportunity in this country; it is the sole public institution that guarantees every child the possibility of upward mobility and full participation in our common civic culture.

Americans must reaffirm their commitment to this ideal and reject the alternatives of both the left and the right. Our nation must insist on a reinvigorated public education system that helps every child learn how to learn, grow up to become a good worker, build a strong family, and become an informed citizen.

Redefining Public Education

To redesign public schools for the 21st century, Americans must reconsider the very definition of "public" education and think again about what a public school should be.

Today, public education is defined by its *governance*—who owns and oper-

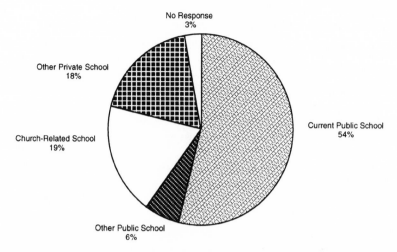

Fig. 6.2. Public school parents' responses to the question, "How would you use a $3,500 voucher?" Data from Phi Delta Kappa/Gallup Poll.

ates it. Schools are public only in the sense that they are funded by public dollars, operated by public school boards, and staffed by public employees.

In the future, public education should be defined by its *purpose* —setting high standards and helping all students meet them. Under this new definition, *any* school would be considered public if it meets these critical purposes and is accountable to a public authority.

In this new system, a school district would most often serve as the guarantor of public accountability. Districts would become purchasers of educational services, holding educational vendors accountable for clearly defined outcomes. Vendors could be groups of teachers, labor unions, nonprofit or for-profit organizations, institutions of higher education, or religiously affiliated organizations.

Such a system would completely reorder the priorities of public education. For too long, Americans have accepted a system that guarantees standardized schools that produce widely diverse standards of quality. It's time to demand a system that allows—and encourages—diverse schools that produce high common standards of quality.

A New Vision of Public Education

What would this new system of public education look like? How must traditional roles change?

As the New Progressive Declaration proposes, "Education, like all public institutions, must operate on the progressive cornerstone of mutual responsibility. Government, citizens, businesses, parents, and students must all play a role."

The federal government must help establish national voluntary academic standards based on a public consensus of what every student should know and be able to do at various points along the educational continuum. No school will truly be able to verify that it is results-oriented until there is common agreement on what the results should be.

In a nation in which one-fifth of all children change schools each year, third graders from Maine to Minnesota to New Mexico should be learning the same core lessons, regardless of how schools and teachers impart those lessons. In a nation in which workers change jobs seven times during a lifetime, a high school diploma must serve as a guarantee that its bearer has achieved a high level of common skills and knowledge.

States must adopt these high common standards and allow schools to achieve them by empowering school districts to become educational purchasers. To make the standards meaningful, states also must require all students to pass rigorous tests to be promoted or to graduate.

States must also target money to ensure that every child has the opportunity to meet these standards; students with special needs must receive extra investments of time and resources. Finally, states must require all schools and school districts to publicly report assessment results in a clear, concise way that parents and communities can understand and trust.

The role of *school districts* must change most dramatically. As districts relinquish their traditional educational service-provider role, they would increasingly become purchasers of those educational services by entering into contracts with vendors. In the early stages of this transformation, these vendors would consist mainly of groups of teachers and administrators already in the public schools. But vendors could also include other organizations— colleges and universities, labor unions, even religiously affiliated schools. Any of these institutions could qualify to receive public dollars by meeting state standards for student achievement and public requirements for health, safety, and nondiscrimination. Religiously affiliated schools would be required to separate religious instruction from the core curriculum.

Beyond these basic regulatory functions, school districts would not further prescribe how schools should operate. Instead, districts would monitor how well each school helps all students meet high public standards. Schools that fail to achieve positive results would lose their contracts, and their students would enroll in better schools.

The roles of *teachers and their unions* must change radically, too. Ultimately, teachers would be accountable for ensuring that all students meet the new rigorous standards. In return, schools would free teachers to use their professional judgment and skills to reach those goals. Unions would continue to serve as teachers' advocates, helping them get the professional training and support they need to help all students and insisting that schools guarantee them safe and stable environments.

Businesses and institutions of higher education must reinforce these efforts by offering a payoff for a high school diploma. They should honor only those diplomas that are backed up by test results that prove students are meeting high common standards.

Parents must become active participants who help define standards for what every student must know and can do. Parents also must become educated consumers who monitor their children's progress toward those goals.

Finally, *students* must invest time and effort in their own futures by working hard to meet standards and becoming active participants in this new education bargain.

Creating this results-oriented system requires a three-part strategy:

- Expand choice and competition within public education systems by transforming the model of charter schools to one of charter districts. School boards would enter into contracts with independently managed schools to educate children.

- Set high common standards for what citizens need to succeed in the information economy. These standards should be national, not federal, and voluntary. Public schools will be defined by their ability to achieve this common core of knowledge. States should make the standards meaningful by requiring students to demonstrate skills and pass tests as a condition for promotion and graduation.

- Make the standards meaningful by linking them to rewards and creating a nation of education consumers. Government must require students to meet high standards to advance in school; business must insist that workers meet high standards to get good jobs. Only then will parents insist on schools that help their children meet these high standards. Schools, in turn, must reward teachers who excel and penalize those who fail. Government must require schools to provide education's new consumers—including chartering districts, parents, and businesses—with clear and easily accessible information that shows whether they are meeting the standards.

Charter Schools, Catholic Schools: Points of Departure

Charter schools, first endorsed and promoted by the PPI in 1990, offer a starting point. Since 1991, citizens and political leaders in twenty-six states and the District of Columbia have eagerly embraced the charter school idea and its results-oriented philosophy. Charter schools are freed from most traditional rules and regulations; in return, they are held accountable to their sponsors for results measured by performance reviews.

Catholic schools offer another reform model. These schools, which must succeed to survive, operate without large centralized bureaucracies. Teachers can be hired without stringent credentialing requirements and can be fired for poor performance. What matters most is their ability to teach.

Charter schools and Catholic schools are also notable for their willingness to take on students with special needs and to serve minorities. The nation's first charter school, The City Academy in St. Paul, Minnesota, was designed specifically for dropouts and students in trouble. Many others also serve children with special needs. In 1996, the Hudson Institute surveyed a national cross-section of charter schools; it found that 63 percent of their students were non-white, and more than half were poor enough to qualify for the federal school lunch program.

In the name of social justice, Catholic schools opened their doors to large numbers of poor and minority students of all religions in the 1970s. They have often succeeded where public schools have failed, helping such students do better on standardized achievement tests and graduating students in high numbers.

What these two models share is a focus on results; they exist only as long as they attract students and satisfy parents. But there are fewer than ten thousand Catholic schools nationwide. Even with backing from the Clinton administration, the charter movement so far numbers only about four hundred schools. The movement has been stymied by turf-conscious school boards and by teachers' unions that fear for their members' jobs. Under current conditions, this handful of innovative schools cannot provide enough leverage to transform this nation's eighty-four thousand public schools into a results-oriented education system.

There is evidence, however, that a heavy dose of public school choice can improve a whole school system. In New York City's Community School District No. 4 in Spanish Harlem, school choice was expanded to all junior high schools in 1983. Teams of teachers were granted autonomy to create distinctive programs to attract students and parents, who then became engaged in the process of education reform. Schools that could not compete were closed. In 1974, only 15 percent of students in District No. 4 could read at grade level;

by 1992, the proportion had risen to 38 percent. District No. 4's ranking among New York City's thirty-two school districts rose from 32d to 22d over the same period.[8]

The experiment produced other measurable results. According to Deborah Meier, former principal of District No. 4's Central Park East school, "We have less teenage pregnancy, less truancy, less absenteeism; we maintain virtually all of our students regardless of handicapping conditions . . ." Meier points out that these schools save the city money "by solving real problems—not to mention the incalculable financial advantage of having better educated young people."[9]

How To Expand Public School Choice

Paul Hill, director of the Center for Reinventing Public Education at the University of Washington, proposes expanding public school choice through a "charter districts strategy." Under Hill's proposal, local school boards would stop running schools directly and would no longer hire and fire school staffs. Instead, they would hire independent contractors to run schools, cancelling contracts with failing schools and offering new ones to groups with successful track records or promising programs.

Because school boards would be charged with offering schools that meet the diverse needs of students and communities, says Hill, they would ensure that communities have "the mix of schools necessary for all children to receive a high quality education." A community with a new software industry, for example, might want a high school with a curriculum that includes an emphasis on software development. A community with a large immigrant population might need elementary schools with special programs to help children develop English proficiency rapidly.

Under this common standards/diverse schools model, schools would hire their own teachers and administrators, either on the open market or from registries of certified professionals. Teachers and administrators could apply for jobs of their own choosing. Salaries would be set by the market; merit pay would provide substantial rewards for excellence; and teachers could demand higher pay for difficult assignments or additional responsibilities.

Using publicly accountable school boards as purchasers of educational services would guarantee two critical elements missing in private voucher schemes: Boards would ensure that no chartered school could discriminate in admissions policies, and they would withdraw public funding from failing schools.

Standards, Not Goals

This bold experiment, however, will fail without high common standards. Absent these standards, a national system of diverse schools will deteriorate into an unregulated, uneven patchwork of boutique schools. Instead of promoting equal opportunity, such a system would likely reinforce educational inequality.

Any true reform must be premised on a basic understanding of what every child should learn and when that child should learn it. Our nation is already moving in that direction. Continuing efforts begun during the Bush administration, in 1994 President Clinton signed Goals 2000: The Educate America Act. The law gives states financial incentives to set their own standards for students. The Goals 2000 initiatives have also helped promote a national dialogue on what all students should know.

But Democratic Governor Roy Romer of Colorado, who chaired the first National Educational Goals Panel in 1990, argues that "goals" will not reform education. "Standards," he insists, must be at the heart of any education reform movement. Albert Shanker, president of the American Federation of Teachers (AFT), agrees. "If we had a system of standards and assessments in place," said Shanker, "then as far as I'm concerned, every school should be a charter school."[10]

Most Americans agree as well. According to the Public Agenda Foundation's 1995 report *Assignment Incomplete,* more than 90 percent of Americans—across racial and socioeconomic groups—consider standards a major priority for schools. Seventy percent of Americans said youngsters will "pay more attention to their school work and study harder" under a system of high standards.

Most Americans also agree that this basic set of common standards should be linked to international benchmarks. The states are moving quickly in that direction. According to *Making Standards Matter,* a 1996 report by the AFT, forty-eight states are already devising standards. The AFT points out, however, that the emerging standards are often vague. In addition, fewer than half the states require students to pass high school graduation exams linked to standards. And few states' standards are internationally competitive.

Without national leadership, there will be no effective benchmarking system that compares state standards with international, world-class standards. A system of national voluntary standards can provide a continually revised benchmark to the world's best educational systems and a means for states to gauge their standards against those of other states and other advanced countries.

Why Standards?

Only a small fraction of high school students can perform at the high levels required for today's knowledge-based jobs. According to national assessments, only about 10 percent of U.S. seventeen-year-olds can draw conclusions using detailed scientific knowledge; just 7 percent can solve math problems with more than one step; and only 7 percent can read and understand specialized materials. International tests continue to show U.S. high school students ranking near the bottom in mathematics and science.[11]

The failure to demand and invest in the high achievement of all students perpetuates inequality. The failure of so many schools to expect high achievement from low-income or minority students means those students are likely to graduate without the skills they need.

When only 15 percent of graduates from inner-city high schools go to college, these low expectations condemn the other 85 percent to unemployment or, at best, low-wage service-sector jobs after graduation. "Few employers offering anything other than dead-end, no-skill jobs will take young people right out of high school, because the diploma provides no useful information about what these young people can actually do," notes Marc Tucker, president of the National Center on Education and the Economy.

In our Information Age economy, geographic mobility is a fact of life. The recent AFT report on the state of standards showed that one-fifth of students move to a new school every year. Without common standards, students lose continuity. They fall behind in schools that are more academically rigorous or they find themselves repeating material in less demanding schools. Common standards would ensure smooth transitions.[12]

High standards and achievement also promote citizenship and sustain democracy. Students who can master a common knowledge base, communicate effectively, and think critically will be better citizens. These citizens will be able to demand sensible policies and higher standards from our political leaders.

The End of the Bell Curve as We Know It

Shifting from a "means-based" approach to education reform to a strategy that focuses on academic content and adherence to standards is a radical transformation. It can only be achieved by measuring achievement objectively.

In their book *The Bell Curve*, Richard Herrnstein and Charles Murray propose that "inequality of endowments, including intelligence, is a reality," and that there is a natural distribution of human cognitive differences.[13] Herrnstein and Murray urge policymakers to accept these natural differences in ability, calling the notion that interventions can make up for genetic or environmental disadvantages "overly optimistic."

To the detriment of children, American public education often adheres to this illogic. Lauren Resnick, director of the Learning Research and Development Center at the University of Pittsburgh, points out that school systems base their expectations on an assumed natural bell curve of aptitude: A certain percentage of students are expected to fail; only a small percentage are expected to excel. Students are compared to one another instead of being compared to a common standard of excellence.

Aptitude-based assumptions about learning allow teachers, parents, and students to accept low expectations. But Resnick offers an alternate approach. She suggests that educators must embrace the idea that "effort *creates* ability;" that people can become intelligent by working at the right kinds of learning tasks. Sol Stern, who has written extensively on the Catholic schools, notes that this effort-based model is precisely what makes Catholic schools successful with all kinds of students. Expectations are high and the prevailing attitude is that "no one who works hard will fail."

Is it possible to design a system of high common national standards without the federal government treading on the states' prerogative to control education? Yes, says Diane Ravitch, senior research scholar at New York University, who proposes that a system of voluntary national standards be adopted by states and school districts.

Ravitch notes that one voluntary national model already exists. NAEP—the congressionally mandated, federally funded examination of fourth, eighth, and twelfth graders—is based on standards for every subject area, and rates students according to four achievement levels. Other important tests, such as the SAT, the Advanced Placement tests, and the International Baccalaureate also are used voluntarily nationwide.

What should national standards look like? According to Ravitch, standards should be clear, easily understood by parents and teachers, and "limited only to what students should know and be able to do so as to be well prepared for subsequent grades, higher education, or technical careers."[14]

Perhaps even more importantly, standards should ensure that all students master the same bodies of common knowledge. Today, the United States has none. Only a common core of expectations regarding what every student must know and can do will offer equal opportunity to all students.

Even while the nation moves toward consensus on standards, a second obstacle looms. Standards are meaningless and will be ignored unless they are linked to consequences. Once we agree on what every student should know and be able to do, we must next agree on a system of rewards for achievement.

Marc Tucker proposes a system based on what he calls a Certificate of Initial Mastery (CIM). It would abandon the current practice of dividing students into the academic, vocational, or general tracks at the high school level. Instead, the CIM would represent the highest standards, combining the best of the academic and vocational standards.

The CIM would not replace the diploma. Instead, it would provide the foundation on which students could pursue either postsecondary education, occupational skills training, or job-specific training. It would be the first tier in a sequential system, setting the general standard of excellence and common knowledge that all students must meet.

At the first tier, if a student obtains this rigorous certificate *before* graduating from high school, he or she would have the option to start college-level work, either through Advanced Placement or International Baccalaureate courses and exams. At the second tier, students could continue to prepare for postsecondary education or become certified in one of twenty to thirty "occupational clusters" standards that would qualify graduates for a range of related occupations. At the third tier, students could enter a system similar to apprenticeship, choosing to master job-specific skills set by individual companies, and perhaps receiving some training from potential employers or labor unions.

Schools would be responsible for constantly "working at finding out what works best with which students to keep them on target as they go through the process," says Tucker. Because all students would be required to master basic knowledge and skills to receive a CIM, they would always have the option of changing their educational or career goals. Students who choose the occupational-cluster system or the apprenticeship model, for example, could decide to attend postsecondary institutions and qualify by taking some additional courses.[15]

Setting High Stakes for Everyone

Under such a system, education would become a high-stakes game with a tangible payoff for success. Students would see a clear link between how well they do in school and their life chances. Social promotions would end. Employers would demand diplomas because these documents would offer proof of real achievement.

The stakes in this new system would be high for teachers as well. If we are to ask teachers to meet these new expectations, there is much to be done. The National Commission on Teaching and America's Future has labeled the quality of teacher training and performance, "a national shame": One-fourth of high school teachers lack college training in their primary classroom subject; 40 percent of math teachers are not fully qualified; more than forty states permit teachers to teach without completing training and passing examinations. America needs a real certification system for teachers that evaluates them on how well they have mastered content and how well they can impart that knowledge to students.

Teachers also need a great deal more help and support in the classroom than they get today. Richard Elmore of Harvard University has studied how one school system is addressing this issue. For the past nine years, New York City's Community School District No. 2 has adopted a radically different approach. Its superintendent, Anthony Alvarado, has one goal: improving classroom instruction. It is the single most important organizational objective for teachers, principals, parents, and administrators.

District management is geared exclusively toward helping teachers in the classroom. No one teaches behind closed doors. Teachers get help when they need it; those who cannot meet the standards are asked to leave. Turnover rates are high: 80 percent to 90 percent for principals and 50 percent for teachers. But those who have stayed have succeeded. Among the city's thirty-two community districts, District 2 now ranks second in both reading and math.

Unions, too, can play an important part in this transformation of teaching into a true profession. Instead of preserving their members' jobs through the collective bargaining process alone, unions can preserve jobs by helping members achieve high professional standards. Unions can insist that only highly qualified individuals are accepted into their ranks; they can offer training for prospective teachers and meaningful professional development for veterans. But most of all, unions can press for professional freedom for teachers, allowing them to decide for themselves how best to teach.

Lauren Resnick suggests that this freedom will allow teachers to break through one of the most intractable barriers to good teaching: They will be able to invert the relationship between time and results. Schools now generally provide a standard amount of time of instruction, and whatever learning that takes place in that time is evaluated. If an achievement standard were adopted instead, students and teachers would get the time they need to succeed. If a student needed two hours a day of math instruction rather than the currently prescribed one hour, he or she would get them. Effort would truly pay.

One California high school achieved success with this approach. In 1989, when Judy Codding became a high school principal in Pasadena, she found a predominantly poor and minority student body, and teachers who generally subscribed to the bell curve theory of differential expectations for poor students. Codding began to insist that teachers and administrators demand that all of their students work hard and perform in school.

Codding set a goal that 80 percent of the school's students would finish with As and Bs, but that the grades be earned honestly. To reach that goal, some students took two periods of math a day and attended the school's Center for Independent Learning for extra help. The school year was extended to give students more time to meet the new standards. By 1993, Pasadena had moved from the bottom quartile on standardized tests to the top quartile, transforming itself from the poorest performing to the highest performing school in the district.

The final thing school districts must do is to ensure that every school is a place where children are safe and teachers can teach well. As AFT President Albert Shanker has long pointed out, courts routinely return violent and unmanageable students to school. "What about all the other students?" asks Shanker. "Does it make sense to destroy the education of twenty-five or more students because we are trying to 'rehabilitate' one?" It's time to require separate educational facilities for chronically disruptive and violent students. The public owes every child an education, but achieving that goal may require separate facilities for some.

Parents are the last ingredient in a system that restores consequences in public education. In the Taylor model, schools are the exclusive domain of educators. Yet private schools and Catholic schools have always sought to engage parents in their children's education. Parents can walk into schools and talk to the principals or teachers, and teachers are directly accountable to the parents. It's time to move away from the model that segregates the responsibilities of parents and teachers. Parents must be reengaged as advocates for their children and as "consumers" of public education.

In Chicago, where Mayor Richard M. Daley took over the city's failing schools in 1995, the school system now uses many strategies to reengage parents. First, the schools ended social promotions and instituted mandatory summer school for failing students, some 100,000 in the summer of 1996. Teachers and administrators no longer wait to let parents know when children are in trouble.

The Chicago schools also turned to a very traditional form of parent engagement: homework. The schools are making homework mandatory and offering parents a "homework guide" with strategies and techniques to help their children study. "What we are saying to parents is that we are all in this together," says Blondean Davis, who supervises the school system's daily activities. "We want to rebuild the partnership that was there for most of us when we went through the public school system, and that has become revolutionary; because it's very, very simple."

To be good consumers, parents need clear and easily accessible information. State legislatures should require all schools and districts to publicly report achievement. Parents will be able to judge for themselves how schools are performing. Public reporting adds yet another layer of pressure for schools and districts to perform at internationally benchmarked levels. Such a system enhances the power of communities to close failing schools and open better ones to serve children.

Conclusion

These changes will not transform every public school into a results-driven institution meeting high common standards overnight. But over time—and in combination—they will accomplish more than all of the tinkering of the past two decades. And they will preserve for America and its children the ideal of the common public school.

Nearly a century ago, educational philosopher John Dewey offered advice that should guide this most critical national undertaking. "What the best and wisest parent wants for his own child," wrote Dewey, "that must the community want for all of its children. Any other ideal for our schools is narrow and unlovely; acted upon, it destroys our democracy."

Notes

1. Robert L. Maginnis, "Violence in the Schoolhouse: A 10-Year Update" (Washington, DC: Family Research Council, 1994), 4.

2. Stanley M. Elam, Lowell C. Rose, and Alec M. Gallup, "The 28th Annual Phi Delta Kappa/Gallup Poll of the Public's Attitudes toward the Public Schools" *Phi Delta Kappan* 78, no. 1 (September 1996).

3. National Commission on Teaching & America's Future, *What Matters Most: Teaching for America's Future* (New York: National Commission on Teaching & America's Future, 1996), 5.

4. National Center for Education Statistics, *The Condition of Education 1996* (Washington, DC: U.S. Department of Education, 1996), 240.

5. National Center for Education Statistics, *National Assessment of Educational Progress* (Washington, DC: U.S. Department of Education, 1994), 12–13.

6. National Center for Education Statistics, *The Condition of Education 1996* (Washington, DC: U.S. Department of Education, 1996), 52.

7. National Center for Education Statistics, *The Mini-Digest of Education Statistics* (Washington, DC: U.S. Department of Education, 1995), Table 3, 11.

8. Seymour Fliegel with James Macguire, *Miracle in East Harlem: The Fight for Choice in Public Education* (New York: Times Books, 1993), 230, 231.

9. Seymour Fliegel with James Macguire, *Miracle in East Harlem,* 189.

10. Sara Mosle, "The Answer is National Standards," *New York Times Magazine* (27 Oct. 1996): 56.

11. Educational Testing Service, *A World of Differences: An International Assessment of Mathematics and Science* (Princeton, NJ: Educational Testing Service, 1989), 17, 38. National Center for Education Statistics, *The Condition of Education, 1995* (Washington, DC: U.S. Department of Education, 1995), 58–60, 64–66.

12. Matthew Gandal, *Making Standards Matter* (Washington, DC: American Federation of Teachers, 1996), vii.

13. Richard J. Herrnstein and Charles Murray, *The Bell Curve: Intelligence and Class Structure in American Life* (New York: Free Press, 1994), 551.

14. Diane Ravitch, "50 States, 50 Standards," *The Brookings Review* (Summer 1996): 8.

15. National Center on Education and the Economy, *The Certificate of Initial Mastery: A Primer* (Washington, DC: National Center on Education and the Economy, April 1994), 6–12.

Chapter 7

Reform and Invest: Reinventing Government's Next Steps

David Osborne

In the long, lackluster presidential campaign of 1996, one issue alone seemed to truly energize the electorate: the disappearance of job security. Brought to the surface by Pat Buchanan, it dropped from view along with his candidacy. President Clinton did address the issue, but in the muted tones of a front-running incumbent. Still, it remains working America's biggest worry.

Call it downsizing, global competitiveness, or just plain unemployment, job security has animated American politics since the recession of the early 1980s. President Clinton has rightly argued that in today's global economy, the only form of job security government can provide is lifelong access to education and training, so people can equip themselves to get the next job when the last one disappears. Toward that end, he has passed or proposed initiatives that every American can use—from school-to-work apprenticeships, to job retraining vouchers, to tax credits for college tuition.

The President says these initiatives are his highest second-term priority. They are the foundation of his bridge to the twenty-first century—a Big Idea he needs to define his final years in office. And they are popular, on both sides of the aisle. All they lack is money. Clinton's proposals would cost up to $17 billion a year by 2002. How can we ever pay for them in this era of balanced budgets?

Vice-President Gore, meanwhile, is floating his own Big Idea. To press his reinventing government initiative forward, he wants to transform many federal agencies into "performance-based organizations" (PBOs). The idea is simple: Give agencies the flexibility they need to improve their performance, then hold them accountable for results. The proposal is modeled after one of the most sweeping and successful reinventing government initiatives in the world, the British "Next Steps" reforms. The British have converted 75 percent of their bureaucracy into Next Steps agencies, trimming civil service ranks by 15 percent and cutting many agencies' operating budgets, while improving performance.

Like Clinton's education and training agenda, Gore's PBO proposal enjoys bipartisan support, at least among members of Congress who care about management issues. Unfortunately, such members are few and far between. Gore faces one of the reinventor's biggest quandaries: How do you get politicians to focus on management reform?

The solution to both Gore's problem and Clinton's is to marry their Big Ideas. It worked once before: In 1994, when Gore asked a Democratic Congress to downsize the federal work force by 12 percent, it did so because it wanted to spend the savings on Clinton's 100,000 new cops on the beat. Three years later, why not offer Congress a PBO bill it could use to fund education and training?

PBOs can save us $25 billion a year—enough to fund Clinton's agenda and more. If we reinvent the federal bureaucracy, we can afford to reinvent our workforce development system.

The Next Step in Federal Reinvention

In its first term, the Clinton administration made progress toward its promise of creating a federal government that works better and costs less. But because Congress never passed the administration's most important reinvention proposals, it still has far to go. In poll after poll, voters have made clear how important this agenda is: They want a smaller, less bureaucratic government, but one that can still address key issues, from crime to environmental protection, Medicare to job training. If New Democrats are to champion effective government rather than simply smaller government, they have a duty to deliver on their promises to reinvent the federal bureaucracy.

Gore's PBO proposal would radically change both the performance and culture of the federal bureaucracy. It offers agencies the most basic deal in the reinventors' tool kit: freedom from red tape in exchange for accountability for performance. Great Britain, New Zealand, Australia, and several American states have already cut this deal.[1] The Vice-President's National Performance Review recommended the same basic approach in 1993. But Congress, which has shown little interest in sweeping management reforms, passed only a few of the relevant recommendations. So in 1995, Gore decided to cut the deal agency by agency: He asked Congress for permission to turn them into PBOs, one by one.

Gore's initiative is modeled on Margaret Thatcher's groundbreaking reforms in the United Kingdom. High in the pantheon of conservative heroes, Thatcher spent her first eight years in office privatizing and downsizing government. But after eight years, she still hadn't made much headway with the remaining civil service bureaucracies. Finally, in 1986, she asked her efficiency advisers to study the problem and recommend the next steps.

Over the preceding 150 years, British politicians had commissioned numerous civil service reform studies. But this study team did something none of the others had done: It asked the civil servants themselves.

The answer came back loud and clear: Untie our hands and let us manage. Hold us accountable for results—not for following silly rules and spending every penny of every budgeted line item.

The reform the study team proposed—which Peter Plastrik and I describe at length in our new book, *Banishing Bureaucracy: The Five Strategies for Reinventing Government*—became known as the "Next Steps" initiative. Briefly, it:

- Separated departments' various service delivery and regulatory functions into discrete chunks, called Executive Agencies.

- Gave those agencies much more control over their budgets, personnel systems, purchasing, and other management practices.

- Let departments pay agency chief executives whatever it took to get the job done, including performance bonuses of up to 20 percent of their salaries—but denied them the normal lifetime tenure.

- Required those chief executives to negotiate a three-year performance contract, called a "framework document," with their department, specifying the results they would achieve and the flexibilities they would be granted.

- Required agencies to negotiate annual performance targets with their departments, and published agencies' performance against those targets.

- Put agencies on trial for their lives every three years. Departments conduct "prior options reviews," asking whether the agency or its individual functions should be abolished, sold to private owners, merged with another agency, or restructured. If the agency survives this scrutiny, the chief executive must reapply for his or her job, against all comers.

By late 1996, Britain had created 126 Executive Agencies, which employed almost 75 percent of its civil service. Although the British extended the time frame for performance contracts and reviews from three to five years, the basic reform is now firmly in place. Agency executives can now manage effectively, but both their pay and their jobs depend on their agency's performance against quantifiable standards. And every employee knows that if the agency doesn't perform, it may be abolished, privatized, or restructured at its five-year review. Since 1988, about a dozen agencies have been privatized.

The results have probably exceeded even Thatcher's expectations. Even the largest agencies have increased their operating efficiency by at least 2 percent per year. And some agencies—which have embraced outsourcing or competition between public and private service providers—have posted annual increases as high as 30 percent.

Overall, the British have shrunk their civil service by 15 percent since they began creating executive agencies (and by a third since Thatcher was elected in 1979). Meanwhile, performance has steadily improved. In 1995, agencies hit an average of 83 percent of their performance targets—many of which had been raised over time—while cutting their planned level of operating costs by an average of 4.7 percent.[2] (Operating costs, known in Britain as "running costs," include all payroll, overhead, rent, and other operating expenses, but not direct program costs such as benefits paid to individuals or grants to local governments.)

Because they are now accountable for their performance, agencies have used almost every tool in the reinventors' kit: contracting out, public versus private competition, performance bonuses, group bonuses, total quality management, customer surveys, business process reengineering, internal markets, "one-stop" offices, and on and on.

The first agency created was the Vehicle Inspectorate, for example. It quickly opened offices on weekends, introduced new services, contracted out others, removed a layer of management, and established group performance bonuses keyed to overall efficiency increases. In its first three years, it reported operating cost efficiency increases of 4.5 percent, 4.1 percent, and 3.6 percent—triggering bonuses of up to £213 per employee.[3]

The Employment Service was one of the largest of the early executive agencies, with forty thousand employees in 1990. Michael Fogden, the CEO, began measuring performance and publishing comparative data about each of his nine regions, to push them to improve. Later, he pushed the comparisons down to the local office level; each now displays its performance record and the records of up to six neighboring offices, for comparison.

At the same time, Fogden gave his regions great flexibility. Many cut waiting times dramatically. The entire agency has eliminated a layer of management and restructured its personnel system—including pay, grading, and recruitment. Fogden has instituted regular customer surveys, customer panels, and customer service standards. The surveys show general improvement, while other indicators show a 40 percent increase in job placements with no new resources, gradual improvements in the accuracy of benefit payments, and 2 percent annual increases in efficiency.[4]

Overall, Next Steps is widely considered a resounding success. In 1991, the Labor Party announced it would keep the reform in place if it won power. The unions have not opposed it. And in November 1994, Parliament's Treasury and Civil Service Committee called it "the single most successful Civil Service reform programme of recent decades."[5]

Performance-Based Organizations

Gore and Clinton propose to do almost exactly what the British have done: divide service delivery and regulatory functions into discrete agencies; hire CEOs; pay them a base salary of $150,000, with another $150,000 in possible performance bonuses; and give them flexibility to manage their own personnel, procurement, budget, real estate, and other affairs—within very broad civil service, procurement, and budget parameters. Using the performance measures each agency is now developing under the 1993 Government Performance and Results Act, departments would negotiate annual performance targets with agency executives, who would receive bonuses only if they met or exceeded the targets. Every five years, the administration would review each agency, as in the U.K.[6]

To be considered, agencies would need clear service or regulatory missions, measurable functions, and proven capacity to measure their performance. (This would exclude policy operations and organizations whose performance is difficult to measure, such as the State Department.) The administration has already named the Patent and Trademark Office (PTO) and the Defense Commissary Agency as provisional PBOs, while awaiting congressional approval. Other early candidates include the St. Lawrence Seaway Development Corporation, the U.S. Mint, the National Technical Information Service, retirement benefit management services, passport services, student aid services, defense printing services, the Federal Supply Service, and the Occupational Safety and Health Administration.[7]

According to John Kamensky, deputy director of the National Performance Review, two-thirds of federal employees work in agencies that deliver services to the public or to other federal organizations. Adding regulatory agencies, it seems clear that the British target of 75 percent also makes sense here. New Zealand has done essentially the same thing with more than 90 percent of its civil servants.[8]

Why do we need PBOs? For the same reasons the British and New Zealanders did: We cannot expect dramatically better performance from federal organizations unless we cut the red tape that binds them and give them clear consequences for their performance. Consider the Federal Aviation Administration (FAA), which has been so hamstrung by budget and procurement restrictions that its efforts to modernize its massive computer systems have fallen a decade behind schedule—and so hamstrung by civil service personnel rules that some of its busiest centers are chronically understaffed. In 1993, the National Performance Review recommended turning the FAA into a public corporation, free from federal budget, personnel, and procurement systems. Congress would not go that far, but in 1995 it finally acknowledged the severity of the problem and freed the FAA to create its own personnel and procurement systems.

The first candidate for PBO status, the PTO, has experienced a doubling in the volume of patent applications over the past decade—and Commissioner Bruce A. Lehman expects volume to double again in the next five. Yet as the *Washington Post* has reported, federal procurement and personnel rules constantly frustrate Lehman's efforts to keep up with the demand. Personnel rules make it so hard to hire and retain qualified patent examiners that the PTO hires people and then pays to send them to law school at night. But after they graduate, the agency often loses them, because private patent attorneys make so much more than the $75,000 the federal personnel system typically allows it for lawyers. Several years ago, when the PTO moved to computerized record-keeping, its proposal to purchase a new computer system took two years to get through the General Services Administration (GSA). By the time the new computers arrived, they were already out of date.[9]

Our federal government does not calculate its operating costs, as the British, Australians, and New Zealanders do. But based on the Office of Management and Budget's (OMB) fiscal 1997 estimates, we will spend approximately $88.312 billion on civilian personnel (including benefits) this year, plus $222.533 billion for "contractual services and supplies": rent, telephones, printing, travel, purchases of goods and contract services from government accounts, medical care, maintenance, and supplies. OMB and National Performance Review officials believe these two numbers, which total $311.845 billion, provide a rough approximation of federal operating costs.

It would take many years to convert functions employing 75 percent or more of federal civil servants into PBOs. The British have done it over ten years, while New Zealand did it in two. Common sense suggests that we split the difference and plan a six-year conversion process.

If every PBO were required to function with 3 percent less operating money each year—to become 3 percent more productive, in other words—this effort would save roughly $25 billion in its sixth year, and more in subsequent years.[10] Why 3 percent? Because businesses typically aim to become 3 to 4 percent more productive every year.

Investing the Savings: Building a Bridge to the Twenty-First Century

In his first term, President Clinton also made limited progress toward another important goal: investing in the education and training every American needs to thrive in today's Information Age economy. The money we save by making the federal government more productive should be invested in building this bridge to the twenty-first century.

In every economic age, one resource becomes dominant. In the Agricultural Age, it was land. In the Industrial Era, it was labor. In the Information Age, it is knowledge. If you have knowledge and skills, you can find—or create—a decent-paying job. If you don't, the odds are against you.

In the 1950s, 70 percent of American job holders worked with their hands, while 30 percent worked with their brains. Today, that ratio is gradually being reversed. A decade ago, a Hudson Institute study found that while only 24 percent of existing jobs required substantial skills in math, language, and reasoning, 41 percent of new jobs did.[11] The Bureau of Labor Statistics tells us that over the next decade:

- "Jobs requiring the most education and training will be the fastest growing and highest paying."

- "Occupations which require a bachelor's degree or above will average 23 percent growth, almost double the 12 percent growth projected for occupations that require less education and training."

- "Although high paying jobs will be available without college training, most jobs that pay above average wages will require a college degree."

- "Eight . . . occupations will account for about half of the new jobs: registered nurses, systems analysts, blue-collar worker supervisors, general managers and top executives, and four teaching occupations— elementary school teachers, secondary school teachers, college faculty, and special education teachers."[12]

Not only will middle-class jobs in the coming century require high skills, they will also be less secure. The global marketplace is changing at a frightening pace. Half the jobs performed today did not exist twenty years ago. Entire industries emerge, grow, recede, and die within the space of thirty years. Consider the minicomputer industry, which emerged in Massachusetts in the 1960s and collapsed in the early 1990s. In 1987, Wang Laboratories had 33,000 employees; six years later, it had 5,000. In 1989, the Digital Equipment Corporation had 120,000 employees; today it has 57,000.

The average American entering the work force today is expected to change jobs seven or eight times. This churning labor market creates the undercurrent of anxiety that Buchanan tapped last winter. Today, many Americans lose their jobs even in good times. And as entire industries shrink and die, many of those jobs don't come back. By 1993, more than half of all displaced workers were still unemployed, or employed in jobs paying less than 80 percent of their former wages, one year after they lost their jobs.[13]

In sum, the new economy is a frightening place for many people. From 1945 through 1975, Americans enjoyed a relatively stable economy; today we have an economy of constant change. During the Industrial Era, we had an economy that was built on brawn and driven by giant corporations that offered virtual lifetime employment; today we have an economy that is built on brains and driven by entrepreneurial firms that expand and contract almost overnight.

In today's global marketplace, quality and innovation are the ticket to a better tomorrow. That's because anything that can be done in the Third World—at low cost and with relatively unskilled labor—will be. In 1960, only 20 percent of goods we produced faced active foreign competition. By 1980, 70 percent did.[14]

With the average American wage eight times the world average, we simply cannot compete at the low end. Our competitive advantage lies in doing things that can't be done in the Third World, and doing them better and faster than our European and Japanese competitors. It lies in using advanced technologies; developing new products and processes; building information-intensive products and services; and producing customized products with flexible, computer-driven equipment.

To do these things, we need the world's most skilled work force. And yet, this is a country in which 25 to 30 percent of the population is functionally illiterate. As former Xerox CEO David Kearns once said, "If current demographic and economic trends continue, American businesses will have to hire a million new workers a year who cannot read, write, or count."[15]

The Solution: A Career Opportunity System

America's unemployment insurance system dates from the 1930s. It assumes that layoffs will be temporary and that most people will eventually get their old jobs back or find similar ones. In the 1940s, Congress passed the GI Bill to help veterans go to college. Since then, it has added Pell Grants, student loans, and dozens of small job-training programs, typically aimed at specific disadvantaged populations such as the poor, the unemployed, migrants, and Native Americans.

This "system," if one is charitable enough to call it that, is completely inadequate today. If Americans are to thrive in an economy driven by technological revolution and global competition, they will need to upgrade their skills throughout their working lives. They will need a lifelong system that helps them find the education and training they need, whenever they need it.

The Clinton administration has created a small school-to-work apprenticeship program, a small national service program, and a small grant program that encourages states to create One-Stop Career Centers. The President has also proposed job-training vouchers; the use of Individual Retirement Account (IRA) savings for education and training; more money for college grants, scholarships, and work-study programs; and tuition tax credits and deductions for postsecondary education.

The media has written these proposals off as mere tinkering. Where, they ask, are the Big Ideas?

The problem is a lack of boldness. It may be a deliberate one, after the debacle of Clinton's Big Idea on national health insurance, but it is a problem nevertheless. If the President wants to capture the imagination of the American people, he needs a Big Idea. He needs to expand these initiatives into a single, highly visible Career Opportunity System. This system would help *every* American get the education, training, or job-search assistance they need throughout their working lives—from the engineer who loses his job, to the housewife returning to the work force, to the welfare recipient trying to provide for her family.

A Career Opportunity System, which would speak directly to Americans' anxiety about the loss of job security, would rest on four pillars:

- Career Opportunity Accounts, which would finance training and education for the poor and dislocated workers and let the middle class save for future education and training needs tax-free.

- Expanded college aid, through tax credits, work-study grants, and a broadened national service program.

- An expanded school-to-work program, in which sixteen- and seventeen-year-olds would combine class work with on-the-job apprenticeships.

- And a national system of One-Stop Career Centers, through which every American could learn which education and training providers, apprenticeships, or colleges were best for them; what jobs were available; and how to get them.

Career opportunity accounts

In March 1994, PPI urged Washington to take the money it now spends on dozens of small training programs and use it instead to provide "job opportunity vouchers" to the more than one million workers who are displaced every year.[16] The vouchers were to buy up to $500 worth of employment services, such as skill assessment and job placement, and up to $2,000 worth of training and education services—from any provider, public or private.

Nine months later, President Clinton made this idea the centerpiece of his proposed GI Bill for American Workers. In December 1994, he proposed consolidating seventy training programs to pay for vouchers worth $2,620, for both displaced and disadvantaged workers.

Clinton was right to broaden the eligible population, but if he wants a Big Idea, he should go even further. *Every American* should have the right to open a Career Opportunity Account at any financial institution that handles IRAs. Citizens should have broad discretion over when and how to use their funds. The government should give vouchers to the poor and dislocated workers to let them open accounts while encouraging the middle class to invest in their own accounts, tax-free. In addition, it should find an effective means to encourage employers to contribute to their employees' accounts.

This last point is critical, because most job training in America is and will continue to be funded by business, for its current employees. Today, 70 percent of that business investment is devoted to retraining only 10 percent of the work force—primarily managers.[17]

Career Opportunity Accounts should be phased in only as states build the infrastructure needed to make them work: One-Stop Career Centers, backed up by systems to measure the performance of all education and training providers (see below). Rather than fund Career Opportunity Accounts immediately, the Clinton administration should push to move the seventy existing programs into a block grant now, to give states the flexibility they need to build these centers and systems. The states should have three years to do so, after which at least 75 percent of their block grant funds should be shifted into Career Opportunity Accounts.

Expanded college aid

To expand opportunities for college education, the President has proposed "Hope Scholarships"—$1,500 in tax credits annually for up to two years of tuition for students who maintain B averages and stay drug-free. He has also proposed a $10,000 annual tax deduction for college tuition (which would be phased out between $80,000 and $100,000 of family income, or between $50,000 and $70,000 of individual income).

This plan, while commendable, has several flaws. First, its proposed deduction is skewed toward those with higher incomes: It would be worth $2,500 a year to people in the 25 percent tax bracket, but only $1,500 to those in the 15 percent bracket. The fairest solution would be to convert both the deduction and tax credit into a single $2,000 credit that would yield equal value for all claimants. The credit would cover tuition, fees, books, and other expenses for up to four years of college or technical school, and would be phased out at the same income levels as the proposed deduction.

The plan's second problem is that it ignores one of the New Progressive Declaration's key themes; namely, that we should replace unconditional entitlements wherever possible with benefits which must be earned. Any new tax credit should require recipients to give something back, in the form of part-time community service. We should also expand the national service program, AmeriCorps, which now has funding for only twenty-five thousand service workers. At a minimum, we should raise AmeriCorps' budget over five years from the current $215 million to $1.2 billion, letting another 100,000 young people pay for college by giving something back to their communities. The new positions should focus on urgent social needs, such as the enormous increase in child care that will be needed if states are to move welfare recipients into jobs. Finally, the tuition assistance that AmeriCorps workers earn ($4,725 a year currently) should be indexed for inflation and should be deposited in their Career Opportunity Accounts.

The third problem with Clinton's plan is that it would encourage colleges to continue raising tuition at almost double the rate of inflation. To make the higher education market more cost-sensitive, the administration should give families more and better information about the comparative quality and cost of different institutions. The upcoming section on One-Stop Career Centers will explain how.

School-to-work apprenticeships

One of the President's most important and least appreciated first-term initiatives was the School-to-Work program, which gives states and communities $400 million a year for apprenticeship programs. For those not planning to attend college, apprenticeships offer a chance to begin acquiring career skills while still in high school. By spending part of every school week working in an area business, students build a bridge to technical jobs that pay well but don't require a college degree. They also gain a powerful incentive to finish high school.

Although the apprenticeship program is working, it is progressing too slowly. By gradually expanding our current $400 million annual investment to $2 billion, we will hasten the day when every young person has access to this powerful bridge to a decent job. These grants should be competitive, however; to receive them, states and communities should have to match them and prove they can perform.

One-stop career centers

During the 1930s, the Roosevelt administration created a national Employment Service to help the unemployed find jobs. Like most public monopolies, it was a good idea that ossified over time. By the time the Clinton administration's Labor Department evaluated it, few Americans thought of it as anything other than a place to pick up an unemployment check or hire a day laborer. According to the 1993 Labor Department study: "Workers feel they are treated as second-class citizens, given inaccurate information about prospects for employment and provided with little guidance that can help them find a job. . . . [W]orkers feel that the staff is poorly trained and unmotivated to provide customer service."[18] Only 30 percent of businesses listed their open jobs at the 1,800 Employment Service offices, and only one in five of the jobs listed were for skilled positions. Less than 7 percent of employers used the Employment Service more than twice a year.[19]

Yet working Americans desperately need help finding the jobs, training, and education that meet their needs. Both the job market and the market for training and adult education are too complex for many working people to navigate on their own. When they feel a need to upgrade their skills, most people have no idea where to turn. And if they haven't lost a job recently, aren't on welfare, or otherwise fail to fit into a "disadvantaged" category, most federal programs are off limits.

To address this problem, the Clinton administration began offering grants to states to open One-Stop Career Centers, where people could find and apply for jobs; learn which training, education, and apprenticeship programs were available, how much they cost, and how well they performed; and learn whether they qualified for public help. Most states are building such systems, although many are simply moving existing offices into a single building and renaming them One-Stop Career Centers.

Bona fide Career Centers are the linchpin of the Career Opportunity System. Career Opportunity Accounts will not work unless Americans have good information about the quality and cost of education and training providers. Indeed, people whose accounts are funded directly by the federal government should be required to talk with a Career Center counselor before they can spend their money. Otherwise, many will train for jobs that will not have openings. Dislocated male workers, for example, often want training to be truck drivers—despite the fact that few new jobs for truck drivers exist. Counselors should not have to approve an individual's choice: Someone who is determined to be a truck driver despite the odds can usually find a way to make it work. But counselors should have to certify that they have talked with the individual and explained the realities of the job market.

Table 7.1

New Spending for a Career Opportunity System, Sixth Year
(The Career Opportunity System would cost roughly $25 billion a year by the sixth year.)

Program	Approx. amount (in billions of $)
Career Opportunity Accounts	6
Remaining Workforce Development Block Grant	2
Hope Scholarship Tax Credits and Broadened IRAs	13.23*
Expansion of Pell Grants, Work-Study, Scholarships and Other College Aid	0.857*
Expansion of National Service	1
Expansion of School-to-Work Apprenticeships	1.6
One-Stop Career Centers	0.075[†]
TOTAL	24.762

*These are the amounts proposed by the Clinton Administration. The President has recommended paying for $2.542 billion of this by raising fees on international flight departures, tightening a loophole multinational corporations can use to decrease their U.S. taxes, and auctioning off 25 megahertz of spectrum reserved for digital audio radio services. We have not subtracted that from this total.

[†]We recommend most of the new spending—$1.1 billion—in years one through five.

Similarly, new tax credits for college tuition will encourage colleges to keep raising their tuitions unless families and students have reliable consumer information. Career Centers should provide good comparative information—on costs, customer satisfaction, professionally rated quality, and performance of graduates in the labor market—on all postsecondary education and training institutions.

The Career Center initiative now costs only $150 million a year. The Clinton administration should extend it for four years, to fund the creation of integrated, One-Stop Career Centers—not simply co-located offices—where all services are handled by one staff. To get the extended grants, however, states should be required to make institutions—public, private, and non-profit—compete for the right to operate Career Centers, as Massachusetts has. No matter how good its intentions, any system created as a public monopoly will eventually deteriorate, because Career Center operators will have little pressure to keep up with their customers' needs or to use the latest technologies.

We should also spend another $200 million next year and an additional $75 million a year thereafter to build the performance measurement system just described and to complete "America's Job Bank"—the Labor Department's online job-listing service, which is already one of the ten most frequently visited content sites on the World Wide Web.

Cutting the Deal

If President Clinton offered Congress the opportunity to spend $25 billion a year on education and training, without increasing the deficit, it might well be interested. Would it be interested enough to pass a sweeping PBO bill? We won't know unless the President tries it.

The boldest route Clinton could take would be to ask Congress simply to pass a bill allowing him to create PBOs, but requiring advance notification of each one and giving Congress ninety days to pass legislation blocking implementation. However, this tactic might not pass political muster in a Republican Congress. The alternative is to ask Congress to renew the reorganization authority most presidents have enjoyed since 1932.

The 1932 law was designed for precisely this kind of restructuring. It requires that the President "from time to time . . . examine the organization of all agencies," to determine changes necessary to better enforce the law and promote more effective management. It allows him to submit reorganization plans—consolidations, transfers of functions, abolition of functions or entire agencies, or delegations of authority—to Congress. Until 1983, when the Supreme Court ruled "legislative vetoes" unconstitutional, one or both houses of Congress (the law was amended over the years) had to pass a resolution opposing a plan to stop it.

Between 1953 and 1980, presidents submitted sixty-five reorganization plans and Congress rejected only eight. After the 1983 Supreme Court decision, Congress amended the act to require a joint House-Senate resolution *approving* the plan before it could be implemented. But it extended the President's reorganization authority only through Dec. 31, 1984.

President Clinton could ask Congress to create a new six-year period of reorganization authority and to amend the act to require that both houses vote on each plan within ninety days, so plans could not die through inattention. (An amendment should also eliminate language that says the President cannot have more than three plans pending at any one time.) The President could then use this authority to submit a reorganization plan for each PBO, and Congress would have ninety days to accept or reject each one.

Conclusion

Americans want and need a new form of job security: the security of knowing that they have the means to keep their skills current, so they can always find the next job when they lose the last one. This is the only kind of job security that makes sense in a globally competitive, twenty-first century economy. To create it, we need to build a Career Opportunity System.

We can fund that system simply by making the federal government more productive. The money is there; we already spend it. All we have to do is make a deal with our federal employees: cut them loose from red tape, but require that they use their freedom to do more with less. The learning they do will finance the lifelong learning system Americans need to thrive in the twenty-first century.

Notes

1. See David Osborne and Peter Plastrik, *Banishing Bureaucracy: The Five Strategies for Reinventing Government* (Reading, MA: Addison-Wesley, 1997).

2. Eighty-three percent of performance targets: *Next Steps Review: 1995* (London: HMSO, 1996), v. Reduction in operative costs of 4.7 percent, telephone interview with the head of the Next Steps Team in the Office of Public Service, Jeremy Cowper, 19 Sept. 1996.

3. *Improving Management in Government: The Next Steps Agencies, Review 1991,*

Cm. 1760 (London: HMSO, 1991), 67. *The Next Steps Agencies: Review 1992*, Cm. 2111 (London: HMSO, 1992), 92.

4. *The Citizen's Charter: The Facts and Figures* (London: HMSO, 1995), 19. *Notes: News of the Employment Service* (June 1993, August 1993, and June 1994), published by the U.K. Employment Service. *Improving Management in Government*, 24–25. *Next Steps Agencies: Review 1992*, 35–36. *Next Steps Review: 1993*, 50–51. *Next Steps Review 1994*, 31–32. *Next Steps Review: 1995*, 50–55. Personal communication from Jeremy Cowper, head of Next Steps Team, Sept. 1996.

5. *Next Steps: Briefing Note* (London: Next Steps Team, Office of Public Service, 26 Feb. 1996): 6.

6. "Creating Performance-Based Organizations," *National Performance Review* (October 1996). Interview with NPR Deputy Director, John Kamensky, October 1996.

7. Ibid.

8. For more on New Zealand, see David Osborne and Peter Plastrik, *Banishing Bureaucracy: The Five Strategies for Reinventing Government* (Reading, MA: Addison-Wesley, 1997).

9. Bill McAllister, "After 205 Years, Patent Office Prepares for Major 'Reinventing'," *Washington Post*, 27 Nov. 1995.

10. The math works this way: 75 percent of $311.845 billion is $233.884 billion. If an average of one-sixth (16.7 percent) of all PBOs were created each year, the savings would accumulate roughly as follows (in constant, non-inflation-adjusted dollars). The total operating cost of $233.884 billion would decline each year because PBO savings would reduce it:

Year 1 savings: 16.7 percent of $233.884 x .03 = $1.1695 billion
Year 2 savings: 33.4 percent of $232.7145 billion x .03 = $2.3318 billion
Year 3 savings: 50 percent of $230.3827 billion x .03 = $3.4557 billion
Year 4 savings: 66.7 percent of $226.927 billion x .03 = $4.5408 billion
Year 5 savings: 83.4 percent of $222.3862 billion x .03 = $5.5641 billion
Year 6 savings: 100 percent of $216.822 billion x .03 = $6.5047 billion

By Year 6, then, total operating costs for PBOs would be $216.822 billion minus $6.5047 billion, for a total of $210.3173 billion. This is a reduction of $23.5667 billion in operating costs. Adjusted for inflation, assuming an annual rate of 3 percent, the sixth-year savings would be roughly $25 billion. These savings would increase thereafter at a rate of about $6.5 billion a year in inflation-adjusted dollars. If the inflation rate were 3 percent, of course, operating costs for PBOs would simply remain flat in current dollars.

11. William J. Spring, "New England's Training Systems and Regional Economic Competitiveness," *New England Economic Indicators* (Second Quarter 1989): iv.

12. "Tomorrow's Jobs." In Occupational Outlook Handbook, Bureau of Labor Statistics [World Wide Web]. Available from http://stats.bls.gov/oco/oco2003.htm; INTERNET.

13. United States Department of Labor, Employment and Training Administration, *The Workforce Security and Re-Employment Act of 1994, Draft* (Washington, DC: November 1993).

14. Twenty percent: *A Strategy for Growth: An Economic Development Program for the Pittsburgh Region*, I (Pittsburgh: Allegheny Conference on Community Development, 1984), 14. Seventy percent: Robert B. Reich, *The Next American Frontier* (New York: Penguin Books, 1984), 121.

15. Adult Literacy Task Force, *Countdown 2000* (Lansing, MI: Governor's Office, March 1988).

16. See Peter Plastrik, "Reinventing the Federal Unemployment and Training System: Helping Millions of American Workers Secure New Jobs" (Washington, DC: Progressive Policy Institute, Policy Report No. 19, March 1994).

17. Robert J. Shapiro, "Bright Ideas: Innovation - Not Higher Savings, Is the Key to Economic Growth," *The New Democrat* 8, no. 5 (Sept./Oct. 1996): 34.

18. Yankelovich Partners and Jobs for the Future, "Summary of Focused Groups," (paper prepared for the U.S. Department of Labor, Washington, DC, 4 June 1993).

19. Plastrik, "Reinventing the Federal Unemployment and Training System," 6. Plastrik cited a nationwide telephone survey conducted for the Interstate Conference of Employment Security Agencies by Ketchum Public Relations, the results of which were summarized in a paper in July 1991: "What U.S. Employers Desire From Their State Public Employment Agencies."

Chapter 8

Community Self-Defense: A New Strategy for Preventing Crime and Restoring Public Order

Ed Kilgore

Public safety traditionally has been thought of as the most local of government responsibilities. But thanks to more than three decades of high crime rates and steadily mounting disorder in our cities, the public is forcing politicians to make public safety a national issue. The subject routinely appears at or near the top of every public opinion survey of national problems, even during periods when "the experts" point to short-term improvements in crime rates as grounds for optimism.

In April 1995, for example, amid reports that violent crime rates were dropping following a boomlet in those rates in the late 1980s and early 1990s, the Times-Mirror poll asked Americans if the United States was making progress or losing ground on twenty-one different issues. Crime elicited the most pessimistic response of all, with 77 percent of respondents saying the country was losing ground, and only 9 percent agreeing with the experts that the country was making progress.[1]

Recent publicity on marginally lower crime rates obscures the cumulative impact of persistently high rates over the lifetimes of most adult Americans. In 1995, a "good" year for crime-fighting, there were nearly 14 million reported crimes, more than four times the number in 1960. The number of reported violent crimes that year dropped below 1.8 million for the first time since 1989—a very positive statistic, but still about six times the number of reported violent crimes in 1960.[2]

Ed Kilgore

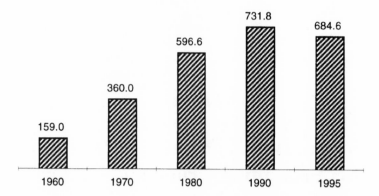

Fig. 8.1. Violent offenses in the U.S., per 100,000 inhabitants, 1960–1995. Data from *Uniform Crime Reports,* U.S. Department of Justice, 1960, 1970, and 1995.

Americans have grown tired of crime and disorder, and they want national leaders, not just police chiefs and mayors, to do something about it.

The State, the Individual, and the Community

The nationalization of the crime issue is a striking counterexample to the conservative assumption that government dysfunction is exclusively the product of excessive federal power. By any measurement, the various elements of the criminal justice system exhibit all the worst features of Industrial Age bureaucracies: lack of public accountability, turf consciousness, self-defined "professionalism," remoteness from the common experience of citizens, voracity for additional resources, and inbred resistance to change. While federal crime policy has contributed to these institutional vices, by no means has it created them.

It is impossible to identify a sole prevailing governing paradigm for the criminal justice system, divided as it is into distinct and largely uncoordinated bureaucracies involved in crime prevention, child welfare, juvenile justice, alcohol and substance abuse, policing, prosecution, adjudication, incarceration, and probation—with overlapping federal, state, and local jurisdictions in each. But by and large, the system is organized around two basic principles: the rights of the state, as expressed in laws and fixed sanctions for their violation, and the rights of the individual, as expressed in constitutional and statutory guarantees of civil rights and liberties. The interests of the *community*, the actual citizens and neighborhoods affected by crime and disorder, are rarely taken into account, or they are assumed to be reflected in the state's prosecution and punishment of crimes, and in the individual's liberty from excessive police powers.

While the national debate on crime and disorder has been driven by citizens concerned for their communities, it has largely focused instead on the twin towers of state power and individual liberty. It has done so, though, with some surprising wrinkles in recent years.

Conservatives generally have championed state power in the form of a single-minded support for longer and harsher prison sentences, sometimes appearing to favor permanent imprisonment of all violent felons and drug offenders. Liberals usually have been identified with individual rights and minority-group grievances against the criminal justice system, frequently suggesting that crime and disorder are lamentable but inevitable consequences of social and economic inequality.

In the 1990s, conservatives, while still arguing for longer stretches for more offenders in more pitiless prisons, have become actively hostile to the state's police power when it is exercised to control firearm ownership or to dissolve armed religious or paramilitary encampments (an attitude typified by the National Rifle Association letter that called officers of the federal Bureau of Alcohol, Tobacco, and Firearms "jack-booted government thugs").[3] The right also has become increasingly indifferent to those parts of the criminal justice system that come into play before a convicted defendant is sentenced by a judge.

For its part, the left, overwhelmed by public hostility to victimization theories about crime, has largely withdrawn from the law and order debate, other than exercising reflexive opposition to measures aimed at longer sentences for criminal acts. As recently as 1988, a Democratic candidate for president proudly claimed membership in the ACLU. Few rising political stars would make that mistake today.

Meanwhile, progressives in both parties, political independents, and police advocates have stimulated an entirely new debate focused not on root-cause remedies or postarrest punishments (though most do support an end to cost-driven "revolving door" conditions under which prisoners serve a small fraction of sentences), but on how police and communities can collaborate to fight both crime itself and the conditions of disorder and anarchy that immediately breed it.

The community policing movement, spearheaded in the 1980s by a handful of local leaders, embraced by the Clinton administration more recently, and scoring a series of high-profile successes in the last few years, reflects more than a fashionable strategy of employing police officers in the cities. Community policing is potentially the opening wedge of a fundamental change in the function, objectives, and structure of the criminal justice system: from a series of uncoordinated bureaucracies waging an abstract, often losing fight for improved crime statistics, to a radically decentralized but highly focused array of public resources aimed at helping communities defend themselves.

This paradigm shift reflects two of the New Progressive Declaration's strategies for renewing our democracy: reconstructing the social order, and returning power to self-governing citizens and communities.

This chapter will explore the history and implications of the movement for community-based crime prevention, and outline key steps that citizens and national, state, and local officials can take to broaden its impact. In particular, it will urge:

- a stronger national commitment to community policing;

- vigorous federal support for the interests of communities in conflicts between the state and criminal defendants;

- a national campaign to regain community control of public spaces;

- making supervised reintegration of criminals into community life a central priority in corrections, probation, and parole decisions; and,

- a comprehensive overhaul of criminal justice bureaucracies to focus them on contributing to community self-defense.

The Police Bureaucracy

No one would be surprised to hear the child welfare, juvenile justice, probation, parole, and corrections systems described as bureaucracies. Even the federal and state court systems, with their adjunct prosecutors and public defenders, are easily viewed as entrenched bureaucracies with their own culture and standards. What is surprising, though, is that our front-line troops, the local police departments, have developed into classic bureaucracies, too. This little-remarked phenomenon goes a long way toward explaining the public's growing estrangement from the criminal justice system.

Throughout the twentieth century, and with growing intensity during the past thirty years, local police have evolved from a traditional, community-based "peace officer" role into a detached and reactive, "professional crime fighter" role. Old-fashioned peace officers, or neighborhood police, were intimately involved in all aspects of civic life, and viewed their responsibility to the community more broadly than simply apprehending criminal suspects. Any threat to public tranquility from virtually any source was considered within their jurisdiction.[4] For example, local police might have become personally involved with clearing a vacant lot filled with trash or admonishing someone who broke a window. Modern police professionals, on the other hand, are expected to strictly limit their activities to the detection of crimes and the apprehension of their likely perpetrators. Essentially, they serve as the entry processing point for suspects into other elements of the criminal justice system, much as local welfare agencies serve as the entry processing point for clients seeking various forms of public assistance.

While peace officers instinctively thought of themselves as integral members of the community and protected it accordingly, police professionals tend to view the community as a neutral site for fighting crime, and of citizens as irrelevant to their work unless they are offenders, victims, or witnesses.

Four developments—one political, one technological, one organizational, and one reflecting both technological and organizational change—accelerated the trend toward the bureaucratization of police:

- In a manner that strikingly parallels the civil service reform movement in other segments of public service, police reformers sought explicitly to minimize officers' contacts with the community, and to insulate police departments from city politics. Both steps were rationalized as inoculations against corruption.[5]

- The advent of motorized patrol quickly eroded the tradition of assigning officers to beats in specific neighborhoods, and increasingly organized their work around responses to criminal incidents, rather than responsibility for general levels of public order.[6]

- In a pattern common to all bureaucracies, police departments almost universally became organized around a promotion hierarchy that made beat assignment an undesirable entry-level position, soon left behind by competent and ambitious officers for detective work and administration. In many cities, unionization of police, while leading to significant improvements in pay and benefits, also tended to harden the promotion hierarchy and make careers in policing similar to civil service occupations, in terms of distaste for performance incentives and public accountability.[7]

- Improvements in crime data collection and dissemination, especially the FBI's Uniform Crime Report, made crime rates a convenient performance measurement, and the severity of crimes an equally convenient determinant for the allocation of resources. This fixation on crime statistics further eroded the police's traditional public-order priorities.

The trend toward removing police from communities and enrolling them in a professional crime-fighting bureaucracy has culminated in the 911 telephone emergency-response system that has dominated policing in most parts of the country since the late 1970s. The 911 systems represent far more than a method for speeding information about criminal incidents to police. They reflect a conscious effort to limit police interaction with the community to incident-related contacts. Fully integrated with the motorized rapid-response method of deployment, 911 systems complete the trend away from the traditional peace officers model. Legitimate police work is now defined as response to isolated incidents, with performance increasingly measured by "response times," and with police attention to underlying community patterns of crime and disorder officially discouraged.

Four warning signs, still relevant today, accompanied the near-universal adoption of the professional crime fighting model:

- Almost everywhere, citizens resisted the abandonment of the old community-based model of policing, and the police's abdication of responsibility for public-order maintenance tasks unrelated to "crime-fighting."

- In most large urban centers, the elimination of regular police-community contact, and the adoption by officers of a paramilitary "strike force" ethic, bred an unprecedented level of suspicion and hostility toward officers, especially in minority communities.

- National crime rates rose sharply to previously unimagined levels throughout the entire period in which police departments focused most obsessively on deploying resources to respond to criminal incidents.

- Fed up with both rising crime rates and police insensitivity to their desire for the maintenance of public order, communities and businesses across America began organizing their own private "security forces." In 1995, American's hired 1.5 million private police officers to supplement public police protection.[8]

Unfortunately, police administrators cited all of these discouraging trends as justification for an even greater emphasis on professionalism and technology-driven responsiveness. Professionalism was actively marketed as the best guarantee of "constituent satisfaction" and as a counter to lingering bias against minorities in majority-white departments, while ever-lower response times were deemed critical to reversing rising crime rates.

The Start of the Community Policing Movement

In a striking example of how ideas often do matter, the countertrend away from the professional crime-fighting and rapid-response models for policing began in academic circles. Beginning in the mid-1970s, the Police Foundation funded a research project by George L. Kelling (the former director of the foundation's evaluation field staff and a research fellow at Harvard University's John F. Kennedy School of Government) aimed at testing a return to police foot patrols on a limited basis in Newark, New Jersey. The experiment was conducted primarily through officers working overtime and did not represent a real commitment of resources or a changed departmental strategy. Nevertheless, Kelling noted impressive improvements in public perceptions of safety and overwhelming public support for foot patrol. The positive reaction appeared to stem from two interrelated factors: the increased visibility of police in daily neighborhood life, and even more important, foot patrol officers' knowledge of and willingness to deal with patterns of physical and behavioral disorder—patterns that citizens were convinced diminished their safety and contributed to crime.

The Newark experiment strongly influenced the document that really launched the community policing movement: "Broken Windows," a 1982 article in *The Atlantic Monthly* written by Kelling with social scientist James Q. Wilson.[9] The article's hypothesis was that disorder did indeed breed crime by driving law-abiding citizens out of public areas and attracting criminal predators. It suggested that police deployed continuously in neighborhood beats—rather than being launched in and out sporadically in patrol cars in response to "incidents"— would be in a far superior position to identify and address disorderly conditions, and to encourage active community participation in "retaking" public spaces.

In effect, Kelling and Wilson argued for a return to the traditional peace officer model of policing. Even more provocatively, they suggested that police served a public order function that was integral to fighting crime, and that deploying resources based on a severity-of-crime standard would often produce *de facto* tolerance for behaviors that diminished public safety from the citizens' point of view.[10]

The article's impact was greatly enhanced by its timing. It appeared near the peak of the long climb in crime rates that began in the 1960s, and amid a nationwide explosion of concern about the deteriorating quality of urban life:

- The "homeless" phenomenon—the sudden, shocking appearance in nearly every major city of aggressive street beggars, caused in no small part by court-ordered deinstitutionalization of substance abusers and the mentally ill—was transforming public transit systems, commercial and retail areas, and parks into threatening places.

- The crack cocaine epidemic was gaining steam, introducing a cheap, violence-inducing drug into virtually every impoverished inner-city neighborhood from coast to coast.

• White and minority middle-class flight from decaying urban centers, a response to declining public order which accelerated during the national real estate boom of the mid-1980s. As these solid citizens left the cities, conditions for those left behind grew even worse.

The time was ripe for a reevaluation of the prevailing assumption that maintaining public order was an illegitimate task for police. A handful of community policing experiments were launched during the mid- to late-1980s in cities ranging from Flint, Michigan, to Atlanta, Houston, Boston, and New York. Like the original Newark experiment, nearly all were small initiatives in limited areas, and occurred amid continuing commitment to the rapid-response model. Even so, these largely superficial efforts attracted strong public support in the affected communities, and significantly improved perceptions of public safety, if not the actual crime rate. In Flint, voters twice approved tax increases to continue foot patrols.[11]

Opposition to Community Policing

Opposition to community policing provides a textbook example of bureaucratic resistance to systemic change.

Police administrators and unions often oppose the strategy for the same two reasons: It upsets long-established, highly valued career-ladder hierarchies, and challenges the professional ethic assumed central to police recruitment and morale. Restoring the peace officer model is interpreted as asking police to become social workers.

Many prosecutors and judges resist community policing as well, for reasons that perfectly reflect the traditional paradigm of state interest versus individual rights.

Trained in and bureaucratically organized around "serious" criminal justice specialties, prosecutors are often ill-disposed to try such "minor" crimes as loitering, disturbances of the peace, public drunkenness, and unlawful entry. Judges are similarly inclined to throw out or mitigate sentences in such cases. Together with prosecutors, they oppose "wasting" police resources on public order functions that tend not to lead to arrests: orders to "move on," intervention in neighborhood disputes, and the like. The purpose of policing, they believe, is to supply them with cases. This mindset helps explain why arrest rates for "lesser" crimes are abysmally low: 9.5 percent for burglary and 7.6

percent for car theft in the nation's seven largest cities in 1995, making these crimes nearly risk-free when committed.

Meanwhile, many public defenders (and many judges) are deeply opposed on principle to the use of police discretion in making arrests that reflect community, not state, priorities. All acts of public drunkenness, they believe, should be treated equally, regardless of community impact. For them, there is no difference between the drunk who intimidates pedestrians and the drunk who quietly sits alone. Among probation and parole officers, selective arrests are resented as a preemption of their authority to determine whether a given offense is grounds for revoking their "client's" status.

The single most important source of resistance to community policing comes from lawyers and judges who inherently oppose the legitimacy of community control of public spaces. Two especially notorious test cases in the late 1980s involved efforts to clear nonresidents from crime-ridden public housing units in Chicago, and to enforce rules of civil behavior on the New York City subways.

Chicago public housing tenants, painfully aware of the nexus between nonresidents and drug-related crime and violence, strongly supported the public-order measures. The initiative ultimately collapsed, however, after the ACLU persuaded the courts to bar police from aggressively searching and screening units for unauthorized persons. The case epitomizes the elevation of individual interests over community interests: Two residents represented by the ACLU were able to halt security measures supported formally by a tenants' association representing thousands of other residents.

The New York subway case, in which George Kelling (as a consultant) and Transit Police Commissioner William Bratton played leading roles, turned out differently. In 1989, between 1,200 and 2,000 persons were sleeping in the subway system each night. Fare-jumpers and fare-thieves were costing the city more than $60 million per year.[12] Felonies on cars and in stations were rising sharply, and virtually all riders—whose numbers were dropping at an alarming rate—feared for their safety.

Under Bratton's direction, transit police began an intensive effort ("Operation Enforcement") to regulate aggressive begging; smoking; public displays of nudity, urination, and defecation; psychotic outbursts; and obstruction of passengers. Homeless persons were directed to shelters or to areas where they would not interfere with transit riders. The initiative succeeded despite attempts by the ACLU and others to claim First Amendment protection for uncivil behavior, and to deny citizens a liberty interest in the peaceful enjoyment of subway transit. Since the beginning of Operation Enforcement, felonies in the subway system have declined by 75 percent, and ridership has stabilized.[13]

The case demonstrated that community order and individual rights could be balanced by carefully emphasizing behavior over status, and through an equally careful effort to provide alternative areas for the use of "street people."

The Politics of Community Policing

At the municipal level, community policing has won support from centrist, reform-minded politicians of both parties, with especially strong commitments being made by Democratic administrations in Baltimore, Boston, and Seattle, and Republican administrations in Indianapolis, New York, and San Diego.

At the national level, the subject drew scant attention from the political parties or from policy groups until the PPI made it a signature idea in 1990. PPI's endorsement, in turn, led to Bill Clinton's campaign pledge in 1992 to support both community policing and a related federal initiative, dubbed COPS, to help cities and counties hire an additional 100,000 police officers over five years.

Before Clinton's COPS initiative became federal law and Democratic orthodoxy in 1994, the national political debate on crime remained stuck in its old ruts.

Conservatives remained convinced that "liberal permissiveness" was the root cause of rising crime. Few viewed policing strategies as being relevant to the crime rate, though some agreed with the status quo belief that community policing was turning police into soft-minded social workers.

On the left, civil libertarians continued to fight Old Paradigm extensions of state power along with New Paradigm approaches to promoting public order. Their role in frustrating efforts to maintain public order and recapture public spaces cannot be exaggerated. In particular, professional advocates for the homeless deliberately encouraged maximum domination of public areas by their "constituents" as a living advertisement for their plight.

With Clinton's election, the goal of strengthening police departments, if not necessarily changing their mission, rose to the top of the national policy agenda as part of a long-awaited federal "crime bill." While the measure that was passed did provide ultimately for the hiring of 100,000 new police officers, it was inadequately funded and also failed to connect the increase in police power to the community policing strategy. (The Clinton administration's Justice Department, however, clearly has been committed to community policing in its technical assistance and research efforts.) Among other shortcomings, the crime bill failed to concentrate the new officers in high-crime communities, and left communities fully responsible for their salaries after five years, creating the risk that those positions will lapse with the federal aid. In the 104th Congress, House Republicans passed legislation (never taken up by the Senate) that would have eliminated COPS and other crime prevention programs authorized by the crime bill in favor of a new, unrestricted block grant to cities and counties.

The real political struggle over community policing in the 1990s erupted in two cities run by mayors with a special commitment to the strategy.

- In San Francisco, Democratic Mayor Frank Jordan, a former policeman, was elected on a platform of reclaiming parks, streets, and the downtown commercial area from panhandlers, prostitutes, and drug and alcohol abusers. Jordan spent much of his term fighting advocacy groups and the courts to implement his "Operation Matrix" strategy for moving street people out of public spaces and into social service and treatment facilities. Key elements of Operation Matrix were struck down by the courts. Jordan was defeated in 1995 by State Assembly Speaker Willie Brown, a liberal Democrat who made opposition to Operation Matrix a central campaign issue.

- In New York, maverick Republican Mayor Rudolph Giuliani in 1994 immediately expanded the community policing initiative begun by his Democratic predecessor, David Dinkins. Giuliani hired William Bratton, who directed the successful New York City subway cleanup, as his police commissioner. Bratton was advised, as earlier, by George Kelling. Using an explicit and aggressive public order strategy right out of "Broken Windows"—enforced by holding precinct captains strictly accountable for results, and enhanced by computerized data on crime in every neighborhood—the Giuliani-Bratton initiative not only increased perceptions of public safety, but produced a sensational reduction in violent crimes. In 1995, the likelihood that a New Yorker would become a crime victim dropped to the lowest odds since 1970; robberies were at their lowest level since 1973; and homicides had been cut nearly in half from their 1990 level.[14] While longer sentences for criminal offenses in New York also undoubtedly contributed to the progress on violent crime, the especially sharp drops in the city's crime rates indicate policing measures have been critical. More recently, Bratton's resignation after a series of clashes with Giuliani and complaints from minority communities about alleged police brutality have made the crime initiative newly controversial on the eve of Giuliani's 1997 reelection campaign.

Beyond Community Policing

As community policing has struggled for acceptance, a few pioneers have
begun to apply the same principles to other bureaucracies in the criminal justice system.

The "community prosecution" movement is now roughly at the same stage
of development and acceptance as community policing was in the mid-1980s.
Actively supported by the Clinton administration's Justice Department and
extensively studied by the American Prosecutorial Research Institute, community prosecution is sometimes adopted as an adjunct to community policing
(as in New York City), and sometimes as a free-standing experiment (as in
Portland, Oregon and Austin, Texas).

Like community policing, community prosecution involves a paradigm
shift in the organization, deployment, and strategic use of law enforcement
resources. It makes the actual impact of patterns of criminal behavior in specific communities the strategic linchpin and measure of success in law enforcement decisions, rather than abstract judgments of a professional elite.

And like community policing, community prosecution requires a significant
change in the professional culture of the criminal justice bureaucracy. Lawyers currently trained and assigned by case specialty are instead assigned to
neighborhoods. Decisions to prosecute cases are based on the impact of a
given offense to public order in the community, not on preestablished and
unvarying indices of a crime's severity.

Prosecutors adopting a community-based approach are encountering the
same kind of support from the public, and the same kind of resistance from
bureaucracies and advocacy groups, previously experienced by community
policing pioneers. For example, State's Attorney Rod Smith of Gainesville,
Florida, aggressively sought public support for a "selective prosecution" initiative focused on a high-crime minority neighborhood in his jurisdiction. He
successfully recruited African-American community leaders to dispute
charges by civil liberties groups that the initiative was racially discriminatory.[15]

In Boston, municipal leaders brought probation officers into a community-
based public order initiative—an especially important experiment given the
power of probation officers over individuals still under the supervision of the
criminal justice system.

Even in the judicial arena, there is an analogous community-based movement seen in the spread of specialty "drug courts," where community-impact
testimony and informal community sanctions are an important part of both
fact-finding and sentencing.

The System Crisis

The glacial movement toward community-based strategies in criminal justice highlights a problem mentioned at the beginning of this chapter: The criminal justice system is, in fact, a wide array of highly fragmented bureaucracies with varying philosophies and governance structures.

This is not merely a problem of public administration. Fragmentation of the criminal justice system is arguably one of the three key factors—along with high crime rates and official indifference to public order—that explains the public's chronic frustration about crime that has forced the issue into national politics.

A compelling, and continuing, example of the problem of fragmentation is the series of perverse and unanticipated consequences proceeding from the so-called "war on drugs" of the early- to mid-1980s.

At both the federal and state levels, a vast array of tougher criminal sanctions were enacted to cope with the trafficking, sale, and consumption of illegal drugs. A criminal justice system that was barely adequate to cope with existing levels of crime was literally overwhelmed by the influx of new offenders.

Already thin police resources were stretched, resulting in lower arrest rates. Prosecutors with unsustainable case loads began to bargain for pleas whenever possible. Supervision of probationers and parolees suffered. And worst of all, federal and state prisons could not accommodate the new levels of convicts.

Hamstrung by federal court orders limiting inmate concentrations, many states undertook drastic measures to create bed space in prisons for the most dangerous offenders, "backwashing" some inmates into local jails, and releasing others long before their sentences were completed. Corrections pressures led many judges to lighten sentences up front. The combined effect of plea bargains, shorter sentences, and early releases was to significantly reduce the ratio of incarceration to crimes, at a time when public sentiment strongly favored longer, not shorter sentences. Early-release and alternative-corrections programs inevitably produced high-profile horror stories of violent offenders committing heinous crimes after serving a small fraction of their sentences.

The "revolving door" phenomenon of repeat offenders, already a major problem, was worsened significantly by a failure to make the resources available to actually implement a "get tough" anti-drug policy.

The backlash to these developments led to a wave of mandatory sentencing legislation at the federal and state levels—most famously, "three strikes and you're out"—aimed at reining in prosecutors, judges, and parole boards, eliminating the local discretion so important to making community impact a significant factor in law enforcement decisions. In fact, the mandatory-sentencing trend is becoming counterproductive, as is best seen with the latest fashionable Republican idea of abolishing parole. While eliminating parole would indeed increase time served in prison, it would also mean that convicts completing their sentences would be released into the community without benefit of continuing supervision by the criminal justice system—a disastrous blow to every community's ability to monitor likely repeat offenders. Longer sentences are entirely possible without abolishing post-incarceration supervision through parole.

An institutional solution to the system crisis is virtually impossible, involving as it would massive constitutional changes at every level of government, and political interference with the judicial system as well.

The most direct, and only feasible, route to reorganization of the criminal justice system is to overcome diverse bureaucratic cultures and philosophies by the broad adoption of a new paradigm for crime and public order that the various institutions could all be encouraged to embrace.

Restorative Justice

There is, in fact, a new paradigm on the margins of social science research and public policy debate on crime that could potentially refocus the criminal justice system on community needs and public order in a comprehensive manner: restorative justice.

The basic concept of restorative justice is that the principle aim of the criminal justice system should be to redress the damage done by criminal offenders to the community in which they live. This approach contrasts sharply with the theory of retributive justice, which focuses on vindicating the state's interests in enforcing its laws, and the theory of distributive justice, which aims at ensuring that offenders are not punished more than is necessary to deter future criminal behavior. As should be obvious, the relationship of restorative justice to its better-known rival theories is very similar to the relationship of community policing to the liberal and conservative paradigms focused on the rights of the individual and of the state.

Developed originally in connection with experiments in offender-victim reconciliation, the restorative justice movement is also the primary theoretical fountainhead of victim's rights programs—embraced during the 1996 presidential campaign by both candidates as a potential constitutional amendment.

If applied as the central principle of the U.S. criminal justice system, restorative justice would:

- Fully vindicate the community policing model, including its key premise that "minor" offenses threatening public order should be addressed;

- Strengthen the rights of citizens to maintain access to public spaces;

- Make community impact a fully legitimate issue in sentencing decisions;

- Strongly enhance the importance of postsentencing and post-incarceration supervision of offenders, to ensure reintegration with the community;

- Refocus crime prevention programs to build strength of community institutions, and;

- Make overall public safety of communities, not crime statistics, the focus of crime policy debate.

The most interesting implication of the restorative justice model is that it would provide the first fresh thinking on the purpose and structure of corrections systems in a generation. Today's prisons, typically operated according to an inchoate hybrid of individual retribution and rehabilitation theories, are often dominated by an inmate culture in which the most violent criminals earn the greatest respect. Parole and other release decisions may focus on good behavior, and even remorse, but rarely take into account the relative socialization of inmates into the value system of the communities in which they are released.

If impact on the community upon release were to become a major concern of prison administrators, then prisons might well be reorganized to make *respect for authority* and *willingness to cooperate* key goals for each inmate, along with specific planning for life after prison. Instead of tolerating inmate-to-inmate violence as a mildly unfortunate element of punishment, administrators would work hard to ensure that predators are undermined in every effort to assert authority over other inmates. In addition, prerelease socialization would be closely coordinated with postrelease parole supervision.

While some elements of the restorative justice theory have been applied in a wide variety of cities, counties, states, and nations—most notably in victim compensation, victim-offender rehabilitation, and alternative sentencing programs—it has been applied comprehensively in just one jurisdiction: the small rural community of Genesee County, New York. First developed fifteen years ago by an innovative sheriff in response to a local jail overcrowding crisis, the "Genesee Justice" program enjoys overwhelming public and bipartisan political support in the community. Its key features include a well established, and very successful, community service-based alternative-sentencing system that has significantly reduced recidivism; intensive victim assistance services; voluntary victim-offender reconciliation; presentencing community impact statements; and even "conscience classes" aimed at developing respect for authority and community among prison inmates.[16]

Regardless of whether restorative justice gains support as a new paradigm for criminal justice in the United States, legally recognizing the community's interests in public spaces is all-important. Otherwise, even such popular and successful reforms as community policing may be stymied by a legal system in which abstract state and individual interests are deemed paramount.

Where to Begin

At first blush, it may appear counterintuitive to suggest that creating a community-based paradigm for crime prevention and maintenance of public order can be accomplished at any level other than that of the local governments closest to the communities themselves.

But recall that the public has nationalized the debate on crime and disorder precisely because state and local bureaucracies have failed to respond, and in part because no single jurisdiction controls enough of the system to force decentralization.

In such circumstances, it is entirely legitimate for the federal government (or alternatively, the states, which control more criminal justice resources than any other level of government) to intervene—*not by creating programs, but by empowering communities to take control of their own protection and their own public spaces.*

Federal policymakers should consider the following suggestions as first steps toward that paradigm shift:

- Fully fund the COPS program, but link federal funding explicitly to full adoption by recipient jurisdictions of bona fide community policing.

- Intervene aggressively in key court cases to support the community interest in public order as a significant factor in sentencing.

- Identify a set of public spaces—parks, downtown commercial and retail areas, public transportation systems, and entertainment facilities— where safe public access should be guaranteed, and launch a national (as opposed to federal) campaign to regain full control of public places in every urban area.

- Direct federal corrections, probation, and parole systems (and parallel state systems that use federal construction funds) to make supervised reintegration of offenders into communities a central priority.

• Expand federal research and technical assistance programs support- ing community policing and community prosecution initiatives, and ex- pand them into community-based models for probation, parole, juvenile justice, and child welfare.

• Offer large challenge grants to a few states to experiment with a comprehensive overhaul of criminal justice bureaucracies on a commu- nity-based model.

Conclusion

Public safety is one area of domestic governance in which the conventional wisdom must be turned on its head. Marginal reductions in "serious crime" rates will not satisfy citizens, so long as they feel endangered in the conduct of their daily lives and prohibited from use of public spaces.

Citizens are demanding national action on public safety not because they want a larger federal bureaucracy or more uniform federal rules governing sentencing, but because they want someone to force state and local criminal justice bureaucracies to defend them. The best way to reduce "serious crimes" is to address "less serious" conditions that breed crime by promoting physical and social disintegration and abandonment of public spaces to predators.

The most effective tool for fighting crime is not a professional crime-fight- ing apparatus with the latest technology, but a police-community partnership based on monitoring and protecting the safety and vitality of our neighbor- hoods. "Wars" on crime, drugs, and gangs will not succeed unless all ele- ments of the criminal justice system are in synch and focused on responding to real-life community needs.

All participants in the criminal justice system—cops, judges, parole and probation officers, prosecutors, prison guards, and yes, criminals themselves when they have done their time—must ultimately be integrated into an effort to make communities resistant to crime, and capable of defending themselves.

Notes

1. Times Mirror Center for The People & The Press, 13 April 1995, News Release, "More Clinton Leadership Wanted: Now the GOP Faces Cynical, Dissatisfied Public," 27, 45.

2. Federal Bureau of Investigation, United States Department of Justice, *Uniform*

Crime Reports for the United States 1995 (Washington, DC: 1996), 5. Federal Bureau of Investigation, United States Department of Justice, *Uniform Crime Reports, 1988,* "Index of Crime, United States, 1960–1987," 1988.

3. *Washington Post*, 28 Oct. 1996, National Weekly Edition.

4. John F. Persinos, "The Return of Officer Friendly," *Governing* (August 1989): 56.

5. George L. Kelling and Mark H. Moore, "The Evolving Strategy of Policing," *Perspectives on Policing*, no. 4 (November 1988) (U.S. Department of Justice, National Institute of Justice, Washington, DC), 2.

6. Ibid., 7.

7. Ibid., 5.

8. Adam Walinsky, "The Crisis of Public Order," *Atlantic Monthly*, July 1995, 40.

9. James Q. Wilson and George L. Kelling, "Broken Windows," *Atlantic Monthly*, Mar. 1982.

10. Ibid., 31.

11. Kelling and Moore, "The Evolving Strategy of Policing," 10.

12. George L. Kelling and Catherine M. Coles, *Fixing Broken Windows* (New York: The Free Press, 1996), 118.

13. Ibid., 125.

14. Ibid., 153.

15. Public Policy discussion on Crime at the DLC Annual Meeting, Washington, DC, November 1995.

16. John Fabian to Ed Kilgore, interoffice memo, 3 June 1996, "Genesee Justice: A Model of Restorative Justice," 5–6.

Chapter 9

Markets and Empowerment: Helping Cities Help Themselves

Fred Siegel and Will Marshall

America's cities are awakening from a decades-long spell of economic de-cline, social breakdown, and ineffectual urban policy. For all the body blows they have suffered, many self-inflicted, they have proven to be remarkably resilient. Unemployment in Detroit has plunged from 18 percent to 8 percent in the past few years, and high-end, service-sector jobs are booming in Chi-cago and Minneapolis.[1] Los Angeles and San Jose, California have become incubators of the Digital Revolution that is giving shape to the postindustrial economy. Serious crime has fallen markedly in nearly all big cities, with New York City leading the way—it recorded a 28 percent decline last year alone.[2]

Immigrants from Asia, Latin America, the Caribbean, and the Middle East are reviving our older cities. Retailers and property developers, having con-verted nearly every available square inch of the suburbs into strip malls, are slowly recognizing that the inner cities are our own Eastern Europe—a vast, virtually untapped market.

And all across America, public housing projects—the most conspicuous symbols of federal good intentions gone awry—are falling to the wrecking ball. Some thirty thousand units were slated for demolition last year alone. But buildings aren't all that is crashing down: The entire intellectual founda-tion for dealing with urban problems is being swept away.

This framework, perhaps best described as the U.S. Conference of Mayors approach, dates to the Depression. At the urging of legendary Mayors James Curley of Boston and Fiorello LaGuardia of New York, Washington responded to the emergency by breaking with old principles of federalism and sending money directly to cities. Some thirty years later as the Great Society began,

129

the framework was given a new rationale: Cities were assumed to be a welter of needs and pathologies that could best be healed by financial therapy from Washington. Accordingly, spending on cities was vastly increased. Then, as the 1960s drew to a close, a final, ominous twist was added: Mayors began arguing for more money as a form of insurance against riots.

In a policy turn with tragic consequences, urban America ceased to present itself as the center of commerce and innovation and instead began to peddle itself as a hopeless victim of racism and economic disruption. Once the economic dynamos of the nation, the cities had become wards of the federal government. We became a nation of dependent cities filled with dependent people. In the words of Mayor Michael White of Cleveland, one of the best of the new wave of market-oriented mayors, our big cities became "a code name for a lot of things: for minorities, for crumbling neighborhoods, for crime—for everything that America has moved away from."[3]

Although the cities-as-victims gambit has failed abysmally, it remains extraordinarily powerful. John Norquist of Milwaukee, another leading new wave mayor, recalls how some fellow members of the U.S. Conference of Mayors were actually heartened by the Los Angeles riots in the summer of 1992. They believed the destruction would force Congress and the governors to pay more attention—and send more money—to all cities. They were disappointed.

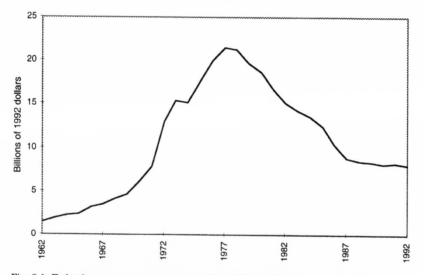

Fig. 9.1. Federal government payments to cities, 1962–1992. Author's calculations based on data from *City Government Finances,* U.S. Bureau of the Census, 1963–1993; and *Economic Report of the President,* 1996.

Bill Clinton's victory in the 1992 presidential election, however, rekindled hope for a federal bailout. For a while, prospects seemed bright: The $16 billion "economic stimulus" program that Clinton proposed in 1993 was based largely on a "ready to go" wish list of construction and infrastructure projects kept by the mayors' conference. But in the end, the program was rejected despite Democratic control of the White House and both chambers of Congress. The old urban policy game was almost over.

A New Strategy for Community Empowerment

Two great American dilemmas—poverty and racial inequality—converge on our inner cities. Our country needs once again to mobilize its energies and resources to vanquish these twin scourges. This time, however, we must take a very different approach, one which reverses some of the key assumptions behind the 1960s War on Poverty.

This chapter presents a blueprint for replacing the discredited approach of bureaucratic paternalism and social-service delivery with a new one based on local initiative, markets, and economic empowerment.

The New Progressive strategy for community empowerment differs from the old urban policy in three critical ways:

- It would stop expanding social programs intended to redistribute wealth and instead pursue a market-based strategy for creating wealth in the inner city.

- It would replace welfare with new empowerment policies that complement the new emphasis on markets and economic development.

- It would shift decisions and resources from central bureaucracies and service providers to community groups and individual citizens.

The new approach assumes that cities must shed their victim mentality and once again become centers of self-sustaining economic activity. It also assumes that Washington's role is not to dispense alms but to help build on the natural vitality of cities. This strategy entails a transition on the one hand from federal to local initiative, and, on the other, from an emphasis on social ills and social services to economic development. Above all, it aims to reintegrate the inner cities into America's market economy and to end the terrible social as well as economic isolation that afflicts Americans in the inner city.

Rather than emphasize income maintenance, the ability to consume, and dependence on public relief, the empowerment strategy emphasizes the classic means by which most Americans get ahead: work, learning, saving, entrepreneurship, and home ownership. The experience of the past quarter century demonstrates that expanded federal social programs are not a short cut to middle-class prosperity and cannot substitute for individual striving.

The new strategy would also leverage the flow of private capital into urban communities, foster small business creation, and build upon the inner cities' competitive advantages, such as their proximity to transportation hubs. Rather than promote color-conscious preferences and minority set-asides that mainly benefit those least in need, the empowerment strategy would advance racial justice by reconnecting the urban minority poor to the economic and social mainstream of American life.

Any credible strategy for urban revitalization must include a dramatic increase in the quality of urban schools and an equally sharp decrease in serious crime. Innovative strategies that build on experiments with charter schools and community policing are detailed elsewhere in this book. This chapter concentrates on how Washington's traditional urban policies should be refashioned to equip urban communities to solve their own problems.

The Urban Exodus

The exodus of jobs and the middle class from America's urban centers began after World War II. "The manufacturing losses in some northern cities have been staggering," Harvard sociologist William Julius Wilson wrote. "In the twenty-year period from 1967 to 1987, Philadelphia lost 64 percent of its manufacturing jobs; Chicago lost 60 percent; New York city, 58 percent; Detroit, 51 percent."[4] In the thirty years after 1950, the central cities lost more than nine million middle- and lower-middle-class whites and gained five million African-Americans migrants, largely from the rural South.

In 1945, city dwellers had higher incomes than suburbanites. But by 1960, suburbanites' incomes were 13 percent higher, and by the end of the 1980s, the gap was 43 percent in cities with populations above one million. Declining population and incomes gave cities declining political clout. In 1970, cities had a four-seat advantage over suburbs in Congress (148 seats to 144). By 1990, Congress had 228 suburban, 79 urban, and 128 rural districts. In the 1992 presidential election, cities with populations above 250,000 accounted for only 12 percent of the vote.[5]

Smaller industrial cities like Gary, Indiana and Camden, New Jersey, were often the areas hardest hit by corporate consolidations and increased manufacturing productivity, trends which produced a drastic decline in manufacturing employment. From 1979 to 1988, steel industry employment dropped from thirty thousand to six thousand workers in Gary, even though more steel is being produced in the city than ever.[6] Camden, now the murder capital of the Northeast, once called itself "the biggest little city in the world." It boasted the Victor Talking Machine Company (which became RCA) and Campbell's, the pioneer of condensed soup. But RCA left after World War II, the shipyards closed in the 1950s, and Campbell's continually reduced its presence in Camden. By 1990, fewer than 100 households in this city of 80,000 had incomes above $50,000, while the nearby suburbs suffered a labor shortage. As a local priest put it, "Everything has flown over the wall that could. What's left are all those with broken wings."

Bad as they were, some of Camden's problems might have been alleviated had it been able to expand its boundaries to incorporate some of its booming suburbs. As David Rusk, author of "Cities without Suburbs," has shown, flexible cities—those able to expand their boundaries—have fared much better than "inelastic" cities. For example, Fort Wayne, Indiana and New Haven, Connecticut, have similar problems and populations. But while Fort Wayne has annexed prosperous suburbs, New Haven, unable to expand, has been overwhelmed by the concentrated poverty trapped within its borders.

The Rise of "Poverty Inc."

The social service industry that attends to problems in cities like Gary and Camden was once hailed for both its therapeutic skills and its financial worth as a pipeline for federal money. Today, it is increasingly derided as "Poverty Inc."—a lucrative business for those who directly benefit by peddling pathology to a willing buyer in Washington.

Rosemary Jackson, a Camden city official, captures the sentiment against social services in the thirty-plus cities across America that have used their building and zoning codes to prohibit the establishment of new "helping" agencies:

> We meet every criteria for poverty, so we always received grants. All it did was create a social service organization bigger than any Fortune 500 company. The money never trickled down to the people. It just created a bureaucracy and allowed the party bosses to control the plantation.

Likewise, Hartford, Connecticut City Councilman Art Feltman rejects Poverty Inc.'s sense of pity toward the poor.

> There's a paternalistic view in the social services community that the poor will always be poor . . . and that if not for us do-gooders, everyone is going to die. I

think we have to have confidence that, given the right opportunity, people can do more for themselves and take more responsibility.

"This city," proclaims Feltman, speaking for older cities across the country, "has a new philosophy: It's jobs, it's homes, it's opportunities."

The Mismatch Thesis: Old Wine in New Bottles

The Rev. Walter Fauntroy, the District of Columbia's former non-voting Congressman, recently gave a rip-roaring speech on how the Capital City's collapse was due to the manufacturing sector's desertion of the district for the suburbs and South China. Fauntroy's evocation of a city victimized by impersonal economic forces was greeted with cheers from the audience. So thoroughly had he expressed the conventional wisdom about the decline of American cities that no one thought to note that D.C., the model city for the U.S. Conference of Mayors' approach, had never had any industry.

In academic circles, Fauntroy's argument is usually referred to as the "mismatch thesis." It argues that the flight of manufacturing jobs from the cities has left masses of willing inner-city workers trapped in poverty. These would-be employees are both unqualified by education to work in the cities' new high-tech professions, and unable to commute to the low-skill, entry-level jobs that have moved beyond even the suburbs.

The thesis, whose most eloquent exponent is Wilson, has the virtue of seeming to explain economic decline in the inner city despite the decline of racial discrimination since the 1960s. Without a doubt, the loss of manufacturing jobs has intensified the cities' economic and social ills. But the mismatch thesis fails as an all-purpose explanation of urban woes because it overlooks the contribution of cultural and political factors, and because its economic analysis is based on two dubious assumptions.

The first is the assumption that the decline of manufacturing jobs represented the end of urban opportunity, particularly in the Rust Belt. One study reported that since the 1960s, there has been a significant amount of "deindustrialization" and erosion in job opportunities especially in the Midwest and Northeast.[7] But the economies of larger, more diversified cities like Chicago and Milwaukee have revived. The Rust Belt as a whole came roaring back in the 1990s in part because of a booming service sector that has spawned high-end jobs.

The second mistaken assumption is that most people work near home. They don't. If the mismatch thesis were correct, the group that should have suffered

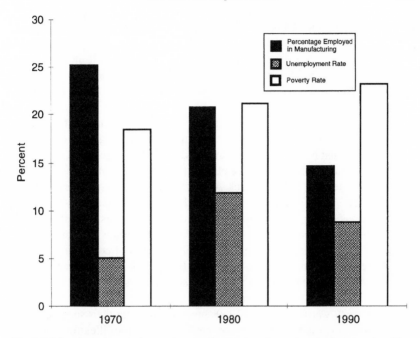

Fig. 9.2. Manufacturing employment, unemployment, and poverty rates in ten major cities, 1970–1990. Data are averages of the individual rates for New York, Los Angeles, Washington, Atlanta, Chicago, Baltimore, Detroit, St. Louis, Cleveland, and Philadelphia; from *County and City Data Book,* U.S. Bureau of the Census, 1967, 1977, 1983, 1994.

most from the loss of manufacturing in the city was the new immigrants, who were heavily concentrated in inner-city industry. Yet they adapted by commuting to where the jobs were, and their employment has continued to grow. During the 1980s when the manufacturing sector shrunk, the immigrant presence continued to expand.

In New York and Los Angeles, job opportunities for low-skilled workers have actually increased in recent years. This is because while the number of such jobs has declined, the number of job seekers has declined even more, due to the massive out-migration of white unskilled and semi-skilled workers. For the most part, immigrants have filled the vacuum rather than African-Americans, who have turned increasingly to the civil service and to the government-reliant health and social service sectors for employment. But clearly, if "the era of big government" is truly over as President Clinton has said, it is imperative for us to draw more African-American inner-city residents into the private sector economy.

The Broken Civil Rights Consensus

For all the encouraging developments, the cities' future is still mortgaged to America's unpaid racial debts. If our cities cannot tackle the problem of intense inner-city poverty, millions will be left in desperation and their own tentative revivals will be jeopardized.

When the civil rights movement and the Great Society moved to redeem the country from its racist past more than three decades ago, no one could have imagined that its efforts would have produced both magnificent successes and dismal failures. Thanks to those efforts, there is now a large black middle class among the four-fifths of black America that lives outside the slums of the inner city. At the same time, however, the number of blacks who live in the ghettos has grown by more than one-third in recent years. And those who are poor tend to be poor longer and to live further beneath the poverty line than in previous generations. Measured solely in terms of consumer activity, the inner cities of America have improved. But that rise in consumption has been accompanied by a social and moral breakdown so severe that the horrors of Dickens's London pale in comparison.

"The poverty warriors" of the 1960s never dreamt that their social experiments could crash amid an unprecedented rise in crime, illegitimacy, teen motherhood, hopelessness, child abuse, and a "gangsta" culture so coarse that it regularly refers to women as "hoes" and "bitches." But they have.

For thirty years, social policy was based largely on two assumptions. The first was that society was required, as reparations of sorts, to give aid and assistance to the politically organized of the inner city on their own terms. In practice, this emphasis on community control and community development often meant that government was funding the continued concentration of poverty in all-black neighborhoods. For example, welfare rolls mushroomed as antipoverty lawyers fought to make it easier to get public assistance and harder to be terminated once on. The political correlate was that government was supporting separatist black politics on the local level.

The second assumption was that, just as urban renewal had been the great task for the cities from the 1940s through the early 1960s, the great new task was human renewal. This meant a vast array of social programs—and hence jobs—designed to ameliorate the past effects of both racism and capitalism. Yet the spread of urban pathologies has dissipated the 1960s faith that social psychologists, psychiatrists, and social workers had both the knowledge and wherewithal to make the wounded whole. Even under the best of circumstances (as in Atlanta, where both the region and the city have boomed), the poverty of the isolated inner city has intensified. "Not one majority black neighborhood [that was] poor in 1970 is measurably less poor in 1990," explains David Rusk.[8] A rising tide, it turned out, didn't lift all boats. That's because the concentration of the jobless minority poor leaves people cut off from connections to work, even as it generates a politics of racial resentment that feeds off isolation.

The violence of the 1960s set in motion a dual secession that severely damaged the cities. On the one hand, many middle-class whites and blacks fled the cities, insulating themselves from the chaos they left behind. On the other hand, black nationalism and the commercial cultivation of racial resentment made the inner city seem more and more alien to the rest of America. As the populations were reshuffled, a new element entered the picture: the arrival of the greatest wave of immigration since the turn of the century. In the case of Miami, Washington, Dallas, and Los Angeles, this has set off a round of black-brown violence that sometimes eclipses the old black-white antagonisms.

For many Americans, the temptation is to flee urban disorder and not look back. But the social costs of such evasions are mounting. Americans today have many reasons to attack with renewed resolve the cycle of inner-city poverty: to right enduring racial wrongs; to reinforce the cities' historic role in assimilating newcomers to our country; to ensure that our cities can compete in global markets; and, to demonstrate to ourselves and to a world that looks to our example that free enterprise is the solution to poverty, not its cause.

The Clinton administration has pointed the nation in the right direction. While the jury is still out on its empowerment zone initiative, the U.S. Department of Housing and Urban Development, under the creative leadership of Secretary Henry Cisneros, has cut bureaucracy, given cities wider discretion in how they use federal resources, promoted community initiative, and launched efforts to expand the supply of credit as well as opportunities for home ownership in low-income communities.

Some prominent Republicans, such as Vice Presidential candidate Jack Kemp, Sen. Dan Coats of Indiana, and Reps. Jim Talent of Missouri and J.C. Watts of Oklahoma, also have begun to advance a serious empowerment agenda. It relies heavily on tax incentives to spur economic development in urban centers, and to shift resources for meeting human needs from public bureaucracies to private charities and churches.

The great political challenge today is to unite left and right around a new, radically different blueprint for revitalizing our cities and reducing urban poverty. Our strategy, reflecting the New Progressive Declaration's guiding principles of equal opportunity, mutual responsibility, and new governing institutions that equip people and communities to solve their own problems, stresses three key goals: making inner-city markets work; moving from welfare to empowerment; and shifting power to people and communities.

Making Inner-City Markets Work

Urban America has had a hard time finding its place in the most rapidly decentralizing, advanced civilization in history. Earlier this century, decentralization was driven by the automobile, the electric grid, and the telephone; today, it is being driven by fax machines, modems, and the Internet. One in ten workers in Los Angeles County is a full- or part-time telecommuter. Already handicapped by high crime, high costs, and hidebound public-sector unions, the central cities must compete not only with exurbia, but also with their own "technoburbs"—growth corridors which are neither city nor suburb and which increasingly define the modern economy.

Public policy, however, has largely ignored the challenge of connecting inner-city residents to markets. Of the $200 billion Washington spends annually to alleviate poverty, only 5 percent is earmarked for economic development.[9] Much of the rest is siphoned off by social service providers. A study of federal, state, and local spending on the poor in Cook County, Illinois, for example, showed that only 37 percent went directly into the hands of its supposed beneficiaries. John McKnight of Northwestern University, a trenchant critic of the therapeutic approach of "helping" professionals, suggests that Washington gradually reverse its priorities by shifting 2 percent to 3 percent of social spending each year toward efforts to lift incomes and promote job creation.[10]

While federal social programs can alleviate some symptoms of poverty, they are almost always too small and narrow in reach to grapple with the underlying causes of poverty. Only by harnessing the power of markets can we create sufficient jobs and wealth in the cities to keep middle-class families from moving out, while giving inner-city residents a chance to move up. The best use for scarce public dollars is to leverage private investment in central cities.

Consider public housing. Instead of perpetuating federal subsidies for the poor (which aid less than one-fifth of those who are eligible and do little to help people "graduate" from public assistance), we should convert some of those dollars into one-time subsidies for community-based efforts to expand the supply of housing, which would lower rents. Likewise, Washington should promote home ownership by converting dollars now spent on rental subsidies (the annual total exceeds $10 billion) into grants to local governments and community groups, which would use the money to clear sites for construction of low-cost housing and to cut mortgage interest rates for owner-occupant home buyers in low-income neighborhoods.

Everyone knows the myriad reasons why it's hard to do business in the inner city: Crime is rampant, the schools are bad, too many people lack basic skills and have poor work habits, transportation and other infrastructure is in disrepair, and municipal taxes and regulations are onerous. Yet important research by Michael Porter of the Harvard Business School suggests the inner city enjoys important competitive advantages. One is central location: Urban enterprises are located close to ports and transportation hubs, storage and distribution networks, and cultural attractions. Another is local market demand: Despite low family incomes, densely packed neighborhoods have high collective purchasing power—$3.4 billion in inner-city Boston alone. A third advantage is the opportunity to integrate into regional business clusters, such as the entertainment industry in Los Angeles or the financial services industry in New York. Finally, the cities are rich in human resources, including highly motivated immigrant workers, as well as entrepreneurial talent, though much of the latter is siphoned off by the social service industry.

Porter argues that government's role should shift from providing social relief and subsidies to creating a favorable business climate in urban areas. Specific steps would include tax breaks for long-term equity investments; one-time subsidies that reduce the cost of processing loans; guarantees for inner-city business loans; the targeting of government preference programs to firms that hire inner-city residents; and deregulation of cumbersome zoning, building code, business licensing, and environmental standards.

President Clinton last fall proposed $2 billion in tax credits for private companies that finance cleanups of mildly polluted urban land, or "brownfields." And cities can put out the welcome mat by opening "one-stop" centers where entrepreneurs can clear all regulatory hurdles instead of spending countless hours scurrying from one agency to another to acquire permits and pay fees. Moreover, it's time to repeal the federal Davis-Bacon law which, by requiring low-cost housing developers to pay union-scale "prevailing wages," drives up the cost of construction in low-income neighborhoods.

One temptation in turning to the private sector will be to look for quick fixes in the form of convention centers, casinos, and sports franchises.[11] In fact, retailing provides the best opportunities today for inner-city employment. A large retail outlet such as the new Pathmark food store in Harlem generates more revenue for the local economy than does a professional football team that plays eight home games a year. With the over-building of suburban malls, developers and retailers are increasingly turning toward the untapped inner-city market. Inner-city Cleveland and Washington enjoy major new shopping centers. There is a new shopping center and movie complex on line for Newark with the help of LISC (Local Initiative Support Corporation). And in forlorn New Haven, a bevy of developers is competing to build one million square feet of shopping in a city that's only twenty-one square miles.

In commercial jargon, the older cities are "under retailed." As of 1995,

New York City, for instance, was at the lowest level of retail employment since 1958. The city, says Planning Commissioner Joe Rose, exports about $3.1 billion of retail activity a year because one-third of households do their major shopping outside the city.[12]

"We think Harlem is retailing's best-kept secret," enthuses a spokeswoman for The Gap, which plans to open there shortly. In recent years, Ben and Jerry's, Rite Aid, and Blockbuster Video have opened in Harlem; Disney, Sony, Home Depot, and Caldor are all looking for sites. Referring to both the managerial and entry-level positions these new outlets can provide, the Harlem manager of Ben and Jerry's sees the new stores as a shot at "our piece of the American dream."

If cities are going to revive, they will need jobs created not only by retailing but by the niche manufacturers that are increasingly important in supplying retailers. Local manufacturing for private labels can be a boon to department stores, which demand quick deliveries on new clothing lines. Similarly, the software, multimedia, jewelry, and banking businesses are also generating demand for specialty manufacturing.

Moving From Welfare to Empowerment

As we focus urban policy on the new goal of strengthening inner-city markets, we must also reorient our social policies around the complementary task of equipping everyone to seize economic opportunities. This requires replacing not only welfare but also other dependency-inducing programs with a new strategy for empowering inner-city residents to find and keep private-sector jobs, to save and build personal assets, and to develop their entrepreneurial capacities through microenterprise.

Connecting welfare recipients to work

Withstanding furious criticism from liberal activists, President Clinton last fall signed legislation eliminating the sixty-one-year-old federal entitlement to cash payments for low-income mothers and their dependent children. In doing so, the President at once redeemed his 1992 pledge to "end welfare as we know it" and opened a new front in the war on poverty.

The old welfare system was geared to maintaining poor families at a low level of consumption. But as Michael Sherraden of Washington University has pointed out, "you can't spend your way out of poverty." Instead of income maintenance, consumption, and dependence, government's efforts to lift the poor should emphasize America's time-tested formula for upward mobility: work, savings, and building personal assets.

Thanks to a host of policy changes championed by the Clinton administration—more money to help mothers pay for child care when they take a job; a dramatic, $21 billion expansion of the Earned Income Tax Credit, a direct subsidy for low-wage workers; and tougher enforcement of absent fathers' child support obligations—work at even entry-level jobs will lift most families out of poverty.

This new "Work First" approach to welfare, however, still lacks a critical component: a job placement and support system that connects welfare recipients to private employers. Inner-city residents often lack the informal networks through which most of us learn about job opportunities. Even after they get jobs, many welfare recipients will need help staying on and moving up the ladder of work. This help can, and should, be provided through nongovernmental, nonbureaucratic means.

Consider the example of America Works, a private, for-profit firm based in New York. The company solicits welfare recipients through word-of-mouth, grooms them for job interviews, and then matches them with prospective employers for a four month trial period. During the trial, the workers stay on the America Works payroll. Significantly, they are also assigned to counselors who help them cope with the many small emergencies that people living on the edge routinely face. If the new worker manages to hold the job for about six months, the state pays America Works a fee.

We should build the bridge from welfare to work with choice and competition rather than government bureaucracies. To stimulate a market for welfare-to-work services, PPI has proposed that states convert welfare payments into vouchers that welfare mothers could use to buy job placement and support services from competing providers: nonprofit organizations, businesses such as America Works, and state and local agencies. Since those providers could only redeem the full value of those vouchers by making sure their clients stay employed, this approach would ensure that taxpayers pay only for success.

Believing that good jobs are scarce in the cities, Wilson and other analysts argue that government must jump-start urban revitalization through large-scale public works. Others dispute their premise, noting that immigrants in the cities have had little trouble finding private-sector work. While it may be possible to justify large-scale public works as an emergency response to chronic inner-city unemployment, the long-term challenge is to link inner-city residents to private labor markets, and to ensure that even entry-level jobs always offer a better deal than welfare.

Encouraging savings and investment

We also need to reorient U.S. social policy around the goals of saving and investment. After all, Washington offers middle-class Americans strong inducements to save and build personal assets, in the form of mortgage-interest deduction and tax breaks for private pensions and savings accounts. These breaks are worth hundreds of billions of dollars annually, yet our welfare policies not only fail to offer similar incentives to low-income families, they often penalize thrift.

To rectify this glaring inequity, Peter Dreier of Occidental College and John Atlas of the National Housing Institute propose replacing the federal income tax mortgage-interest deduction with a refundable tax credit to increase home ownership. "The current mortgage-interest deduction is a government subsidy that goes primarily to the affluent," they write, noting that the $51 billion cost of the deduction is double the entire HUD budget.[13]

Michael Sherraden has proposed another way to promote asset-building: Individual Development Accounts (IDA) for low-income families whose deposits can be matched by government as well as local businesses, churches, and community groups. IDA savings should be restricted to uses that help low-income people become upwardly mobile and accumulate assets: paying for college or job training, starting a small business, or buying a home.

Community-run IDA demonstration projects are proliferating. For example, Eastside Community Investments, a nonprofit venture in Indianapolis, Indiana, sets up accounts for low-income people and matches every dollar they contribute with up to nine of its own. It helped Tina Moynihan, a nineteen-year-old single mother, fulfill her fantasy of owning her own home. "If it wasn't for the IDA money, I never could have done it," she says. "I was horrible with saving. Now I have a savings account and a checking account."[14]

The State of Oregon has made asset-building an integral part of its attempts to replace welfare with work. It urges employers to hire welfare recipients as trainees and converts their welfare payments into wages. In lieu of wages, the employers contribute $1 per hour into individual savings accounts set up for the trainees.

The new welfare reform bill encourages IDAs by, in effect, waiving federal limitations on the amount people can save and still receive public assistance. Asset-building would get an even bigger boost if the federal government were to give IDAs the same tax-exempt treatment accorded Individual Retirement Accounts, and invest in IDA projects in order to leverage private contributions. The Clinton administration should embrace a bipartisan proposal by Sens. Coats and Carol Moseley-Braun, Democrat of Illinois, for a five-year demonstration project that would create fifty thousand IDAs for low-income families at a cost to the federal government of $100 million.

Finally, by helping the minority poor in the inner city save and build personal wealth, IDAs would offer a new way to advance the cause of racial equality in America. According to the U.S. Census Bureau, the distribution of personal assets (property, savings, and investments) by race is even more skewed than the distribution of income: whites possess 92 percent of Americans' total net worth while blacks have only 3.1 percent.[15]

Microenterprise

Like everyone else, low-income Americans must learn how to compete in today's more entrepreneurial economy. The rapid growth of the "microenterprise" programs—which offer low-income people small loans (typically less than $10,000) to start their own business—strongly suggests there is an abundance of latent entrepreneurial talent in poor communities.

Just in the last decade, more than six hundred microlending programs have sprung up around the country, from Chicago's ghettoes to rural North Carolina. Bob Friedman of the Corporation for Enterprise Development, a leading proponent of microenterprise, estimates that as many as thirty thousand low-income Americans have become self-employed through microloans.[16] For example, loan recipients have gone into business making and selling T-shirts, operating ice cream trucks, planning weddings and parties—even offering financial services. Some groups, like the Women's Self-Employment Project in Chicago, use a system of peer-group lending to produce low default rates that any commercial bank would envy.

Microenterprise is more than a lending program, it is an investment in developing the human capital of poor neighborhoods. Projects offer budding entrepreneurs not just credit, but training in business and accounting techniques, and a better understanding of how markets work. In fact, the high costs of training and technical assistance are a greater obstacle to the spread of microenterprise than a lack of credit (most of which comes from private sources, as it should).

Washington can help by shifting some of the money it spends on education and job training to microenterprise projects. "We ought to train people to make jobs, not just to take jobs," Friedman notes. Moreover, President Clinton's proposed $3.4 billion plan for job creation, placement, and tax credits to employers who hire welfare recipients should be modified to permit refundable credits to welfare mothers who choose self-employment. Local governments can pitch in by easing regulations that stymie entrepreneurial behavior, such as bans on home businesses and limits on entry to certain occupations, such as taxi driving.

Shifting Power to People and Communities

A new vision for America's cities springs from the simple recognition that bureaucracies in Washington cannot supply the moral inspiration and leadership necessary to salvage distressed communities. That can come only from within. While Washington can play an important supporting role, top-down decision-making must yield to bottom-up strategies designed not by "experts" but by local problem solvers who know their neighborhood's needs, who have the greatest stake in finding solutions that work, and who are equipped to confront both the moral and economic dimensions of the urban crisis. Empowerment in its profoundest sense means convincing poor Americans that they have the capacity to make their own choices, and, with the community's help, to overcome obstacles to opportunity and independence.

One example is the growing trend toward tenant management of public housing. Experience shows that when residents manage their own affairs, they are more likely than their bureaucratic overseers in local housing authorities to insist on responsible behavior by fellow tenants. Cicero Wilson of the Corporation for Enterprise Development notes that, in Washington's Kenilworth-Parkside project, a long-running experiment with tenant management led to an increase in monthly rent collections from $55,000 to $144,000. Welfare rates in that project dropped by 30 percent, teen pregnancies by 75 percent, and crimes committed by residents by 95 percent.[17] Residents even started a college fund—an unimaginable leap for many until the experience of taking charge of their immediate surroundings widened their horizons.

Washington cannot devolve responsibility into an institutional void. Public policies, therefore, ought to stimulate the proliferation of homegrown institutions for community self-help that can map practical strategies for reviving neighborhoods from the inside out. A promising model is the community development corporation (CDC) movement.

Over the last fifteen years, more than twenty-two hundred CDCs have sprouted up in urban neighborhoods. These private, nonprofit groups have concentrated mostly on rehabilitating and building affordable housing for low-income families. Their growth was originally spurred by federal policy, especially the 1977 Community Reinvestment Act, which requires banks to extend credit to inner-city communities, and the low-income housing credit, which gives a tax break to private investors in affordable housing.

CDCs are undoing the worst legacy of nearly fifty years of federal housing policy: the packing of extremely poor families in particular neighborhoods and buildings. The Columbia Heights Community Development Corporation in Washington targets run-down apartment buildings where tenants who receive rental subsidies are concentrated. After renovating the buildings, it rigorously screens tenants to ensure that a solid majority of them will be responsible working people.

In Chicago, nonprofit groups and a for-profit community bank, South Shore Bank, emphasize home ownership as the most effective strategy for reviving decaying inner-city neighborhoods. That's because owners have a powerful motive—maintaining the value of their property—to keep their communities clean and safe. And businesses are more likely to locate in neighborhoods spruced up and protected by homeowners.

The National Housing Service (NHS) works block by block in Chicago, offering low-interest loans to potential buyers or to existing owners to fix up their homes rather than fleeing to another neighborhood. While NHS receives some money from government, it has a major private partner in the Bank of America-Illinois, which has invested $40 million in the nonprofit group. "This is an attractive piece of business for us," says bank vice president William Goodyear, who notes that NHS makes small loans that the commercial giant can't make because transaction costs are too high. The big bank's insistence on making a profit on its investment introduces market discipline that has been conspicuously lacking in government's attempts to expand the supply of low-cost housing.

Community-based groups like CDCs do more than put together complicated financial packages for developing housing. They also help identify and train community leaders and encourage them to form block associations, neighborhood-watch groups, and other mutual aid organizations. In short, they help stricken communities replenish their stock of "social capital"—the networks of civic, religious, ethnic, and business associations that are a healthy community's antibodies against urban decay.

The next frontier for CDCs and other "third-sector" organizations is economic development. Many already have begun to focus their lending on small retail businesses: supermarkets, drug stores, dry cleaners, and the like. With the advent of genuine welfare reform, community-based groups also need to turn their attention to preparing the inner-city workforce and providing connections to labor markets.

How can the federal government's resources be redeployed to assist? One way would be to replace HUD with a new Community Empowerment Agency. Its job would be to transform the federal government's long-established relationship to cities—to make Washington an investor in, and facilitator of, community-based economic and human development projects, rather than a designer and dispenser of top-down programs and categorical grants.

Conclusion

With the Cold War behind us, the greatest moral and economic challenge facing our society is ending the isolation and intense concentration of the minority poor in the inner city. New Progressives believe there is a compelling national interest in assisting the economic and social reconstruction of our central cities. But the federal government's role must change. In recent decades, America's big cities exhibited what John McKnight calls a "cargo cult" mentality—scanning the skies, like South Sea islanders during World War II, for parachutes bearing pallets of aid from Washington. Today, sparked by new urban partnerships that include community groups, local businesses, and reform-minded mayors, many cities are determined to shed this debilitating dependence and rebuild themselves from the ground up. Washington can and must help by replacing central decision making, social services, and welfare with a new strategy based on local initiative, markets, and individual empowerment.

Notes

1. *New York Times*, 21 July 1996, Business and Finance section.
2. Mayor's Management Report [1996], New York, N.Y.
3. Jonathan Walters, "Cities on Their Own," *Governing* (Apr. 1991): 29.
4. William Julius Wilson, *When Work Disappears: The World of the New Urban Poor* (New York: Alfred A. Knopf, 1996), 29–30. "In absolute numbers, these percentages represent the loss of 160,000 jobs in Philadelphia, 326,000 in Chicago, 520,000— over half a million—in New York, and 108,000 in Detroit."
5. NBC, ABC, CBS and CNN, "National President Total # of Respondents - 15232 Exit Poll Horizontal %'s for All Voters," (Voter Research & Surveys, General Election, 3 Nov. 1992).
6. Robert Caitlin, "The Decline and Fall of Gary, Indiana," *Planning* (June 1988): 14.
7. Wilson, *When Work Disappears: The World of the New Urban Poor*, 29.
8. David Rusk, telephone conversation with author, Report to the Atlanta Regional Commission, 15 Aug. 1996.
9. Professor Michael E. Porter, conversation with author, Washington, DC, 17 Oct. 1995.
10. John McKnight, discussion with Vice President Gore's taskforce on Urban Empowerment, 30 July 1993, transcript, Vowell & Jennings, Inc.
11. The problem is not only that there have been too many such facilities built in too many cities, but they involve ordinary taxpayers subsidizing wealthy developers with little payback. The economic returns of tourism have been wildly exaggerated. Convention centers, like stadia, are justified on the grounds that every dollar put into

the economy generates the spending of four or five more dollars. True enough, but most of that spending simply shifts revenues from preexisting businesses to those that benefit from the new center. Casinos bring in both new revenues and new problems like gambling addiction. The casinos of Atlantic City are wildly successful, but the city, which went from fifty-fifth to first in per capita crime, is not.

12. Joe Rose, New York City Planning Commission Report [1995], New York, NY.

13. Peter Dreier and John Atlas, "How to Expand Home Ownership for More Americans," *Challenge* (March/April 1992).

14. Marilyn Werber Serafini, "Dream Machine," *National Journal* (27 April 1996): 932.

15. Will Marshall, "From Preferences to Empowerment: A New Bargain on Affirmative Action" (Progressive Policy Institute, Policy Report, 3 Aug. 1995), 15.

16. Robert Friedman, telephone conversation with author, Corporation for Enterprise Development, 14 Oct. 1996.

17. Cicero Wilson, meeting on Urban Empowerment: New Strategies for Saving America's Cities, Washington, DC, 18 Mar. 1996.

Chapter 10

A Progressive Family Policy for the Twenty-First Century

William A. Galston

During the past generation, our country endured what some have called a culture war, and the family was one of its most contested fronts. In universities and think tanks, in social movements and public debate, competing diagnoses of the causes of family change became weapons in an ideological contest. Proponents of economic explanations dueled with proponents of cultural analyses; calls for increased social responsibility were matched by calls for increased personal responsibility. Demands for personal and gender liberation warred with demands, based on history and theology, for the restoration of what many regard as traditional family patterns.

On the eve of the twenty-first century, the dust of battle appears to be settling and it may be possible to work toward a truce. While the extremes are unreconciled, and probably irreconcilable, there are reasons to hope that a coalition of the center can coalesce around a progressive approach to family policy consistent with emerging economic and social realities.

President Clinton has done much to foster such an approach and to alter the tone and terms of public discourse. To address the economic problems of working families, he has pushed for a large increase in the Earned Income Tax Credit, signed the Family and Medical Leave Act, and toughened child support enforcement. His comprehensive education agenda, partially enacted into law, offers new opportunities for families—from Head Start, to postsecondary edu-

The sections on second-chance homes and foster care are based on the work of PPI's Vice President for Domestic Policy Kathleen Sylvester and research analyst Stephanie Soler.

cation, to job retraining for displaced workers. On the cultural front, he has pressed for laws upgrading children's television programming; enhanced parental control and choice through the television "V-chip" and a related television rating system; and, reinforced parental authority as well as child safety by supporting curfews and public school uniforms. To strengthen family structures, he has vigorously supported both public and voluntary sector efforts to reduce teen pregnancy and out-of-wedlock births. And although the law of divorce is principally a state rather than federal question, both the President and Hillary Rodham Clinton have called for a reconsideration of easily accessible divorce when minor children are involved.

These steps, while important, are only a beginning. During his second term, the President should bring new clarity and urgency to the challenge of fortifying families. He should offer a new paradigm for understanding this challenge, and a new agenda of public, private, and voluntary initiatives to meet it. In short, he must build on the foundation he laid during the past four years to create a progressive family policy for the twenty-first century.

Basic Elements of a Progressive Family Policy

The *goals* of this policy are clear: First, strengthening intact, two-parent families to maximize the number of children who have the opportunity to grow up in such families; second, providing new supports for the millions of children in single-parent families, to create the closest possible functional equivalent of intact families; and third, radically changing our policies for children who lack even one caring, competent adult in light of what we know about the minimum conditions for normal child development.

The *scope* of a progressive family policy is equally clear. It must attend to the economic underpinnings of healthy family life, to its cultural preconditions, and to questions of family structure.

The *principles* of this policy have not changed significantly since they were stated four years ago in PPI's *Mandate for Change*: Public programs cannot substitute for healthy families; neighborhoods, communities, and the voluntary sector must continue to provide essential supplements to both parents and governmental programs; the private sector cannot shirk its distinctive responsibilities. When government acts, it must minimize bureaucratic complexity and intrusion, working instead to broaden individual opportunity and choice.

This chapter sketches a handful of key proposals. They do not represent a comprehensive family policy, but rather materials from which such a policy must be constructed. (A truly comprehensive policy would include not just public sector actions, but new responsibilities for America's corporations and every other important sector of our society.)

A New Family Policy Paradigm for a New Society

To develop this new paradigm, we must get beyond the outdated debate between conservatives and liberals. Conservatives must understand that the economic and social changes of the past generation have rendered traditional gender roles unrealistic and confining for an increasing number of Americans. Liberals must understand that in the economy and society of the next century, stable intact families will not be obsolete, but more necessary than ever. Conservatives must accept the legitimacy of government efforts to strengthen the capacity of parents to raise children; liberals must discard the hope that government programs can somehow substitute for functioning families.

As we enter the twenty-first century, both mothers and fathers will be struggling to balance work and family and to nurture children for a new society in which educational achievement and good character will be crucial. Parents understand how powerfully our culture shapes and limits their ability to reach these goals. Public policy can alter culture directly (for example, by imposing reasonable regulations on children's television) and indirectly, by aligning the moral premises of government policies with the values we hope to nourish.

The Historical Setting of the New Family Paradigm

As the New Progressive Declaration makes clear, the transition from the Industrial to the Information Age is profoundly altering not just modes of production, but social relations as well. Over the past generation, technological innovation and global competition have exerted continuing pressure on wages. The days when single wage earners with modest skills could comfortably support a middle-class family are probably gone for good. Upgrading education and training can help, of course. But for the foreseeable future, most families will need two adults with wage-earning capacities to remain securely in the middle class.

During the past two decades, median family incomes have barely budged. But this familiar economic aggregate conceals a more complex social reality: While the incomes of families headed by single parents or lower-skilled workers have fared badly, the incomes of better educated two-parent families have surged. From an economic perspective, the two-parent family is not less necessary, but more necessary, than it was in its heyday forty years ago.

This conclusion is reinforced by another feature of the new economy: insecurity. Recent studies suggest that job loss at all levels—but especially among managers and white-collar workers—is higher than a generation ago. Families with more than one adult wage earner serve in effect as informal insurance systems against economic catastrophe. While the family temporarily retrenches, the partner who remains employed eases the other's transition to new employment opportunities.

In the new economy, education is a necessary (though not always sufficient) condition of success. All other things being equal, children from intact families enjoy higher levels of educational achievement and are more likely to internalize the skills and virtues required for lifetime learning. Individual opportunity is increasingly a function of individual knowledge and character rather than social rules and institutions.

This fact points to a broader phenomenon, perhaps the most fundamental difference between the new and old economies. During the Industrial Era, government and the private sector provided relatively stable security structures. Individuals could obtain economic security from large corporations that offered job continuity as well as health and pension benefits within a framework of hierarchically administered rules. And they could find social security within publicly funded, government-managed institutions in which all were able (or required) to participate.

In the Information Age, however, these older structures of stability are eroding. The share of unemployment attributable to permanent dismissals rather than temporary layoffs is increasing, and older white-collar workers are being hit harder than in previous economic cycles. Pension and health care coverage by private corporations is declining. Meanwhile, public social insurance programs are coming under intense pressure and probably cannot maintain their current structures and levels of benefits. In these circumstances, well-functioning families are needed both to enhance security and reinforce the strengths of character on which lives of self-reliance depend. Success in the new economy means shoring up the oldest of social institutions.

Adverse Trends

At a moment in history when strong families are more important than ever, numerous forces are converging to weaken them. In middle-class communities, economic changes have presented many parents with tough choices between family income and family time. Too often, parents have less time than they would like to invest in their children. Many kids come home after school to empty homes, a development that increases opportunities for unsupervised teens to get into trouble and reinforces the power of television over younger children. (There is no longer a reasonable scholarly basis for doubting the causal link between televised violence and antisocial behavior among young people, and evidence is accumulating in the case of televised sex as well.)

In many urban areas, the consequences of economic change for families have been even more severe. Harvard sociologist William Julius Wilson argues that, with the disappearance of manufacturing jobs from our central cities, employment opportunities for young, low-skilled black men have dwindled, adversely shifting the balance between legal and illegal sources of income. While aspects of his thesis remain controversial, (see chapter 9), few doubt that higher unemployment rates among inner city men have contributed to family breakdown. As these men have become less desirable marriage partners (and scarcer through incarceration and early death), the formation of traditional families has all but ended in many areas. In turn, these economic and social developments accelerate cultural change that has deinstitutionalized marriage and destigmatized out-of-wedlock birth. At its points of greatest concentration, this complex of pathologies has produced a new generation of superpredators—young people almost wholly lacking in empathy and impulse control, prone to inflict and receive violence.

Far from being aberrant, these problems are intensified versions of trends clearly visible throughout our society. In 1960, only 5 percent of America's children were born out of wedlock; by 1995 that figure had topped 30 percent. Between 1960 and 1980, the rate of divorce more than doubled before stabilizing at the highest rate, by far, in the industrialized world. More than 40 percent (by some projections, 50 percent) of marriages undertaken today will end in divorce. Not surprisingly, the rate of children living apart from their biological fathers has risen from 17 percent to 36 percent in the past three decades; close to half of these children have not seen their fathers during the past year. Since the 1960s, the number of children directly touched by divorce each year has risen from 485,000 to one million. The odds that a child born in the 1990s will reach age eighteen living with both biological parents have dropped below 50 percent (for African-American children, below 10 percent).

As public attention has focused on the problems of the single-parent family, a new and even more troubling phenomenon has emerged: the rise of the no-parent family in which, for reasons of AIDS, drug addiction, or other problems, neither biological parent is able or willing to care for the children. The result has been a surge in foster care—a system built with the best of intentions, but so dysfunctional in its operation and so perverse in its results as to verge on publicly sanctioned child abuse.

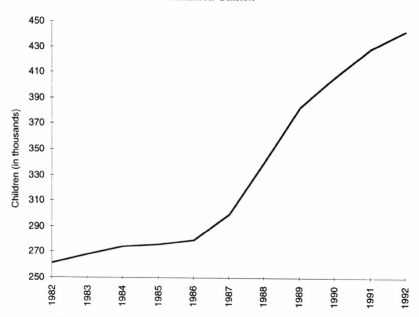

Fig. 10.1. Number of children living in foster care, 1982–1992. Data from Tashio Tatara, *Characteristics of Children in Substitute and Adoptive Care,* 1993; and *Statistical Abstract of the United States,* U.S. Bureau of the Census, 1994.

As recently as the beginning of this decade, PPI felt compelled to offer a detailed scholarly argument in defense of what was then an unfashionable thesis among progressives, that changes in family structure during the past generation were working against the interests of children.[1] Today, that debate is all but settled. Children born out of wedlock, especially those born to young parents who never marry, are likely to labor under economic, educational, and emotional disadvantages throughout their lives. Leading researchers have found that the negative consequences of divorce for children cannot be fully explained by either parental conflict pre-divorce or income decline post-divorce. Divorce itself, frequently followed by the attenuation or termination of contact between fathers and children, has an independent negative effect on school performance, emotional development, and long-term psychological well-being. While young boys are hit early and hard by their father's absence, the long-term consequences for girls appear to be significant as well.[2] Both out-of-wedlock birth and divorce are correlated with increases in crime among young people. Due in part to changes in family structure, violent crime rates have soared for teens and young adults over the past decade; during this time, homicide among fourteen- to seventeen-year-olds has nearly tripled.

Policy Recommendations

The new paradigm of family policy seeks to yoke together three potent forces—economics, politics, and culture—on behalf of children and their parents. To help advance this paradigm, we should consider taking the following steps: create a family-friendly tax code; reform divorce law to put children first; enlist one million mentors for vulnerable kids; create "second-chance" homes for young mothers; and end foster care as we know it.

Create a family-friendly tax code

For the most part, gains in family income will hinge on implementation of the broader economic proposals presented elsewhere in this book. But there is a step we should take right now: creating a family-friendly tax code.

Although Democrats and Republicans frequently say they favor such a code, we still don't have one. We continue to tax away the resources parents need to raise their children; to penalize marriage; and to unduly restrict benefits for lower-income families.

Since 1945, the real value of the federal income tax exemption for dependents has eroded by nearly three-quarters. To reverse decades of neglect, we should replace the current dependent exemption with a $750 per child tax credit (which would be equal to a $5,000 exemption for average families). To permit low-income families to claim the new credit, it should be made refundable. If budgetary constraints make full funding unavailable, the full credit could be limited to families with incomes below a designated ceiling and targeted to younger children.

We also should reduce the tax disadvantages of marriage. We must reexamine both the standard tax code and the Earned Income Tax Credit to reduce—in a manner compatible with affordability and basic progressivity—both disincentives to marriage in the first place and the tax penalties that married couples now shoulder.

Finally, the tax code should create a more level playing field between dual-earner and "traditional" families. We must find sensible ways of recognizing the special social contributions and financial sacrifices of parents who choose to remain home with their young children for extended periods.

Reform divorce law to put children first

As recently as thirty years ago, every state had fault-based divorce laws. The standard grounds for divorce included adultery, physical abuse, mental cruelty, desertion, imprisonment, addiction, and insanity. The nation's first no-fault divorce statute was signed into law by then-Gov. Ronald Reagan of California in late 1969. By 1974, forty-five states had adopted some form of no-fault; ten years later, every state had done so.

These legal changes coincided with large cultural shifts. Compared to thirty years ago, the pollster Daniel Yankelovich finds, today's Americans place less value on obligation, sacrifice, and self-restraint; instead, we emphasize individualism, self-expression, and personal choice. We are far more likely to say that marriage is first and foremost a means to personal happiness. And we are less inclined to believe that parents in a less than fully satisfactory marriage ought to make an effort to stay together for the sake of their children. (In the early 1960s, about one-half of Americans thought they should; today, that figure is about one-fifth.)

Cultural change, though, is not the whole story. Evidence is accumulating that legal change helped accelerate the pace of divorce. A fifty-state survey recently published in the *Journal of Marriage and the Family* concluded that the "switch from fault divorce to no-fault divorce law led to a measurable increase in the divorce rate." A rigorous statistical study presented at the 1996 annual meeting of the American Political Science Association supported this conclusion: "both no-fault divorce laws and general divorce law permissiveness have a strong positive impact on state divorce rates."[3]

States should move to change the current legal regime. To the extent that states retain no-fault divorce, it should for the most part be by mutual consent only. States should eliminate easy unilateral no-fault divorce for couples with minor children and institute an updated fault system that takes into account what we have learned over the past two decades about spousal abuse. As an alternative to fault in unilateral cases, states could establish a five-year waiting period before a nonconsensual no-fault divorce is allowed to occur. Even in cases in which both parties consent, there should be suitable braking mechanisms: a mandatory pause of at least a year for reflection, counseling, and mediation. States should also provide legal backing for couples who wish to enter into premarital agreements that make marriages harder to terminate.

Even if divorce involving minor children cannot be prevented, steps can be taken to mitigate its consequences. Recent research indicates that divorce harms children in three principal ways: diminished income (roughly a 30 percent drop for children and the custodial parent); diminished parenting time (both from the noncustodial parent, usually the father, who detaches himself from his children, and from the custodial parent who must combine work inside and outside the home); and disruption of established social ties to friends, neighborhoods, and schools.[4] Each of these sources of harm can be addressed through the law.

With regard to the economics of divorce, we should adopt (following Mary

Ann Glendon, professor at Harvard Law School) a "children first" principle. Property division should not even be discussed until adequate provision is made for the economic needs of children. And child support should cover a reasonable share of postsecondary education and training, at least until age twenty-one.

With regard to maximizing post-divorce parental involvement, there should be a legal presumption in favor of joint legal custody whenever feasible. When it is not, noncustodial parents should enjoy the most liberal possible visitation rights, strictly enforced.

Finally, with regard to the disruption of vital social ties, minor children should be allowed to remain in their predivorce neighborhoods and communities whenever possible. The goal of allowing children to remain in the family home during the period of greatest emotional vulnerability should trump the goal of immediate property division. Judges should have the option of excluding the home from the property settlement for an extended period—perhaps even until the children have left for college or entered the work force.

There is no federal law of divorce; states must take the lead (reform efforts have already surfaced in four states during the past year). Still, as part of a second-term effort to strengthen America's families, the President and Mrs. Clinton should build on their past statements to catalyze a long-overdue national conversation. If they do, they will find the public is more supportive than they might have imagined. Gallup polls show that three out of four thirteen- to seventeen-year-olds believe it's too easy for people in America to get divorced. A significant shift is underway even among their parents. A recent *Los Angeles Times* poll found 42 percent of adults favoring tougher divorce laws, compared to only 9 percent who think they should be eased. In these circumstances, the moral authority of the presidency (and the example of the first family, which has remained intact despite hard times) could be deployed to great effect.

Enlist one million mentors for vulnerable kids

For more than ninety years, Big Brothers/Big Sisters of America has brought matched adult volunteers with young people from single-parent homes. The volunteers are carefully screened, as are the young people; professional staffs work hard to make good matches. All parties are expected to make substantial time commitments, meeting two to four times a month for at least one year; a typical meeting lasts four hours. The goal of the relationship is not so much to ameliorate specific problems as it is to create a framework within which healthy development toward adulthood can occur.

In November 1995, Public/Private Ventures, a highly respected evaluator of social programs, released a comprehensive study of Big Brothers/Big Sisters, using a rigorous random-assignment technique. The results were astounding. Compared to youth not in the program, young people who met with their mentors regularly for a year were 46 percent less likely to start using illegal drugs; 27 percent less likely to start drinking; 52 percent less likely to skip a day of school; and more trusting of their parents or guardians and less likely to lie to them. According to the study, two elements of the program were crucial to its success: the nature of the one-on-one relationship, and the programmatic infrastructure for screening, matching, and monitoring these relationships.[5]

It is time to expand this effort dramatically. The President should commit his administration to the goal of creating one million mentoring relationships by 2000. The infrastructure and organization needed to create an effective program costs about $1,000 per match. The goal of one million mentors would thus cost about $1 billion annually when fully phased in.

The federal government should not go it alone. The well-being of our young people is a national (not just federal) and community (not just public) issue. Therefore, we should create a mentoring partnership: one-third of the costs to be borne by the federal government, one-third by states and localities, one-third by the voluntary sector. The incremental costs of this program could be reduced if the national service program, AmeriCorps, were to make a significant commitment to the mentoring goal.

The President has already called for a national volunteer effort to promote early reading. That is a good beginning. But we have a large cohort of teens whose troubles extend well beyond impaired literacy. We should not—and need not—write them off.

Create "second-chance" homes for young mothers

The national debate over welfare reform brought into public view two groups of vulnerable young people who need society's help—the children of teenage mothers, and the mothers themselves.

Who are teenage mothers? Most come from homes strained by poverty and dysfunction. Most do poorly in school; many drop out before they become pregnant. They have been badly nurtured: Many have been subjected to neglect or physical violence. As many as two-thirds may be victims of rape or sexual abuse at an early age—crimes often committed by males living in the same household.

As a result, many of these young women suffer from mental and emotional problems. They need more help than a welfare check—or even a job—can provide. They need the support and structure that a functioning family provides—needs typically not met in the homes in which they were raised.

It's time to revive an old institution—the maternity home—in a new form. In 1995, PPI proposed "second-chance" homes, community-based group homes for teen mothers. These homes offer the three elements that teenage mothers need to change their lives: socialization, nurturing and support, structure and discipline. And they all offer a genuine social contract: The mothers who live in these homes must stay in school or job training. They must stay drug free and abide by curfews. They learn to cook and clean, to manage money, to get along with one another, and resolve conflicts. In return, they get help with day care and health care and schoolwork. Most important, they learn how to nurture their children.

The young women in the Teen Parent Residence in Albuquerque, New Mexico, for example, are products of childhoods that were anything but safe and stable. Many had been sexually abused by relatives, beaten by boyfriends, or left homeless and forced to live on the street. The residence's goal, says Barbara Otto of the state's Teen Parent Program, is to turn these fragile young women and their needy children into "sturdy little family units." In many cases, the program succeeds. Its graduates are able to support themselves and be good mothers to their children.[6]

This idea has attracted broad support. In President Clinton's new book, *Between Hope and History,* he writes that for teens who can't go home, "I have proposed seed money for 'Second-Chance Homes,' like those already established in several American communities, that provide safe and supportive community organized and operated residences for teen mothers and their children." Indeed, prototypes for such homes already exist in communities as varied as Washington, D.C., New Albany, Indiana, and Wheeling, West Virginia. Massachusetts, Maryland, and Iowa have passed legislation to create or explore the idea; New Mexico has increased its budget for that purpose; and other states, including California, Wisconsin, Minnesota, Michigan, and New Jersey, are actively investigating it.

The recently enacted welfare reform bill supports this approach as well. It requires unmarried teenage parents to live in adult-supervised settings to receive Temporary Assistance for Needy Families. When families are abusive or neglectful, the law says that state agencies should place teen mothers in second-chance homes.

The time has come for the next step. By 2000, every state should establish a network of second-chance homes. Working as partners, the state and federal governments and communities can give young mothers and their children a chance to stabilize their lives and move forward.

End foster care as we know it

The aim of second-chance homes is to help young women become the caring and competent adults their children need. But what should society do about the individuals for whom these homes don't succeed—and about the children who have no suitable biological parents to raise them? The answer is to ensure that these children find stable and loving families soon enough to meet their developmental needs.

That's not what's happening today. Congress passed the Adoption Assistance and Child Welfare Act in 1980 with the best of intentions. Yet today, too many needy children are consigned to wait to return to biological parents who will never be able to care for them. They wait until they are too old or too troubled ever to be adopted.

This is a tragedy, because the best way to give a child a good start in life is to make sure that the child forms a secure attachment to a caring adult before his or her first birthday.[7] Yet on any given day, nearly half a million children in our country languish in foster care without permanent families.[8]

The foster care system was designed as a short-term, one-time intervention to protect children at severe risk. But all too often, it is neither short-term nor one-time. More than half the children in foster care end up in more than one foster home; eight percent are placed in six or more. Minority children suffer the most: The average time spent in first-time foster care by African-American children in Illinois was almost fifty-six months, while Latino children in New York stay more than twenty-two months.[9]

The conclusion is inescapable: All too often, foster care itself has become the obstacle to what children need most—permanent relationships with caring, competent adults. We must end foster care as we now know it, changing it from a damaging long-term experience to a short-term, one-time bridge to stable families for all children.

We must put the needs of children first. The story of One Church, One Child illustrates how barriers to adoption can be overcome when children's needs guide the process.

In 1980, officials of the Illinois Dept. of Children and Family Services approached the Rev. George Clements, leader of an African-American congregation on Chicago's South Side, to help them find parents for their long waiting list of black children ready to be adopted. Citing the long tradition among blacks, dating from slavery, of taking in homeless children, Clements urged his parishioners to adopt. At first, no one came forward, so Clements himself adopted a thirteen-year-old boy named Joey.

Other parishioners soon followed suit, and One Church, One Child was born, based on the idea that each of the city's churches would find at least one family within its congregation to adopt a child. By engaging ministers and communities, One Church, One Child inspired Illinois's child welfare bureaucracy to change its policies. Most importantly, One Church, One Child publicized the tragic plight of parent-less black children to the black community. Hundreds of potential adoptive and foster parents responded enthusiastically. The program continues to be successful because it not only recruits parents, it also supports them throughout the tedious placement process. To date, the idea has spread to thirty-six states, and at least twenty thousand children, mostly African-American, now have permanent loving families.[10]

All children deserve loving, stable homes. To accomplish this goal, the child welfare system should make intensive efforts to help natural parents become competent nurturers of their children. The system should also formalize "kinship care" by giving relatives who can care for children the same benefits that unrelated foster and adoptive parents now receive. But if biological parents or relatives cannot meet the needs of a child, the foster care system should transform itself into an adoption system that matches every child with a competent and caring adult.

Whatever the outcome in specific cases, time limits in this new system must reflect children's developmental timetables, not those of adults. Time is of the essence in the life of a child. A child cannot wait for a parent who needs time to kick a drug habit, to unlearn patterns of violence—or to just grow up. A child must not be held hostage to an overcrowded court docket. As a nation, we must commit ourselves to a goal that is no more than what simple decency requires: No child should spend more than one birthday without a permanent home in a stable, loving family. And we should, without delay, begin making the hard choices needed to achieve this goal.

Conclusion

Democratic Sen. Daniel Patrick Moynihan of New York draws a suggestive parallel between family policy today and the economic policy our country adopted in the wake of World War II. The Employment Act of 1946 did little more than create the Council of Economic Advisors. Yet it had a far greater impact than did any jobs bill. The reasons, Moynihan notes, is that the act declared a national policy and marked the acceptance of a previously disputed public responsibility. Similarly, he suggests, it would be a significant step forward "for a national family policy to declare that the American government sought to promote the stability of well-being of the American family; that the social programs of the federal government would be formulated and administered with this object in mind; and finally, that the President, or some person designated by him, would report to the Congress on the condition of the American family."[11]

This was a sensible proposal when Moynihan first offered it in 1990; it is no less sensible today, and even more urgent. It could serve as a focal theme for the social policies of the President's second administration. And it could well become a key part of the legacy his presidency can leave to our country.

Notes

1. William A. Galston and Elaine Ciulla Kamarck, "Putting Children First: A Progressive Family Policy for the 1990s" (Washington, DC: Progressive Policy Institute, 1990).

2. For a summary of this new evidence, see William A. Galston, "Divorce American Style," *The Public Interest* no. 124 (Summer 1996): 12–26.

3. James C. Garand and Pamela A. Monroe, "Does the Welfare State Increase Divorce Rates in the American States? A Pooled Test, 1960–1984" (Paper delivered to the Annual Meeting of the American Political Science Association, San Francisco, CA, August 1996), 13.

4. See especially Sara McLanahan and Gary Sandefur, *Growing Up with a Single Parent: What Hurts, What Helps* (Cambridge, MA: Harvard University Press, 1994), 79–133.

5. See Joseph P. Tierney, Jean Baldwin Grossman, and Nancy L. Resch, "Making a Difference: An Impact Study of Big Brothers/Big Sisters" (Philadelphia: Public/Private Ventures, 1995).

6. Kathleen Sylvester, "Second-Chance Homes: Breaking the Cycle of Teen Pregnancy," (Washington, DC: Progressive Policy Institute, 1995), 11.

7. Kathleen Stassen Berger and Ross A. Thompson, *The Developing Person Through the Lifespan* (New York: Worth Publishers, 1994), 187.

8. Rebecca Maynard, ed., "Kids Having Kids" (New York: The Robin Hood Foundation, 1996), 8.

9. The Chapin Hall Center for Children at the University of Chicago, "An Update from the Multistate Foster Care Data Archive: Foster Care Dynamics, 1983–1993" (Chicago, 1994), Table 4, 22.

10. John Herbers, "The Innovators: Where Are They Now?" *Governing* (October 1989), 34–35.

11. Daniel Patrick Moynihan, "Family and Nation Revisited," *Social Thought* 16 (1990): 52.

Chapter 11

Easier To Be Green: The Second Generation of Environmental Action

Debra S. Knopman

"It ain't easy being green."
—Rep. John Boehner, Republican of Ohio, quoting Kermit the Frog

In December 1994, soon after the Republican takeover of Congress, the prospective House Majority Leader, Dick Armey of Texas, opined: "[I]f we don't close down the Environmental Protection Agency, we at least put a snaffle bit on them and ride the pony down. They're out of control. There's no doubt." So began the headlong Republican assault on federal environmental, health, and worker-safety regulations. In March 1995, when asked if there were any federal regulations he would keep, House Republican Whip Tom DeLay of Texas replied, "Not that I can think of." A month later, Republican Sen. Slade Gorton of Washington speculated about the consequences of his bill to rewrite the Endangered Species Act: "It doesn't undo everything that's been done. But I suspect it would end up having that effect."[1]

In a textbook case of overreaching, the Republican leadership thought that general public mistrust of bureaucracy would translate into support for weakening environmental protection. As DeLay read public opinion, "The EPA, the Gestapo of government, simply has been one of the major claw hooks that the government has maintained on the backs of our constituents." Further, he boasted, "We're in charge. We don't have to compromise with the Senate. We don't have to compromise with the President. We're only going to fund the programs we like."[2]

DeLay and his colleagues were in for a rude awakening. By the end of 1995, they would discover that over the course of twenty-five years, concern for the environment had become an enduring American value—a fact not lost

163

on President Clinton and many other candidates of both parties who played the environmental card to their advantage this past November.

The GOP's ham-fisted assault on all things green, however, has set back an urgent national task: revamping the nation's outdated "command and control" environmental regulatory apparatus to take on the new challenges of the twenty-first century. Misinterpreting public rejection of the Republican slash-and-burn campaign as support for the regulatory status quo, many environmental activists are now unwilling to concede that change is needed.

The Clinton administration has at least acknowledged the flaws in the "first generation" of environmental laws and rules adopted since the 1970s. By and large, these laws and rules demand that businesses and local governments adopt federally preordained technological solutions to reduce pollution and manage resources. To its credit, the administration has corrected some of the glitches in the Endangered Species Act, the wetlands program, and other regulations. There are even signs of progress in Congress. Recent changes in the drinking water and pesticides laws show it is possible to forge a bipartisan consensus on priority-setting and cost-effective reduction of health risks.

Still, the bottom line going into 1997 is that the frustration with the first generation environmental approach remains a sore point, especially for those most directly affected by regulation. If we ignore these persistent frustrations, 1996 could well turn into a hollow victory for the environmental movement.

It is time for a "second generation" environmental strategy, one which transcends the "us versus them" mindset of the current debate, and which achieves higher levels of protection than the old top-down approach by using more democratic and efficient means. Without such a decisive policy shift, we will never come to closure on the old environmental agenda, nor will we build the political will or free up the resources necessary to prevail over the more complex environmental challenges of the future.

The Changing Nature of the Environmental Challenge

Environmental protection is one of the biggest governmental success stories of the past half-century. Cleveland's burning Cuyahoga River of the 1960s—an enduring symbol of the environmental abuse wreaked by the post–World War II industrial boom—is now a model of urban waterfront renewal. An overwhelming majority of Americans say they want both a strong economy *and* a clean, healthy environment. Today, we enjoy cleaner air, safer drinking water, safer food, and more parks and wilderness for recreation than most every other nation. Fatal illness from polluted air has declined fourfold since 1970. With further assistance for small communities, total elimination of serious illness from drinking water is within our grasp. America protects more natural lands than any other nation.[3] Still, we have not accomplished all we set out to do twenty-five years ago, and new challenges demand our attention.

While factories can do more to improve water quality, in most places improvement will come only by reducing pollution from farms, suburban development, aging urban storm sewers, and abandoned mines.[4] Air quality in cities like Los Angeles and Denver will improve dramatically only if we curb automobile emissions. Conserving the habitats of endangered and threatened species will progress only when we engage private landowners in the business of conservation. Dangerous exposures to hazardous chemicals will decline further only when we learn which chemicals pose the greatest risks and target them for reductions. Cleaning up hazardous waste sites and disposing of nuclear waste have proven to be more difficult challenges than we ever imagined, and these problems demand fresh responses.

Recent studies show that indoor air pollution from radon, molds, carpeting, and wall coverings may be far more serious for some people than outdoor air pollution, particularly because most of us spend 90 percent of our lives indoors. An accumulating body of evidence suggests that some man-made chemicals in the environment are disrupting normal development and reproduction of wildlife and humans.[5]

Most scientists agree that the buildup of carbon dioxide in the atmosphere from the burning of fossil fuels could have a disruptive effect on our climate.[6] In some places in the world, species like frogs are disappearing more rapidly than would be expected naturally because of changes in climate, destruction of habitat, or exposure to chemicals. Finally, the effects of natural disasters like fires, hurricanes, floods, drought, earthquakes, and volcanoes are only now being considered in terms of their environmental consequences. For example, in a January 1996 flood, the Chesapeake Bay received six times more nitrogen pollution and seventeen times more sediment than typical for the entire month.

Today's environmental challenges are more vexing than their predecessors in that they cannot be easily traced back to a smokestack or pipe running into a river. Instead, they may be particular to a region like the Everglades or the Pacific Northwest; more diffuse in their geography like the runoff of pollutants from farms; or more subtle in their appearance and effects like climate change and the ozone hole above the Antarctic. Their different character demands different problem-solving tools.

The Inadequacies of the First Generation Approach

Our constant vigilance is needed to protect the environmental gains already made. There is no turning back. Still, the first generation of environmental

Debra S. Knopman

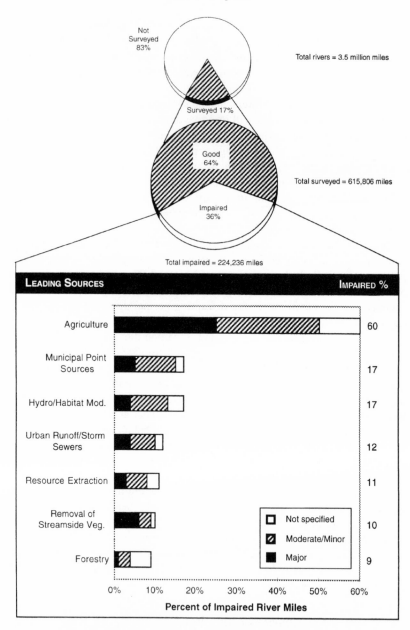

Fig. 11.1. Summary of national water quality conditions and leading sources of impairment based on assessments conducted by states. States survey only 17 percent of the nation's 3.5 million miles of streams and rivers. Data from U.S. Environmental Protection Agency, Office of Water, *National Water Quality Inventory: 1994 Report to Congress* (Appendixes).

laws and rules, and the centralized agencies that enforce them, simply are not up to current political and scientific challenges. Today's great problems arise from the everyday activities of all of us, which puts them beyond the capacities of top-down regulation from Washington. Consider the following:

- First generation laws and rules, while appropriate for the easy-to-pinpoint industrial problems of the past, do little to prevent pollution in the first place. They also are ill-suited for dealing with pollution from cars and trucks, indoor air pollution, and global problems like greenhouse gas emissions and ozone depletion.

- These laws emphasize control of pollution after it has been produced and conservation of species after they are endangered. The lack of incentives for pollution prevention and enlightened conservation efforts has the perverse effect of slowing down environmental progress. Existing laws and rules actually encourage the continued operation of aging industrial plants (in part because new sources of pollution must meet stricter standards), and encourage the destruction of habitat (as landowners dodge the regulatory bullets that come with endangered species).

- Each law focuses on a single issue, so that the system misses important connections to other environmental and economic values and choices. As experiences from the Everglades, Chesapeake Bay, and San Francisco Bay have shown, some environmental problems can only be solved by looking at the functioning of biological systems as a whole.

- Because we fail to set clear national environmental goals and priorities, we are not applying our considerable public and private resources—$135 billion annually for pollution control alone—to the areas of greatest need: safe drinking water for smaller communities, reducing greenhouse gas emissions, and lessening risk from chemicals that cause significant harm to human and wildlife development, to name a few. The current system locks us into spending on the old agenda, no matter whether it is cost-effective or environmentally beneficial.

- Central rule-making and the concentration of power in Washington has spawned a culture of litigation and political favor-seeking that undermines the ethic of civic responsibility and consensus-building among local and regional stakeholders.

New Tools for New Challenges

As the New Progressive Declaration suggests, Information Age technologies and organizational principles enable us to both tackle lingering environmental problems more effectively and to refocus on new challenges. The second generation of environmental activism should be based on five key steps: setting clear goals and priorities; decentralizing decisions to communities and individuals; harnessing market forces to curb pollution and increase conservation; adopting more flexible means to achieve environmental goals; and measuring actual results, rather than focusing narrowly on compliance with rules and regulations.[7]

Setting realistic goals and priorities

We need to know where we want to go with the environment before we can decide how to get there. The current system is the regulatory equivalent of flying blind: ten of the twelve laws that guide EPA programs have *no explicit environmental goals* (for example, how clean a toxic waste site needs to be). Instead, the laws are laden with prescriptions for control and details about process (the Clean Water and Clean Air Acts are the two exceptions). Few explicit goals are found in the laws governing natural and biological resources. The nation's environmental goals and priorities should be set through a democratic process fully informed by sound science and economics, and construed broadly to encompass changes needed in the financial, transportation, energy, and agricultural sectors, as well as national accounting and tax policy.

Decentralizing decision making

How and where decisions are made has everything to do with whether solutions to environmental problems are sustainable in the long run. In an age in which information technologies are breaking central institutions' monopoly on vital information, there is no reason to be bound by the past conviction—justified at the time—that every important environmental decision should be made in Washington. Many of today's problems, particularly those related to land use, are addressed most effectively at the state and local levels. Further, expertise at the state level has greatly increased from two decades ago. Washington has much to learn from the experiences of communities across the country, which are working creatively and cooperatively to solve long-standing environmental problems. Beneath the radar of national politics, communities like Chattanooga, Tennessee; Henry's Fork, Idaho; Wichita, Kansas; Seattle, Washington; and the New York City region are finding innovative solutions and partnerships outside the boxes drawn by the first generation of environmental laws. The President's Council for Sustainable Development recently documented how many communities across America are solving their own environmental problems, and doing their part for national and global needs as

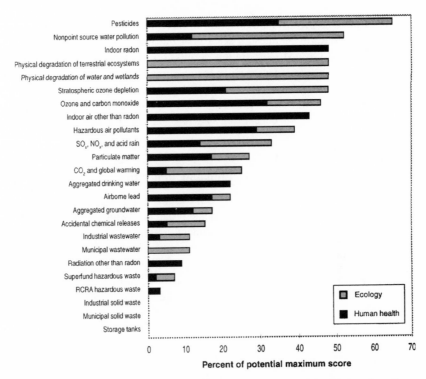

Fig. 11.2. Combined human health and ecological risk, rankings by ten EPA regions. Data from Office of Technology Assessment, U.S. Environmental Protection Agency.

well.[8] To its credit, the Clinton administration initiated efforts in the Everglades, the Pacific Northwest, and the San Francisco Bay-Delta to solve problems on a regional scale with the involvement of states, communities, and other stakeholders. However, their progress may only be transitory unless a more systemic change occurs in laws and bureaucracies. It remains to be seen how enduring these efforts will be when a new administration with different interests and priorities arrives.

Promoting flexibility to improve environmental performance

We need a new compact between regulators and environmental managers—public and private—that rewards responsible stewardship with flexibility. Flexibility in the way in which goals are achieved opens the door to the use of market-based incentives as alternatives to command-and-control tools. It has the potential to substantially lower compliance costs, foster cooperative partnerships, and encourage innovation in meeting environmental goals. For example, the state of Minnesota set a goal but did not prescribe a process when it granted the 3M Corporation permission to modify production processes at its St. Paul tape factory—as long as the company remained within a total air emissions cap.[9] Through a conservation agreement, the federal Bureau of Land Management (BLM) granted Lemhi County, Idaho, the authority to devise its own means of conserving valuable habitat on public lands within its borders.

Harnessing market forces and stimulating innovation

Our current regulatory system is both too prescriptive and too narrow in scope. To spur innovation, and to stimulate broad environmental progress, we must give individuals, firms, and government direct, self-interested economic incentives for reducing the amounts of waste and pollution they generate and non-renewable resources they consume. For example, markets for trading allowable amounts of air and water pollution can help solve regional problems by encouraging the most efficient sources to reduce their emissions as much as possible. Further, efficiency gains can be used to buy additional environmental improvements. Deposit-refund programs can work for hazardous products such as car batteries and old tires. Pollution taxes on solid and hazardous waste can reduce waste generation. Property rights for species and habitat conservation, such as conservation easements, capture some of the economic value of environmental services.

Focusing on the measurement of environmental results

We need far better ways than we now possess to measure progress toward meeting environmental goals. The second generation strategy depends on national support for scientifically sound, consistent environmental monitoring and research. These strategic functions, prerequisites for rational public debate of goals, priorities, and results-oriented policies, are properly the province of the federal government. Congress will need better information if it is to move toward a broad policy-setting role and away from micromanagement. For example, recent studies by the U.S. Geological Survey have documented the dominant contribution of runoff from farms and suburbs to water pollution in comparison to sewage treatment plants and other point sources. Despite such evidence, the Clean Water Act—untouched by Congress since 1987—continues to focus on point sources. Communities, too, need access to better information to play a more active role in setting their own goals and priorities and understanding what is happening within their boundaries.

From Mandates to Markets

When Congress drafted its first pollution control laws in the 1970s, it directed firms and cities to use the same technologies, regardless of local conditions. This one-size-fits-all regime was relatively easy to administer and seemed fair because it treated everyone equally. Moreover, Congress had to rely on technology mandates because we lacked sufficient information about environmental conditions in specific places to custom tailor control strategies.

While highly effective at first, over time this system has evolved into a time-consuming, process-oriented maze of rules and court decrees in which the goal of environmental improvement sometimes gets lost. In one case, the EPA ordered an IBM plant in Vermont to use a costly technology to reduce the concentration of alcohol in certain liquid wastes to 0.0001 percent, rejecting a cheaper process that would have reduced concentrations to 1 percent. The extra reduction was meaningless in terms of reducing public health risks, considering that under another EPA regulation, alcohol in concentrations below 24 percent is not regulated at all. The technology mandate overrode the criterion for negligible risk in the remaining waste.[10]

It is now clear that mandates tend to freeze in place technologies that existed when the rules were written. They offer businesses few incentives to develop new, cleaner production methods.

Environmental economists have long argued that market incentives are potentially a far more powerful tool than central regulation. A critical missing ingredient for markets, however, is credible information about the costs and particularly the benefits of meeting environmental targets. Most businesses, for example, aren't even sure how much they spend on pollution controls and energy consumption, so it is hard for them to estimate the savings from shifting to cleaner, more efficient techniques. Recent studies indicate that certain companies could reduce their operating costs by as much as 30 percent by carefully evaluating how they use energy and control wastes in their manufacturing processes.[11]

Information on the consumer side is weak as well. Because regulations revolve around technology mandates, the environmental debate quickly gets bogged down in arcane, technical issues dominated by lawyers. Lacking reliable, independent information about public health risks and environmental conditions, opposing parties independently define the "facts" for the public. A veritable industry has sprung up to debunk claims made by the environmental community—on pesticides, endangered species, global climate change, and hormone-disrupting chemicals. While the government is now making limited environmental data widely available on the Internet, they still do not offer much that is particularly useful to ordinary citizens.

So we are stuck in a dilemma: Without more and better information, we cannot move to a more flexible, publicly accountable approach to environmental performance and enforcement. But there is too little demand from the regulated community or the states for better data on environmental conditions because the current regulatory regime too often rewards compliance with procedures, not better environmental outcomes.

In 1995, under the motto, "Cleaner, cheaper, smarter" the Clinton administration launched dozens of "reinventing environmental regulation" initiatives.[12] So far, the changes are only skin deep. Its signature reform initiative, Project XL (for excellence and leadership), is intended to "throw away the rule book" for any company or community that is committed to achieving "superior environmental performance." Environmental activists, understandably suspicious, have criticized Project XL for a lack of public accountability. For Project XL to flourish, the EPA will need to seek legal authority to clarify environmental goals, waive existing regulations when necessary for participating companies and communities, and establish guidance for public involvement.[13]

Regardless of the outcome of the Project XL experiment, the real challenge is to make the bargain implicit in it —more flexibility for firms and communities in return for higher standards of environmental performance—the organizing principle of the EPA and other regulatory agencies.

The Clinton administration should move aggressively to shift the basis of government regulation from mandates to markets—from prescriptive rule making to environmental performance agreements, partnerships, and the strategic use of information. It should strike a new bargain in which communities and businesses get relief from mandated solutions in return for the chance to solve their own problems with better environmental performance and more public accountability. For communities and businesses, this would mean lower compliance costs, greater freedom to design their own ways to reduce pollution and conserve resources, and a chance to win public recognition as environmentally responsible actors. It would open the door to creating markets for trading pollution reduction and conservation credits to achieve overall environmental goals at lower cost.

Public information is the key to this shift. For example, when Congress a decade ago created the Toxics Release Inventory, a simple public listing of air, water, and land emissions of hundreds of toxic chemicals by industry, it had no idea what a powerful tool for progress it unleashed. Although the inventory is incomplete and silent on the actual risks of exposure to these emissions, public scrutiny combined with new standards sparked a 43 percent reduction in toxic emissions in six years.[14]

Another, more familiar precedent for using public information to spur voluntary action is the U.S. Surgeon General's campaign against smoking. Jawboning by respected public officials, consumer product safety labels, and curbs on advertising brought the number of smokers down from 42 percent of the adult population in 1965 to 25 percent in 1993, at relatively little cost to the public.[15]

Citizens and communities could use the new base of environmental knowledge to set realistic goals and priorities, work cooperatively to protect public health, provide for open space, and conserve natural resources. With better information, they may discover, for example, that forcing a factory to further reduce air emissions of nitrogen oxides will do little to improve local air quality because of excess automobile emissions at rush hours. Or, they may find that their water quality problems come primarily from runoff from suburban lawns and malls, and not their local treatment plant.

Investors, bankers, and insurers—now mostly in the dark on the environmental performance of the companies and communities in their portfolios—could routinely use public information to judge the credit worthiness, profit potential, and management competence of businesses and public agencies, large and small.

In a performance-based system, regulators would be rewarded for working cooperatively to encourage higher levels of overall environmental performance, not for the number of citations written, lawsuits filed, or fines collected. Moreover, by using independent firms to conduct environmental audits of businesses and communities seeking to achieve higher levels of performance, and publishing the results, EPA and other regulatory agencies could rely more on public pressure to obtain routine compliance and concentrate its limited enforcement dollars on chronic problems and offenders. And, it would create incentives for businesses and local governments to continually improve their energy efficiency and environmental performance, and self-correct deficiencies in their operations, rather than fight regulations or just do the bare minimum.

How do we get from here to there? Here are four key tasks for the federal government:

Initiate a process to set national goals and priorities

Every other year, Congress should consider a joint resolution outlining the nation's environmental and natural resources goals and priorities. And every year, to clarify the choices about how Congress should allocate federal resources for the environment, a single subcommittee of the Senate and House appropriations committees should act on appropriations for all environmental, natural resources, and energy programs.

Stimulate better environmental performance through incentives

Using the national goals and priorities as a foundation, Congress should require EPA, the Interior Department, and the Agriculture Department to enter into performance-based compliance and conservation agreements with companies (individually or collectively), states, communities, and special water and conservation districts. The federal agencies should offer a variety of incentives—flexibility, third-party auditing, bundling federal program funds for public bodies, fast-track permitting, and technical assistance for small communities and businesses—in return for legally enforceable commitments to exceed current environmental performance. EPA's performance partnership agreements with the states are an important first step in this direction.

Invest more in improving the quality of environmental information

To help states and communities make better decisions, Washington should spend an additional $500 million annually to improve the systematic, scientific study of the environment in specific locales, along the lines of the U.S. Geological Survey's National Water Quality Assessment. The object would be to study how ecosystems work at local and regional scales; make better use of remote sensing technology to monitor land use changes, emissions, and discharges; and improve economic analyses of environmental policy choices. Further, an additional $100 million should be invested in improving information about the health effects of chemicals in commerce.

Empower Americans with reliable information about environmental conditions and actions to reduce risks

Congress needs to overhaul current reporting requirements on industries, states, and local governments to focus on performance measures that are meaningful to average citizens. The statistical and scientific staffs of such agencies as EPA, the U.S. Geological Survey, the National Oceanic and Atmospheric Administration, the Agriculture Department, and the Bureau of Labor Statistics should be charged with providing intelligible information to the public about worker health and safety, environmental conditions in their community, consumer products, and food safety. The Clinton administration's recent calls for an environmental report card and increased spending on environmental monitoring are steps in the right direction. But their efforts need to be raised by an order of magnitude. Regulatory authorities should post company and community performance measures on the Internet and in local newspapers. Congress should direct EPA to resolve the conflicting rules on confidential business information, and make some of EPA's confidential information about toxic chemicals more readily available to responsible state authorities.

An Acid Test: Western Public Lands

The federal government owns more than half of the land in the twelve western-most states, including Alaska. Public land management in the West, a source of perennial political conflict and discontent, is one area of national environmental and natural resources policy where second generation strategies are especially crucial.

The United States has critical environmental, fiduciary, and security interests in its Western lands. At this stage in our history, protecting lands of ecological, cultural, historic, or aesthetic significance is the central concern. In addition, the minerals beneath public lands are vital national assets. However, we should strongly favor farsighted, ecologically sensitive management of these resources over exploitation for short-term deficit reduction. Finally, the federal government's western energy holdings figure prominently in our nation's control over its fossil fuel needs, particularly as our consumption of foreign oil continues to soar.

Of the 630 million acres of public lands in the West, fewer than one-quarter consist of parks, national forests, wilderness areas, and wildlife refuges. The rest is managed by law for multiple uses, commercial uses such as ranching, timber, and mining, and for noncommercial activities such as hunting, fishing, and hiking. Set by law in 1976, the national policy is to retain public lands in public ownership.

In the past, the national interest in the West was clearly defined as resource exploitation in the service of economic development. In the 1800s, Washington could not give away western land fast enough—to individuals for homesteading, to states as land grants, and to corporations for mining, ranching, timber, and railroads. Only American Indians lost out. Laws were passed that enshrined the federal bias toward commercial exploitation of these lands.

These laws—dubbed the "Lords of Yesterday" by the historian Charles Wilkinson—linger even though the West's economy has grown less reliant on mining and oil and more dependent upon diversified growth linked to the land's beauty and well-being. The West is the nation's fastest growing region and, contrary to popular perceptions, its most urbanized. States in which the federal government is the principal landowner—Nevada (83 percent), Utah (64 percent), and Arizona (43 percent)—are projected to have the nation's highest economic growth rates. Aggregate income from service-sector jobs is greater than the income generated from all the natural resources industries

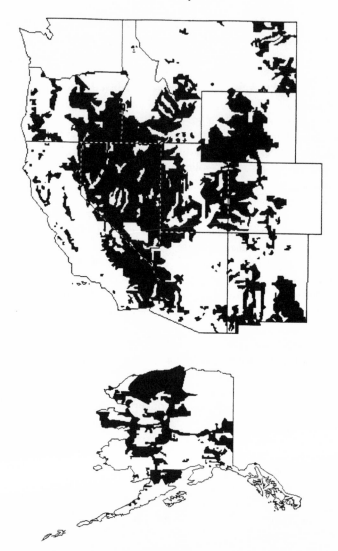

Fig. 11.3. Bureau of Land Management lands in the western states. Reprinted, with permission, from Sarah Bates, *The Western Lands: An Introduction* (Natural Resource Law Center, University of Colorado, 1992).

combined. Livestock grazing on public land accounts for only one in seventeen hundred jobs in the West; metal mining, for less than one in twenty-five hundred. Only three out of two hundred jobs in the economically robust Pacific Northwest are generated by logging on federal land. Between 1988 and 1992, as the controversy over cutting old-growth forests erupted, the region's employment grew 2.4 times faster than the national average.[16]

In 1993, the Clinton administration tried to align federal policies to these new realities by raising grazing fees on public lands to levels comparable to state and private land fees. This seemingly modest reform evoked furious protests throughout the region, from Democrats and Republicans alike. Interior Secretary Bruce Babbitt, an Arizonan, was even hung in effigy. Related efforts to eliminate federal timber, energy, and water subsidies in the West were snuffed out, too. Even the blatant giveaway of minerals on public lands under the 1872 federal mining law could not be stopped.

The heart of the dispute between Washington and the West is not federal subsidies, but control of the land. Current federal land management policies satisfy virtually no one in the West. Proponents of greater state and local control of public lands dislike centralized federal management. The so-called "private property" movement, funded largely by mining, ranching, and timber interests, is a powerful political factor in much of the West. Western conservatives advocate privatization of public lands, or at least divesting the federal government of its holdings and transferring them to the states.[17] Meanwhile, many environmentalists consider the federal land-managements bureaucracy as a lapdog of the commercial interests it supposedly regulates. Grazing and clear-cutting on lands bordering streams and rivers have exacerbated both silting and loss of habitat. Federal dams have been the major culprit in landing dozens of aquatic species on the endangered list.

Democratic Mayor Daniel Kemmis of Missoula, Montana, characterizes the governance problem this way:

> I do not believe the federal government has the capacity to manage the West. I do not believe, either, that any solution coming from one end of the political spectrum or the other is going to have the capacity to do what this landscape requires. The danger is that one ideology or another will win a temporary victory because we did not work hard enough to find our common ground. The bottom line would be to say that we want and need control over our own land. We do not expect to be given that control until we get our own act together.[18]

Many western communities *are* getting their act together. Public and private interests in Henry's Fork, Idaho, have joined to manage land use in the watershed and conserve valuable habitat. Ranchers and conservationists in Gunnison, Colorado, are jointly improving land management practices to conserve species and protect their magnificent landscape. The Natural Resources Law Center at the University of Colorado documented over seventy collaborative watershed protection efforts throughout the West, some of which are working better than others. The keys to success appear to be: a consensus that the status quo is no longer tenable, visionary leaders among each of the interests, and a common understanding of the problems to be solved.

Community Stewardship of Public Lands

To support this growing trend toward regional problem solving, the Clinton administration should engage Western states' leaders in a historic shift of responsibility from Washington to communities for public lands now used mainly for grazing and timber. It should replace federal overlordship with a new concept of "community stewardship." A community stewardship group—like the many watershed councils already in existence—is a balanced consortium of local and regional interests committed to decision making by consensus.

Under this approach, the BLM and the Forest Service would offer to lease selected lands to communities for up to fifty years.[19] Community participation would be entirely voluntary. In return for flexibility to manage the lands in harmony with local needs (and the chance to earn some rent along the way), community stewards would commit themselves to meet or exceed national environmental standards. These legally enforceable conservation agreements—subject to prior public review and comment within the state—would be renewed every ten years. The citizen-led Resource Advisory Councils recently established by the Interior Department in each Western state could be used as a forum for public review of conservation agreements. As a non-negotiable precondition for leasing, continued public access would be assured and certain land uses like waste sites prohibited. In addition, the federal government and the communities would jointly measure and publicly report every three years on environmental and economic indicators of progress.

Existing national parks, wildlife refuges, and wilderness areas would not be included in community leases, nor would congressional action on future wilderness or park designations be impeded. Control of water rights by the states would remain unaffected. Existing federal permits would be honored, but communities participating in the new bargain would have the flexibility to retract, amend, or extend the permits as they expire. For example, a permit could be amended to require sustainable forestry practices and prohibit clear-cutting. Only timber and grazing rights, not mineral rights, would be conveyed by the lease.

The first fifteen years of the lease would be a trial period to determine whether community stewards are managing the resources properly and executing the assessment and monitoring strategy. After fifteen years, the lands could be deeded to the community group with the approval of Congress. If conservation goals are not being met, as determined by an independent assessment of environmental conditions, then the federal government would not exercise the transfer option. In cases of total breakdown, Washington would revoke the lease.

Federal funds now used to manage these lands would be transferred to the communities, and these areas would continue to receive the federal payments now made in lieu of property taxes. The BLM currently spends about $650 million annually and takes in about $1.4 billion in revenues, more than half of which is returned to the states. Net revenues from timber, mining, and grazing would be split equally between the federal treasury and the communities, which could use their share only for conservation or other environmental purposes.

Over time, as federal subsidies for these commercial uses are phased out, revenues might increase and thus lessen the need for direct appropriations. Additional income generated from tourism, recreation, and other nonextractive uses would continue to accrue entirely to the community. To sweeten the pot, Washington would grant participating communities a one-time allowance to use perhaps up to $10 million from the $11 billion Land and Water Conservation Fund (now being used mostly for deficit reduction) to buy conservation easements, negotiate land swaps, and purchase environmentally valuable private lands.

Community stewards could sublease to private parties or conservation organizations, or manage lands themselves as recreation or wilderness areas. But they would always remain legally responsible for the execution of the conservation agreement. When these ten-year agreements come up for renewal, the state and federal governments could expand the lease's boundaries to address larger-scale problems of a watershed, river basin, or ecosystem.

Community stewardship offers numerous advantages over the current system. Public and private lands could be managed for conservation purposes more effectively and efficiently. Public lands could be better integrated into communities' overall economic development plans, boosting their revenues from economic development spurred by a healthy landscape, "ecotourism," and recreation. The communities would gain access to a new stream of federal funds to apply to conservation. By virtue of their proximity, community authorities would be more effective than distant federal regulators at driving home the point that free markets do not create the right to do harm to others, their property, or the community at large. Finally, community stewards would be able to bypass the federal land management bureaucracies and work directly with the spectrum of interests vested in the land.

Community stewardship would not absolve the federal government of responsibility for its public lands, or for overarching environmental concerns that cross political boundaries. There is a critical need for national conservation goals; for money to help communities achieve them; for data collection and dissemination to determine progress toward them; and for enforcement actions when goals are unmet.

Complex and long-standing laws and rules govern public lands, minerals, and water in the West, and hence numerous legal issues would need to be worked through before this initiative could be fully implemented. Indeed, community stewardship should be accompanied by other steps:

- Mining law reform is urgently needed to end both preferential treatment of mining claims on public lands, and the public subsidy to mining interests.

- The Endangered Species Act should be amended to give private landowners incentives to conserve species and habitat on their lands.

- The federal government should support regional efforts to establish regulated water markets, which would create financial incentives for water conservation. Water thus saved would be put to more productive economic and environmental uses.

- The Forest Service should stop setting timber cutting goals from Washington, and funding for local Forest Service offices should be disconnected from timber cutting revenue.

Conclusions

By switching from mandates to markets, and from centralized to community decision-making, America could finally move beyond the outdated, first generation environmental agenda and focus on the new challenges using the powerful tools of the Information Age. Community stewardship creates a platform for addressing national conservation goals that is far more conducive to problem-solving than our current Washington-centric arrangements.

While many of the details still need to be filled in, the initiatives outlined above are viable ideas that build on experiments already underway. For each, the litmus test of success is greater environmental progress achieved with efficiency, equity, and comity. As an environmentalist recently speculated about congressional action on environmental laws in 1997, "It's a jump ball." Let's hope that the tip goes to creative, forward-looking problem-solving, and not to more confrontation and gridlock.

Notes

1. House Republican Leader Dick Armey (R-TX), interview by David Brinkley, *This Week with David Brinkley*, American Broadcasting System, 18 Dec. 1994. *Wall Street Journal*, 3 Mar. 1995. "Gorton Unveils Bill to Kill Major Provisions," *Greenwire* (13 Apr. 1995).

2. Patrice Hill, "EPA Cuts Defeated in House," *Washington Times*, 29 July 1995, A1.

3. Organization for Economic Cooperation and Development, "Environmental Performance Reviews: United States" (Paris, France: OECD, 1996).

4. United States Environmental Protection Agency, "The Quality of Our Nation's Water: 1994" (Washington, DC: U.S. Environmental Protection Agency 841-S-94-002, 1995).

5. Theo Colburn, Dianne Dumanoski, and John Peterson Myers, *Our Stolen Future: Are We Threatening Our Fertility, Intelligence, and Survival?—A Scientific Detective Story* (New York: Dutton, 1996).

6. Intergovernmental Panel on Climate Change, *Climate Change 1995: The Science of Climate Change: Contribution of Working Group I to the Second Assessment Report of the Intergovernmental Panel on Climate Change* (Cambridge, U.K.: Cambridge University Press, 1996).

7. Debra S. Knopman, "Second Generation: A New Strategy for Environmental Protection" (Washington, DC: Progressive Foundation, Apr. 1996).

8. President's Council For Sustainable Development, "Task Force Report on Sustainable Communities" (Washington, DC: President's Council for Sustainable Development, Oct. 1996).

9. United States Congress, Office of Technology Assessment, "Industry, Technology, and the Environment: Competitive Challenges and Business Opportunities" (Washington, DC: U.S. Government Printing Office OTA-ITE-586, Jan. 1994), 275.

10. George S. Hawkins, "The Eagle Agenda: An Agenda for the Future of Environmental Protection," unpublished manuscript, 1996.

11. Daryl Ditz, Janet Ranganathan, and R. Darryl Banks, eds., *Green Ledgers: Case Studies in Corporate Environmental Accounting* (Washington, DC: World Resources Institute, 1995).

12. President William J. Clinton and Vice President Albert Gore, "Common-Sense Strategies to Protect Public Health: A Progress Report on Reinventing Environmental Regulation," *National Performance Review* (Washington, DC: U.S. Environmental Protection Agency, 29 Mar. 1996).

13. Rena Steinzor, "Regulatory Reinvention and Project XL: Does the Emperor Have Any Clothes?" *Environmental Law Reporter* vol. 26 (Oct. 1996): 10527–10537.

14. United States Environmental Protection Agency, "1993 Toxics Release Inventory Public Data Release" (Washington, DC: U.S. Environmental Protection Agency 745-R-95–010, 1995).

15. Centers for Disease Control and Prevention, Data compiled by the Office of Smoking and Health from National Health Interview Surveys 1965–1993, 1995.

16. Thomas Michael Power, "The Wealth of Nature," *Issues in Science and Technology* (Spring 1996): 48–54.

17. Robert H. Nelson, *Public Lands and Private Rights: The Failure of Scientific Management* (Lanham, MD: Rowman & Littlefield, 1995).

18. Lisa Jones, "As a last resort, Westerners start talking to each other," *High Country News* (13 May 1996): 1.

19. Marion Clawson, *The Federal Lands Revisited* (Washington, DC: Resources for the Future, 1983). Marion Clawson proposed that the BLM and Forest Service enter into long-term leasing directly with commercial and conservation interests. The arguments Clawson makes for departing from the status quo of public lands policy are as compelling today as they were in the early 1980s.

Chapter 12

Restoring Upward Mobility in the Knowledge Economy

Robert J. Shapiro

The American economy presents a curious paradox: Employment is high and inflation is low; yet many Americans feel growing economic anxiety.

By most traditional measures, the economy is healthy and strong. Joblessness is at its lowest point in two decades; prices have been rising more slowly than at any time in three decades; and a larger share of Americans are working today than at any point in our history. But for tens of millions of people, having a job doesn't provide the security it once did. A recent survey by Harvard University, the Henry J. Kaiser Family Foundation, and the *Washington Post* found that three-fifths of Americans say they don't earn enough to save. One-third report that a family member had to take a pay cut or work fewer hours to keep his or her job, and one-quarter report problems with bill collectors.[1] Even many Americans who don't face such problems doubt they will ever live as well as their parents.

In certain respects, the generation that went to work in the 1950s and 1960s did enjoy greater opportunities than its children. In those decades, the economy grew an average of 3.5 percent to 4 percent a year—as it had for the century from 1870 to 1969, when our annual growth averaged 3.7 percent—and people at every economic level could roughly double their real incomes by working for twenty years.[2] But since the early 1970s, annual growth has slowed to barely 3 percent, a rate insufficient to support broad upward mobility. The typical middle-class American who worked from 1970 to 1990 barely held his own, after accounting for inflation; most lower-class families saw their real incomes fall. Only the most affluent one-fifth continued to make

183

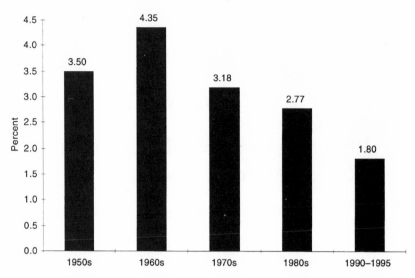

Fig. 12.1. Average annual growth rates of real GDP. Data from *Economic Report of the President,* 1994, 1996.

healthy income gains, with the richest 1 percent achieving the largest in-creases by far.

Thus the paradox of the U.S. economy: Even as it generates new jobs and stable prices, other forces retard its growth and concentrate its benefits.[3]

To help restore strong growth and broad upward mobility, our economic policies must recognize that the wealth of a nation like ours depends less today on traditional, physical forms of economic power, such as the number of workers and the stock of plant and equipment. Rather, higher growth in an advanced and knowledge-based economy depends mainly on factors that are less tangible but more powerful: How much and how well our firms innovate, and how competent our workers are.

President Clinton's prime economic challenge in his second term is to en-sure that as many American firms as possible have the incentives and means to develop new and better ways of doing business, and that as many American workers as possible have opportunities to continuously improve their skills. Four steps can begin this process:

- *A Cut-and-Invest Budget.* The President and Congress should trans-form the priorities of the federal budget to strengthen innovation and expand economic opportunity. Together, they should launch an all-out campaign to repeal some $60 billion to $80 billion a year in spending and tax subsidies for influential industries. The six-year savings of between $350 billion and nearly $500 billion should be used not only to reduce the deficit, but also to underwrite sound tax reforms and national investments in education and training, basic research and development, and our economic infrastructure.

• *A Pro-Growth Tax System.* The President and Congress should reform the tax code to reward economic innovation and efficiency, while preserving progressivity. By closing loopholes that distort the way people and firms earn, save, invest, and spend their money, we could reduce tax rates and enable families to retain the resources they need to raise and educate their children, obtain health insurance, buy a home, and save for retirement.

• *Open Trade.* The United States should press every country to open its markets and welcome foreign competitors into our own. Freer trade makes every nation's economy more efficient, by letting each concentrate where it has a comparative advantage. In addition, it can drive greater economic innovation by giving our firms access to all the world's new ideas and the impetus to stay competitive by innovating themselves.

• *A New Bargain Between Workers and Business for Higher Growth.* Labor and management should forge a new relationship that expands workers' opportunities to improve their skills and their incentives to come up with new ideas. The tax code should continue to provide companies tax benefits for their costs to upgrade employees' skills and to reward new ideas with stock bonuses, but only if *all* full-time workers are eligible. At the same time, workers who accept training from a company should have to stay with the firm for a set period of time, and should have to earn any tax-preferred bonus with a superior performance.

The Failings of Conservative and Liberal Growth Policies

By contrast, the traditional conservative and liberal programs for growth are of little use, because they are still attached to outdated prescriptions from the old industrial economy.

The conservative credo for growth is simple: More business investment and less government. Many conservatives are still recycling theories of business investment from the 1920s (or more charitably the 1950s), when growth seemed to depend on how much General Motors and U.S. Steel spent on new plant and equipment. But as we will see, the growth benefits from higher business investment are at best modest. Moreover, tax cuts have become conservatives' preferred way to spur investment, and this approach actually dampens investment by expanding the budget deficit.

Apart from business investment, less government is the right's favorite remedy for slow growth—even though government spending as a share of the economy has barely changed at all over the last two decades. Conservatives acknowledge, for example, that innovation and skills enhancement can spur growth, but reject the idea that government could promote either. Apart from tax cuts, deregulation is their main strategy for innovation, and they haven't pressed for it very hard, while their answer on worker training is to let GM and U.S. Steel do it.

On the left, the liberal program hearkens back to the 1930s, looking to government to save the day. Whenever the economy cools, government can pump up demand with more federal spending and lower interest rates. Throughout the business cycle, strict government regulation can prevent marauding corporations from shedding their proper obligations to workers and consumers. And trade protection is the best answer to competition from lower-wage foreign workers. In their traditional commitment to more education and training, liberals come closer to what the new economy needs. Yet, they also stalwartly support current entitlement programs which leave few budgetary resources for any new initiatives in these areas.

With President Clinton and the Congress, Americans face a choice. We can stick with the old prescriptions for growth and content ourselves with low unemployment, low inflation, and modest income gains. Or we can adopt a new strategy more attuned to the needs of an advanced, knowledge-based economy. And if we do that, we will find that the American economy is already primed for faster growth. Compared to other advanced countries, our markets are less restricted, our economic culture is more entrepreneurial, and our scientific establishment is larger. Moreover, President Clinton, the Federal Reserve Board, and Congress already have rebuilt our macroeconomic framework through sustained fiscal discipline and sound money. The new challenge is to systematically reorder the rest of national economic policy around the imperatives of the new economy, promoting both innovation in all its aspects and education and training for all Americans.

The Revolution in Economic Thought and Economic Life

Research and experience teach us that the heart of economic growth lies not in how much plant and equipment we have or even how many workers, but in the knowledge imbued in them. To produce as much income tomorrow as we do today, we will have to replace any machines and workers that wear out.

But a better life depends on improving the quality of people's work and the capital they work with, by increasing their skills and by innovating relentlessly. The key to creating new value and national wealth, therefore, is not how many factories we build, but our capacity to develop new products, materials, and production methods; new ways of financing, marketing, and distributing goods and services; and better ways of organizing the workplace and managing a business.

Apart from such knowledge, everything in economic life is subject to the dismal law that the more you do of anything, the less additional reward you get for it. The first piece of equipment any company buys will be whatever produces the highest return, as the first employee hired will be assigned the task that generates the most profit. After that, each successive purchase or new hire will be put to uses that produce relatively *lower* or diminishing returns, because the more profitable uses have been taken.

But knowledge has unique economic qualities, as Paul Romer, the country's leading thinker about innovation, has noted.[4] Unlike a piece of equipment or a worker, an idea can be used by any number of businesses simultaneously. Moreover, once we incur the cost of coming up with a new idea, it can be used freely again and again. Finally, knowledge builds on itself, so that one innovation reduces the cost of the next—as the invention of the internal combustion engine paved the way for the automobile. Not only are new economically useful ideas immune from the law of diminishing returns, they may even exhibit *increasing* returns.

Economic innovation is not limited to exciting new technologies and hot new industries. A mature company like GM, for example, can grow faster not just by developing a new product line, but by using new management ideas to reorganize itself. Flattening the corporate hierarchy and introducing quality teams may eliminate some positions at first. But by making more workers into decisionmakers, these changes can help drive innovations and higher returns that ultimately produce more jobs.

Economists can quantify how innovation and other factors affect growth. Nobel laureate Robert Solow, for example, analyzed America's economic record from 1909 to 1949. He found that apart from the larger work force, seven-eighths of the growth during that period could be traced to technological progress and improvements in the skills and use of workers.[5] The expanding stock of business plant and equipment accounted for only the remaining 12 percent or so.

Another distinguished economist, Edward Denison, reached similar conclusions after analyzing our strong growth in the postwar years of 1948 to 1973.[6] Technological progress, he found, accounted for 37 percent of the nation's 3.8 percent average annual growth in our Gross Domestic Product (GDP), and another 29 percent of the growth was traced to workers' rising education levels and work experience. Of the rest, 15 percent of the growth was traced to increases in business plant and equipment, and about 10 percent each to greater economies of scale in corporations and shifts of labor and capital to more efficient uses.

The way we drive growth affects not only its rate, but also who benefits from it. We can increase growth modestly by raising business investment, but most of the gains will go to the owners of business capital. If we increase growth instead by enhancing workers' skills and capacities, the gains should be larger (if longer in coming) and will be shared by the workers themselves and those who own the business capital they use. By focusing on innovation, we can achieve the greatest gains in growth; and the rewards will be shared among the workers who generate it, the owners of the businesses where they work, and everyone who uses whatever is produced.

We can move beyond the current Hobson's choice in economic policy. We no longer have to choose between narrow business investment policies that mainly benefit wealthy people, and income transfer programs that put money in more people's pockets but fail to strengthen the economy that produces the income. Instead, we can pursue policies that encourage investments in human capital and the factors of innovation, because, to paraphrase Willy Sutton, that's where the real growth is.

Why People and Firms Innovate

If the relationship between innovation and economic growth is well under-stood, why haven't we tailored our policies accordingly? The answer is that, based on a classical view of how markets work, most economic policymakers believe that there's little they could do to increase innovation.[7] Here's the puzzle: If well-oiled markets ensure that all capital and labor are already used efficiently, why would anyone incur the additional cost of coming up with a new idea, especially when the return is uncertain? The answer for traditional economists is that innovation happens when someone happens to have a bright idea and applies it, not because he or she has a rational economic incentive for doing so, but simply for personal reasons. In technical terms, economic innovation is seen as *exogenous*, which is a fancy way of saying that the central factor in growth arises not from the dynamics of the economy, but from personal psychology.

This answer sacrifices common sense and experience to a theory of mar-kets. In the process, it has left us virtually powerless to increase growth by any means except higher business fixed investment. Yet every day, thousands of firms and people behave as if they have good reasons to innovate. They're not daydreaming; they merely understand that being first has its own rewards. It creates a pocket of monopoly that raises an innovator's potential returns by holding back normal competitive pressures.

As a general rule, if a company tries to sell its product for more than its production costs, plus a normal rate of profit, competitors will undercut that price. But when a software developer creates a powerful new program that enables people to do more than any other product, normal market competition cannot force him to sell each copy at its marginal cost of production. Or when a fast food chain first figures out how to market in the high schools, it can sell its burgers for a nickel more than at the mall, because its innovative marketing insulates it from normal price competition. For a time, no one can compete with an innovator, and the price he charges can include a monopoly profit that enables him to recover the costs of development, and more.

The more innovative the economy is, the more it departs from the traditional ideal of pure market competition. That's why innovation has posed such a puzzle to classical economists.

This doesn't explain, however, how anybody but the innovator ever benefits. So long as its monopoly holds, an innovating company can capture most of the new value produced by its new idea—which is why the stock of a firm like Netscape will soar when it introduces a powerful new product. At the same time, its rivals lose ground, and everybody else has to pay the price demanded by the monopoly to get the new product. And copyright and patent laws prevent other companies from simply appropriating Netscape's idea, duplicating the product, and selling it at a lower price that doesn't include the development costs.

Innovation has the capacity to drive broad growth, because it is a dynamic process: Competition drives Netscape's rivals to study the new product and learn from it—and unlike a piece of equipment or a worker, the new idea can be used by more than one firm at the same time. The growth comes when those rivals not only learn from the original innovation but go beyond it. Either a competitor produces a product that does what Netscape's did in a different way and sells it for less, or it learns enough to advance beyond it.

The economic power of innovation lies in the additional value created by these competitive forces and spillovers. For example, when competitors overtook Henry Ford's early dominance in the automobile industry, the economy grew not only because people and products could move more quickly, but also because of the countless spinoffs based on early automotive innovations. Moreover, Ford's economic breakthrough depended as much on reorganizing the workplace for mass production, as on his engineers' innovations. And growth in the 1990s and beyond will probably come as much from new ways of organizing offices and factories—new teamwork strategies that build people's skills, or employee participation plans that encourage workers to contribute their ideas—as from technological breakthroughs.

Still, economic innovations almost always involve losses as well as gains. When a new product or process displaces an existing one, the value of firms and the income of workers falls if they cannot fully make the transition. When IBM introduced the desktop computer, for example, other office equipment manufacturers and their workers were forced to retrench. In time, Compaq, Dell, and others developed clones at lower prices. But even then, thousands of companies and millions of workers were left with obsolete technologies and out-of-date skills.

Sometimes, innovations come in such rapid succession that many people never realize any benefits. The extraordinary pace of development in computer software and microchips, for example, enables some manufacturers to introduce new generations of products before competition has caught up with their previous innovations. Workers without the education and skills to adapt to each new round of progress lose some of their market value, and so have to settle for lower pay. And consumers are forced to either ante up round after round of high prices, or operate at a technological disadvantage.

Nevertheless, the largest share of the growth and income progress we do achieve comes from workers and companies developing new ideas and using those of others. The first priority for national growth policy is to actively promote this process in all of its aspects, and ensure that as many Americans as possible can take advantage of it.

The Value of Education and Training

In the calculus for higher growth, improving the skills and education of the work force comes close behind innovation. And in the working world, the two factors are not entirely distinct, since innovation often requires some form of intellectual expertise, and a company's ability to use new methods and technologies depends on its employees' knowledge and training.

The economic value of educating and training ourselves is no mystery. In fact, our growing income inequality largely follows from our patterns of investment in education and training. Most of the top 15 percent to 20 percent of American workers, whose incomes have grown at healthy rates over the last twenty-five years, are products of a higher education system that is the envy of the world. Once on the job, these managers and professionals also receive some 70 percent of all training expenditures by private businesses. On top of that, their jobs require them to continuously evaluate new information and solve new problems, thereby expanding their knowledge and skills further. Typically, they know more at the end of every year than at the beginning, and so are more productive and efficient—and more highly paid.

By contrast, most office and factory workers have been educated only in our public elementary and secondary schools, which are subjects of national despair. Moreover, after their initial orientation, most of these workers receive little or no additional training on the job, and their work rarely exposes them to new information or demands new thinking. In fact, by *not* building new knowledge and skills, many working people see their economic capacities slowly depreciate over the course of every year, leaving them relatively less productive and efficient—and less well-paid.

Why don't firms better equip their workers for the new economy? After all, since better-trained workers are usually more productive, markets should provide all the incentives that firms need to make economically efficient training decisions. But in the real world, American business invests *less* in training their employees than economic logic would demand, essentially because workers have the freedom to change jobs.

If McDonald's trains a burger flipper to use a computer to monitor inventory, for example, the employee's new skills may enable him to win a better position with Red Lobster or Kmart—and the competitor reaps the benefits of McDonald's training investment. This market failure particularly affects average workers. Large corporations spend whatever is necessary to ensure that their executives and in-house lawyers are up-to-date on management techniques and legal developments, because improving the decisions of supervisors and professionals produces higher returns from all the workers they direct. In addition, many professionals and managers sign agreements that oblige them to stay with their employer for a period. Finally, executives and professional employees have more reason to demand that their company help them upgrade their skills, because they often receive bonuses for improved performance.

The result is that workers at the top of the ladder generally receive the education and training they need to prosper, while most everyone else receives less than they or the economy could profitably use. In the end, growth is less than it could be, and inequality is greater than it need be.

Over the next twenty-five years, information technologies could ease these inequalities—or exacerbate them. Computers have become ubiquitous across the American economy. Already, most firms and new jobs require some form of computer literacy. On the hopeful side, these technologies rely on standard protocols and procedures, so that a worker with computer-related skills can use them in any number of companies and positions. The downside is equally obvious, since anyone who does not continuously improve his computer skills to keep up with the technologies will fall behind.

The Difference That Capital Makes

While growth may depend mainly on our commitments to innovation and education and training, the new economy still needs traditional savings and business fixed investment. The issue for economic policy is how to affect them.

In the 1950s, when international capital flows were relatively small and not much noticed, it was reasonable to assume we could invest no more than we saved. Today, our capital markets are part of a global system that makes the whole world's savings available to any American firm willing to pay the price to borrow it. Saving more for ourselves is still better for the economy than saving less.[8] But how much our businesses invest depends primarily not on how much we save, but on a sound macroeconomic environment that keeps interest rates low and on how productive our businesses are. And that, in turn, depends on how innovative, educated, and well-trained we are.

Yet, for the last two decades, our economic policies have chased the illusion that we could restore strong growth by subsidizing higher personal saving and business capital. By 1990, roughly 80 percent of all personal saving received some form of tax preference.[9] In addition, from 1970 to 1990, federal revenues from corporate taxes as a share of GDP fell by half, from 3.2 percent to 1.6 percent.[10] And from 1977 to 1990, the federal tax burden on the top 10 percent of Americans who own most corporate stock declined by more than 8 percent.[11] Including both corporate and individual taxes, the total effective tax burden on capital income is now roughly 16 percent, or less than two-thirds of the tax burden on labor income.[12]

By any measure, these strategies have failed. Since 1980, as tax benefits for saving have expanded, the personal saving rate has fallen from roughly 6 percent of GDP to 4 percent. Nor has business investment been much more responsive: After replacing worn out plant and equipment, U.S. companies took on additional capital investments at a slower rate than before, despite the tax inducements. Moreover, the entire economy's growth rate has continued to erode, and most people's real incomes have risen by less than 1 percent a year.

The best policies for business investment in the new economy are fiscal discipline and sound money, so the cost of borrowing can remain low, and the repeal of tax subsidies for particular kinds of investments, so companies will allocate their investments based only on the economics of the alternatives available to them. And the best program for business profits is not another tax cut, but measures to help make the economy more productive. That depends on what our current policies generally neglect: the capacities of firms to innovate, and the skills and knowledge of their workers.

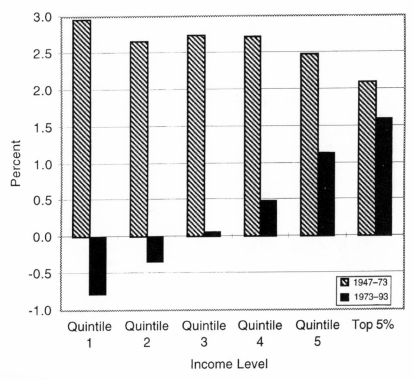

Fig. 12.2. Annual real income growth, 1947–1973 and 1973–1993. Data from U.S. Bureau of the Census, *Current Population Reports: Series P-60.*

A New Growth Policy for the New Economy

Economic growth comes not from new government programs, but from people in private businesses working harder or better to create new value. The government's only role is to foster the most favorable climate and conditions for this enterprise, primarily through its budget, tax, trade, and monetary policies.

A Pro-Growth Budget: Cut and Invest

President Clinton's next budget can help support this enterprise in three ways. First, the next round of federal spending cuts should start with scores of special-interest subsidy programs—from the construction of special roads for timber companies and payments to U.S. companies that advertise abroad, to crop supports and below-market sales of electrical power to private utilities. Such "corporate welfare" not only transfers income from average taxpayers to the industries and firms with the most clout in Washington. It also impedes innovation and growth. By artificially raising the rate of return for politically favored sectors and companies, these subsidies reduce those sectors' and companies' need to figure out new and better ways of competing. Special-interest subsidies also create an uneven playing field that leaves every other industry and business at an economic disadvantage, making the entire economy less efficient.

Since PPI first raised the issue of industry subsidies in 1992, Congress has reduced these programs by less than 10 percent.[13] To eliminate the rest, they will have to take on much of the Washington establishment. To break the hold of the special interests that protect these provisions, the President and Congress should establish a Commission on Industry Subsidies and National Growth modeled on the Military Base Closing Commission. The new Commission would evaluate all industry-specific programs, recommend reform or repeal of those serving no overriding national purpose, and present the package of changes to the President. The President could submit the package to Congress, which would have to vote the recommendations up or down without amendment.

Second, the next budget should shift some of the resources claimed today for corporate welfare to new public investments, especially in areas crucial to growth. Fiscal discipline is not an end in itself, but merely a means for achieving stronger growth; and efforts to roll back our commitments in education, training, R&D, and the nation's infrastructure defeat this purpose. The federal government has crucial roles to play in promoting greater educational and training opportunities, supporting basic research at the frontiers of science, and maintaining and modernizing the economy's infrastructure, from airports and interstate highways to connecting schools and other public facilities to the information superhighway. Yet, since taking office, President Clinton's calls for greater national investments in these areas have been thwarted by conservative opponents in Congress and by the commitment to reduce the deficit. From 1993 to 1997, real federal investment actually declined by more than 4 percent for training programs and by 5 percent for infrastructure, and rose by merely 1 percent in education and by less than 3 percent in non-defense R&D.[14]

A new, cut-and-invest fiscal program would meet the demands of the new economy. It would remove the dead hand of obsolete subsidies from workers and companies, halt legally mandated transfers from average people to the shareholders of influential industries, and provide an economically sound alternative to the balanced budget amendment. And its public investments would promote faster growth, which is the best support the government can provide any industry or firm.

Third, the next budget must sustain the financial environment for private investment by strengthening fiscal discipline. Every dollar off the deficit is a dollar added to the national savings available for business investment. More importantly, budget policy must maintain the expectations of the financial markets that the era of big deficits is over, so that long-term interest rates can remain low and long-term investments in innovation can increase.[15] Meeting these expectations will require not only the repeal of many corporate subsidies, but also serious reforms in Medicare and Social Security, the two federal programs that mean so much to so many Americans (see chapters 4 and 5).

A Pro-Growth Tax Code

Tax reform is not a magic potion for the economy, and neither are tax cuts. But like a cut-and-invest budget, tax reform can make a contribution to growth policy.

Two principles should guide the next round of tax reforms: Simplify the system, and preserve its progressive character. As liberals and conservatives have both long argued, a simpler tax system is generally more efficient and fair. Most of the code's current complexity reflects special tax treatment granted to certain influential industries and constituencies. Since markets usually do a better job than government in allocating the economy's resources, eliminating special provisions that affect how firms and people earn and use their resources would allow them to make better use of those resources. Many of these provisions also favor the most profitable firms and most affluent people, since the value of a tax deduction or exclusion increases with a person's income and tax rate.

Simplifying the tax system, especially on the business side, could promote growth in other ways. While some of the complications in the corporate tax code reflect real complexities in economic life, others testify to the ability of influential industries to win special treatment. Like the spending subsidies in the budget, industry tax subsidies can inhibit innovation, because they reward companies for using their capital and labor in the same ways they have in the past. When an energy firm can reduce its taxes by drilling in certain geological formations, or a corporation can earn a special tax credit by shifting a profit-making operation to a Puerto Rican subsidiary, these firms have less reason and fewer resources to consider new ways of doing business. Congress could promote innovation simply by repealing these subsidies. By so doing, they also could find resources to reduce tax rates—and lower rates are better for the economy's efficiency than higher rates.

Simplifying personal income taxes is also desirable. But income tax reform should maintain special tax treatment for the basic needs of middle-class families. This system would resemble neither the current one with its profusion of tax preferences, nor conservative alternatives like the flat tax that favor investors over wage earners. Instead, it would provide limited tax credits for the five basic constituents of middle-class life—the resources an average family needs to raise its children, send them to college, provide health insurance, own a home, and save for retirement. Tax simplification is also not a reason to abolish progressive tax rates, as would the flat tax, since higher tax burdens on higher-income families help pay for lower tax burdens on the majority of Americans. Finally, tax cuts cannot substitute for tax reform. While lower taxes are generally better for the economy than higher taxes, tax cuts that also bring higher deficits can sabotage growth and innovation by raising interest rates.

Open Markets and Open Trade

Faster growth also requires that Americans embrace the world through open global markets and open trade. The traditional case for free trade always stresses efficiency: Every economy can gain when everyone can buy the products they need at the lowest prices, regardless of who produced them. The catch for an advanced economy is that business captures more of those efficiency gains than workers. In an open global economy, American firms can invest wherever costs are low and profit outlooks are bright; but American workers cannot sell their services wherever in the world they might be used most efficiently. The result has been general progress toward more open international trade, with industries and workers most vulnerable to foreign competition holding on to various forms of trade protection.

The new economy does not change these dynamics or the dilemma. But it raises the costs of protectionism, because innovation and human capital know no national boundaries. Open markets and open trade allow us to learn, borrow, and improve on the ideas and advances of firms throughout the global economy, in effect placing the whole world's human capital at our disposal. Open trade also directly encourages greater investment in R&D, because a firm can allocate the costs of developing a new product over a larger base of potential sales.

Despite the warnings of protectionists, America can benefit *more* from an open global economy than other nations. As the world's most advanced and efficient economy, we are best able to develop new ideas conceived elsewhere. As the world's biggest exporter and largest direct investor in foreign countries, we also have the most to gain from building on the innovations of foreign competitors. However, as our stake in open trade increases, so does our responsibility to ensure that as many Americans as possible have the means to compete effectively.

Strike a New Bargain for Higher Growth between Workers and Business

To meet this responsibility, government and business must work together to provide average working Americans greater opportunities and incentives to improve themselves and become innovators on the job. Ours is already the world's most successful economy when it comes to generating cutting-edge technologies or educating and training managers and professionals. But U.S. growth is relatively slow and economic inequality is increasing, because only people at the top rungs of our society enjoy real opportunities to innovate and improve their skills on an ongoing basis.

The answer lies not in vast new government programs, but in artful new strategies to encourage firms and their employees to work together to advance their mutual interests. Take the problem of on-the-job training for the great bulk of workers who receive little or none of it. Millions of Americans who will never see the inside of a lab or attend a management seminar want to improve their skills, and their employers know that better-trained workers can be more productive and profitable. But today, most workers can't afford the time or the fees to train elsewhere, and companies can't afford to train employees who might just move on to another job. And the federal government doesn't have the resources to provide ongoing training for 130 million working people, nor could it do so efficiently even if it did. That's checkmate, and everybody loses.

Our growth policy addresses this problem from a new direction, beginning with a well-established rule of tax policy. Today, when any company provides tax-free compensation such as health care coverage or pension contributions to its employees, it cannot discriminate by excluding any significant group of its work force. Otherwise, everyone would end up contributing to the favored tax treatment of the few. Yet the training that many executives and professionals receive is clearly a tax-free form of compensation. The first part of our strategy is to apply the non-discrimination rule to employer-provided training. This change in tax treatment would not require that companies train all their workers, but it would force them to weigh the potential benefits of providing all full-time employees the opportunity to improve themselves.

But workers who take advantage of this opportunity should have an obligation to the company that provides it. Today, stockbrokers and lawyers who receive extensive training often sign employment contracts to remain where they are for a time. The second part of this strategy would apply this procedure through model agreements that would oblige any worker accepting additional training to not change jobs for a year.

Using a similar strategy, we can encourage more workers to be innovators. Today, many large corporations encourage their executives and professional employees to come up with new ideas by rewarding superior performance with stock or stock options. Some of the U.S. economy's most innovative industries, such as software and investment banking, go further: They use performance-based bonuses to give all employees a stake in figuring out how to do a better job.

Since anyone can come up with a new idea, growth policy should encourage every worker to develop ideas that can help his or her firm earn more money. Once again, we would apply the non-discrimination rule: When a company provides tax-favored, performance-based bonuses, the opportunity should be available to *all* full-time employees. This change would not force companies to give everyone a bonus, but it would require that they allow all their workers to participate in any performance-based compensation system. In this way, the incentives for innovation that now apply to most executives would be available to all working people. We could even consider enhancing the incentive, as Great Britain does, by exempting from income tax a part of any cash bonus from an approved, performance-based compensation plan.

Conclusion

America's growth policies are still caught up in the images and lessons of an economy of the past. Many conservatives offer the 1920s and 1950s as proof that faster growth would follow if only federal taxes were lower, especially on traditional business investment. Many liberals, remembering the ascendancy of their creed in the 1930s and 1960s, insist that government prime the pump and guarantee everyone more economic benefits.

In the new economy, the decisive factors for growth are not how much business invests in plant and equipment or how much government spends, but how productively our firms and workers use the resources available to them and how effectively they invent new ways of using those resources. The key to higher living standards is to expand our knowledge and imaginations in every aspect of our economic lives. Supporting the efforts of American workers and firms to do this is the central task of new growth policy.

Notes

1. Clay Chandler and Richard Morin, "Prosperity's Imbalances Divide U.S.; Disparity Grows Wider for Winners, Losers," *Washington Post*, 14 Oct. 1996.

2. The U.S. real gross national product (GNP) grew at an average rate of 3.7 percent a year from 1870 to 1969. From 1950 to 1969, real GNP grew at an average rate

of 3.9 percent a year. Bureau of the Census, *Historical Statistics of the United States, Colonial Times to 1970,* (Washington, DC: 1975), Table F, 10–16.

3. For example, while globalization expands markets for American products and enables U.S. firms to invest around the world, it puts pressure on the wages of American workers who now have to compete in a worldwide labor market. Or even as new information technologies give their American developers an edge in world markets that increases profits, the broader productivity benefits often associated with these advances go mainly to highly educated people.

4. See Paul M. Romer, "Endogenous Technological Change," part 2, *Journal of Political Economy* 98, no. 5, (1990): S71–102.

5. Robert Solow, "Growth Theory and After," *The American Economic Review* (June 1988): 307–317.

6. Edward F. Denison, *Trends in American Economic Growth, 1929–1982* (Washington, DC: The Brookings Institution, 1985).

7. This discussion is indebted to Paul Romer, "Increasing Returns and New Developments in the Theory of Growth," NBER reprint No. 1690, reprinted from *Equilibrium Theory and Applications: Proceedings of the Sixth International Symposium in Economic Theory and Econometrics,* eds. William A. Barnett, et al., (Cambridge, UK: Cambridge University Press, 1991), 83–110.

8. If our people and businesses saved enough to meet our investment needs, the profits earned by the lenders as well as those earned by those putting the loans to use would stay here, where they could help raise our living standards.

9. C. Eugene Steuerle, *Taxes, Loans and Inflation: How the Nation's Wealth Becomes Misallocated* (Washington, DC: The Brookings Institution, 1985).

10. Calculations from data reported in *Economic Report of the President,* Feb. 1996, tables B-1, B-76.

11. House Committee on Ways and Means, "Tax Progressivity and Income Distribution," prepared by its Majority Staff, 101st Cong., 2d sess., 26 Mar. 1990, table I, 12.

12. Jane G. Gravelle, *The Economic Effects of Taxing Capital Income* (Cambridge, MA: The MIT Press, 1994). Steuerle, *Taxes, Loans and Inflation.*

13. See Robert J. Shapiro, "Paying for Progress: A Progressive Strategy for Fiscal Discipline" (Washington, DC: Progresssive Policy Institute, 24 Feb. 1991). Robert J. Shapiro, "Cut-and-Invest to Compete and Win: A Budget Strategy for American Growth" (Washington, DC: Progressive Policy Institute, Policy Report No. 18, Jan. 1994). Robert J. Shapiro, "Cut-and-Invest: A Budget Strategy for the New Economy" (Washington, DC: Progressive Policy Institute, Policy Report No. 23, Mar. 1995).

14. Measured in 1992 dollars, federal spending for training programs fell from $3.3 billion in 1993 to $3.1 billion in 1997; spending for infrastructure fell from $26 billion in 1993 to $23.8 billion in 1997; spending for education increased from $23.1 billion in 1993 to $23.3 billion in 1997; and spending for non-defense related research increased from $27.9 billion in 1993 to $28.7 billion in 1997.

15. High interest rates discourage firms from innovating by making it more expensive to finance R&D. In turn, this reduces the net value of R&D's future returns, and increases the current return on less risky investments.

Chapter 13

Democratic Realism: A New Compass for U.S. Global Leadership

Robert A. Manning and Will Marshall

Foreign policy, at the center of presidential politics throughout the post–World War II era, nearly disappeared from the nation's radar screen during the 1996 campaign. Some analysts attributed this lack of interest to the absence of a palpable external threat; others to the widely held feeling that it is time to attend to domestic problems that piled up during the Cold War.

Whatever the reason, Americans can ill afford to adopt a stance of benign neglect toward the rest of the world. Foreign affairs touch the daily lives of Americans now more than ever. Economic globalization moves manufacturing jobs to Mexico and China, fostering insecurity even as it provides plentiful, cheap consumer goods and produces new jobs in export-related industries. The decisions of currency traders in Tokyo and Bonn affect our mortgage rates and national budgets. Conflicts in the Middle East set off a murky chain of events punctuated by the terrorist bombing of a New York skyscraper. From Colombian-produced drugs in our neighborhoods, to cross-border pandemics, to pollution of the world's atmosphere, there is nothing remote about the link between foreign policy and our domestic well-being.

In the late 1940s, the specter of a powerful, aggressive, and ideologically confident Soviet Union united liberal anticommunists and conservative nationalists behind the mission of containing communism. That policy spawned not only the North Atlantic Treaty Organization (NATO), but also a host of

Steven J. Nider provided an invaluable contribution to the writing and preparation of this chapter.

economic and political institutions designed to advance collective security and prosperity. The liberal postwar order, featuring unprecedented economic co-operation through the International Monetary Fund (IMF), the World Bank, global trade accords, and other transnational institutions, fostered free trade and investment, human rights, and the diffusion of democratic norms—eventually even to the communist East.

Now we face the dilemmas of success. As the New Progressive Declaration points out, "The end of the Cold War has weakened the domestic consensus behind vigorous U.S. leadership, leaving us uncertain of our role in the world, torn between the impulse to lead and the temptation to turn inward." Without an overarching national purpose connecting our actions abroad, the rationale for each policy move—intervention in Haiti, deals with North Korea, peace-keeping in Bosnia, free trade expansions—eludes the public. This strategic vacuum invites ethnic constituencies and special interests to play a larger role in shaping U.S. foreign policy, from our efforts to mediate the conflict in Northern Ireland to trade disputes with Japan.

As the bipolar world recedes, there has been a revival of this century's long-running debate between internationalists and isolationists. In general, liberals lean toward international cooperation—some even to the point of substituting multilateralism for strong U.S. leadership. While some conservatives have re-verted to "America First" isolationism, others have embraced a "go it alone" course based on a more narrow definition of national interests.

Even as the old fault lines reemerge, there are new twists as well. The most important change is the challenge to the old free-trade consensus, which has spilled over partisan lines to include such diverse figures as Ross Perot, Pat Buchanan, Ralph Nader, and Jesse Jackson. The new "economic nationalists," who see globalization as a threat to U.S. living standards, vehemently oppose such trade-expanding treaties as the North American Free Trade Agreement (NAFTA). Some argue further that the global struggle for economic suprem-acy is replacing ideological and military rivalries as the dominant theme of international politics.

New Progressives believe that the internationalist path chosen by Franklin D. Roosevelt, Harry S. Truman, and John F. Kennedy, updated to new circum-stances, remains the way of enlightened self-interest for America. Our last experiment with protectionism and isolationism, in the 1920s and 1930s, ended in depression and world war. In contrast, postwar U.S. leadership rallied democratic forces throughout the world and led to unprecedented prosperity. As the world's strongest economy and military power, America remains the linchpin of the liberal democratic order that emerged triumphant in the Cold War. Our aim now should be to strengthen and extend the community of mar-ket democracies as we enter the twenty-first century.

Democratic Realism

Our challenge is to adapt old strategic assumptions and institutions to a messy, multipolar world in which yesterday's foes are potential partners and in which military allies are also tough economic competitors. This requires a new way of thinking about how America leads, about how we organize our military forces, about the role of nuclear weapons in national security, about the various diplomatic tools at our disposal, and about setting priorities in a world that is at once less dangerous and more volatile. We call this approach democratic realism.

Democratic realism builds on the time-honored principles of liberal internationalism. At the core of the post–Cold War world is a growing zone of democracies committed to relatively open markets and free trade, political relations based on agreed-upon rules and norms of behavior, and institutions to cooperatively manage and enforce those standards. Extending that democratic community furthers both our national interests and values. Moreover, by grounding American foreign policy in our democratic values, we can gain the broad bipartisan domestic support needed to sustain credible, U.S. leadership.

At the same time, democratic realism impels us to maintain America's commitments to uphold crucial balances of power in Europe, the Middle East, and Asia. Outside the zone of democracies lies a violent and chaotic zone of turmoil. Democratic realism requires that we maintain military forces capable of deterring and, if necessary, repelling aggression.

This approach to foreign policy also calls for a thorough revamping of the institutions of postwar internationalism, to ensure a more equitable sharing of the burdens of upholding peace and stability. The international system is not self-regulating; major powers must shape its rules. As we saw in the Gulf War, the United States is stronger to the extent it can pursue its objectives in concert with other leading nations. Moreover, in the absence of an overriding threat, the United States must be more selective about intervening in foreign crises.

Democratic realism seeks to fill the strategic vacuum in U.S. foreign policy in three ways: by focusing on central priorities rather than peripheral conflicts; by adapting our Cold War policies and institutions to new conditions (rather than merely perpetuating them as the Clinton administration has, or rejecting them as many Republicans have); and by redefining U.S. leadership, yielding neither to multilateral myths nor unilateral dreams. Our new role in the world must be that of first among equals, with others gradually assuming more power and responsibility.

Global Confusion

In the past seven years, we have gone from the collapse of the Berlin Wall to savage tribal violence in the heart of Europe; from predictions of a new age of democratic harmony to forecasts of civilizations in conflict and neo-Malthusian chaos. This confusion arises from the push and pull of forces that, paradoxically, seem to point simultaneously toward greater global integration and disintegration:

- The instantaneous flow of capital, information, and ideas has become a powerful force in world politics. The globalization of financial markets, trade, and production knits the world together. At the same time, these trends weaken the power of central banks and national governments to uphold traditional social bargains. Fortunately, global markets and communications seem to favor open societies over authoritarian regimes, which risk economic backwardness if they seal themselves off from the world. On the other hand, the rapid diffusion of knowledge and technology gives terrorists easier access to sophisticated weapons.

- For the moment, no ideology rivals liberal democracy as a system of universal appeal. The post–Cold War trends of market-oriented economics and democratization are approaching the status of universal norms. A 1996 study by Freedom House found that 117 of the world's 191 independent nations are now democratic (61 percent, up from 42 percent a decade ago).[1] Yet these gains are often fragile. Democratic values are challenged by religious fundamentalists, as well as by Asian proponents of a "Confucian capitalism" that combines authoritarianism with free markets.

- There are no overtly adversarial relations among the major powers—the United States, the European Union (EU), Japan, Russia, and China. Yet it is not clear whether these latter two "transition states" will choose partnership over obstruction. Staunch allies, Germany and Japan, have become more independent and assertive. Meanwhile, trouble is brewing in a turbulent arc of conflict-prone or failing states, stretching from Africa to Southwest and Central Asia. Easier access to commercial technology with military applications, along with the spread of nuclear and other weapons of mass destruction, gives smaller states unprecedented military capabilities.

- Ethnic and nationalist tensions submerged by the Cold War are prime sources of potential instability. This new quest for communal identity is partly a response to the unraveling of old empires and nations concocted by colonial mapmakers. It stems as well from a sense of powerlessness and cultural loss caused by unaccountable economic and technological forces that are driving global integration.

- While the Cold War is over, the global and national institutions it spawned have yet to be readjusted to cope with a world of multiple, unequal power centers, in which neither economic superpower status such as Japan's, nor nuclear superpower status such as Russia's, necessarily translates into political clout. Even the nature of conflict is changing, with a growing share of it occuring not between states, but between factions and clans within states.

The Democratic and Republican Responses

The Clinton administration has responded to these new, confusing realities by hewing faithfully to the internationalist agenda it inherited, as evidenced by its commitment to free trade, the promotion of democracy, strengthening the United Nations (UN), maintaining traditional alliances in Europe and Asia, and supporting the Middle East peace process.

Yet the administration's failure to set strategic priorities, coupled with well-intentioned humanitarian impulses and special interest pressures, led to early missteps in Somalia, Bosnia, and Haiti. Critics of Clinton's foreign policy have failed to acknowledge his administration's subsequent rise up the learning curve, as manifested in its efforts to halt the fighting in Bosnia and check the North Korean nuclear program.

Nonetheless, the administration's failure to articulate clear strategic goals and priorities has often resulted in a reactive, in-box approach to foreign policy. Moreover, the administration has not moved with sufficient dispatch or imagination to adapt our Cold War policies and institutions to America's new roles and missions in a fast-changing world. This inertia has fed public doubts on both the left and right about the risks, costs, and rewards of U.S. global engagement.

Among Republicans, support for internationalism is waning and unilateralism is on the rise. On one extreme is Pat Buchanan, reprising the old "America First" themes of isolationism and nativism. On the other stand self-proclaimed neo-Reaganites, who call for the United States to establish single-handedly a "benevolent global hegemony."

Somewhere in between fell the Republican-controlled 104th Congress, which sought to slash the State Department's budget, eliminate the U.S. Information Agency (USIA), and cut our contributions to the UN, even though our nation is already some $2 billion in arrears. While adding $6 billion for defense above what the Pentagon requested, congressional Republicans directed the State Department to shut down some thirty embassies and consulates along with twenty-five USIA libraries overseas. [2] In addition, they sought to cut funds for UN peacekeeping and to limit U.S. involvement in such activities. Even GOP presidential candidate Bob Dole, a free trader with a long, consistent record of support for internationalism, got into the act, vowing at one point "not to let our national sovereignty be infringed" by the World Trade Organization (WTO).[3]

Missing: A Conceptual Framework

Missing from the foreign policy debate is a conceptual framework that marries our democratic values to a tough-minded strategy for advancing U.S. interests in a new era. Democratic realism seeks to fill that vacuum by identifying a hierarchy of priorities, and by redefining U.S. leadership from Cold War superpower to first among equals.

The need to establish priorities may seem obvious. But in the real world, governments are often driven by events. To decide when and how to act requires a scale of priorities: what is vital, what is very important, what is less important. The logic is that of writer Walter Lippmann's notion of a solvent foreign policy aimed at keeping aspirations and resources, means and ends, in rough balance. As John F. Kennedy said, "To govern is to choose." Or to put it in more workaday terms, foreign policy means making trade-offs. These choices must be articulated and there must be follow through. We cannot fix all problems. We must live with—and enforce—a hierarchy of priorities.

Too often in recent years, foreign policy has seemed driven by horrific television images beamed into our living rooms. Without a clear scale of priorities, the natural American impulse to solve problems can become a recipe for indiscriminate global activism. Leadership requires public candor about the risks and benefits of U.S. intervention. Even when heart-rending images flood our homes, we must resist the impulse to intervene purely for the sake of "doing something." Americans may want to consider what James Clad and Jonathan Clarke call an art of "masterly inactivity" in their book *After the Crusade.*[4] Foreign policy must stay sharply focused on strategic priorities.

Preventing the domination of Europe or East Asia by any hostile power or coalition, and maintaining freedom of navigation and open commercial access, are abiding, first-tier American interests. Preventing the spread, and deterring the use of weapons of mass destruction; preventing catastrophic failure in the global trade and financial systems; and preventing environmental catastrophes and threats to our energy supplies rise to the level of vital American interests.[5] The United States has important interests in regions such as Latin America, Southeast Asia, and Africa that require different levels of involvement, and where multilateral cooperation is essential to maximize our leverage.

Managing relations among the great powers should be at the top of our list of priorities, particularly weaving a democratizing Russia into the fabric of an integrated Europe. China presents another great challenge. Because of its sheer weight and burgeoning growth, if China ceases moving toward integration into global institutions and acceptance of international norms, our attempts to extend the liberal community of nations will falter, whether the issue is trade, environmental protection, nuclear proliferation, or population control. At the next level, major regional powers, particularly in areas vulnerable to conflict and instability, such as India, Turkey, and Indonesia, should be accorded sustained high-level focus and balanced policies.

The Middle East offers a good illustration of where and why the time and resources of U.S. foreign policy should be spent. The strategic importance of energy resources, the survival of a democratic Israel, and the challenge of Islamic fundamentalism pass the fundamental interest test. Indeed, slain Israeli Prime Minister Itzhak Rabin's vision of a new Middle East, which the peace process is aimed at producing, melds our interests and values.

Aiding democratic transitions is a strategic objective of the United States. Here again, however, we must think strategically and set priorities. We must concentrate our limited resources where the strategic payoff is likely to be highest: Russia and Ukraine, for example. Nor should the United States try to impose democracy on any country where powerful internal forces of reform are not already at work. We tend to be most effective when facilitating free market and pluralist forces already in motion, such as efforts to support fledgling non-government, prodemocracy groups in Indonesia, to write commercial codes for Hungary, and to help China prepare and conduct village elections. The United States should leverage its democracy and market promotion efforts by working closely with key regional actors, such as South Africa, and regional bodies, such as the Organization of American States (OAS).

While there is no substitute for decisive U.S. leadership, our relationship with other major powers must be redefined as one of first among equals. In other words, we must shape new partnerships and share responsibilities with our friends and allies in Europe and Asia.

The leading democracies at the core of the expanding liberal order must assume new tasks. We must extend the diplomatic equivalent of an equity stake in the global system to other major regional players (i.e., India, Turkey, and the Association of Southeast Asian Nations [ASEAN]), building on shared interests, proportionately shared responsibilities, and shared values. This approach does not presume the "end of history" or an outbreak of fraternal feeling among sovereign states; as former Secretary of State Henry Kissinger has suggested, a realistic aim would be a "balance of dissatisfactions" in which the minimum needs of major and regional powers are met sufficiently to provide more incentive to participate than to obstruct.

To sum up, the new strategy of democratic realism rests on seven pillars: Forging a new transatlantic partnership; meeting the Pacific challenge; expanding global trade; revamping our Cold War military for new challenges; controlling proliferation of nuclear and other weapons of mass destruction; overhauling U.S. foreign policy institutions; and adapting global institutions to new realities. Let us take each of these in turn.

Forging A New Transatlantic Partnership

Consolidating America's Cold War gains in Europe is the first imperative of democratic realism. Much as the United States firmly anchored Germany and Japan in the West after World War II, we must now extend the liberal order to the new democracies of Central Europe and, eventually, to the former Soviet Union. The history of the twentieth century—in which the United States has been involved in two world wars and a half century of Cold War—underscores the indissoluble ties of interest, culture, and history that bind us to Europe. That U.S. leadership remains essential today was demonstrated in the crisis over "ethnic cleansing" in Bosnia. Only when the Clinton administration took charge by pledging U.S. peacekeepers was a fragile truce reached. Nonetheless, as we confront the historic task of incorporating the former communist states in a new Europe, our allies must assume a greater role.

The United States and its partners face a threefold challenge in Europe: forging a new relationship with Russia; redefining NATO as a pan-European security organization capable of responding to new challenges; and anchoring the new European democracies in the liberal camp by linking NATO expansion with economic integration.

A new relationship with Russia

Europe's stability and security ultimately hinges on the outcome of Russia's dramatic transformation. The United States has rightly offered consistent support for Russian reform, nurturing its evolving markets and democratic processes. However, the administration's decision to set a fixed date for NATO expansion risks inflaming Russian nationalism and paranoia. Therefore, President Clinton should give equal billing to parallel talks with Moscow aimed at formalizing a relationship between NATO and Russia and specifying the steps leading to the inclusion of a democratic, market-oriented Russia into the new Europe.

Redefining NATO's mission

The question of Russia's place in the new Europe leads directly to the issue of NATO's mission. The prospects of a serious military confrontation with Russia are remote. The evaporation of the Warsaw Pact and much of its arsenal removed any major military threat for at least the next ten to fifteen years. Over the next two decades, threats to European security are far more likely to be local ethnic conflicts like Bosnia, fundamentalist threats from North Africa, or turmoil on its southeastern flank.

The administration's pledge to expand NATO into Central Europe by 1999 is the largest new security commitment the United States will make in the years ahead. There is a broad consensus that a democratic Poland, Hungary, and Czech Republic are culturally and historically part of the West. But we need to bring them into the transatlantic community without unnecessarily antagonizing Russia.

Link EU and NATO expansion

The debate over NATO expansion has obscured the equally important question of providing market access to the emerging democracies of Central and Eastern Europe. Unfortunately, the EU is dragging its heels in offering membership to these nations; no eastward expansion is envisioned before 2002. As former Sen. Sam Nunn, Democrat of Georgia, has argued, NATO and EU expansion should be pursued simultaneously in a two-track approach:

> One track would depend on national economic and political developments in Europe. When countries came to be eligible for EU membership (which is what they really need) they would be eligible for Western European Union [an inter-European cooperative defense arrangement] membership and for NATO membership. These emerging democracies are not threatened by the Russian military, but by insufficient economic development to sustain the political movement towards democracy . . . The second track would respond to threats.[6]

The Clinton administration should draw a more explicit connection between NATO expansion and economic integration. It should press the EU to grant Poland and the other emerging democracies interim membership by 1999.

Meeting the Pacific Challenge

History and geography have made America both a Pacific and an Atlantic power. Moreover, an important thread links Europe and Asia (as well as the Middle East) in our strategy: our large military presence in the Asia Pacific region (about 100,000 U.S. troops as well as the Seventh Fleet), which guarantees stability in what is fast becoming the world's economic dynamo. In Europe through NATO, and in Asia through our network of bilateral alliances (with Japan, South Korea, and Australia), the United States has been and remains, in President Clinton's words, "the indispensable nation," the balancer of last resort.

The absence of multilateral alliances or institutions in the Asia Pacific region, however, has made the U.S. network of bilateral alliances the *de facto* regional security system. One need look no further than the North Korean nuclear crisis of 1993–94 or the March 1996 showdown with China in the Taiwan Strait to illuminate the continued centrality of the U.S. role.

Whether the measure is population, economics, military capabilities, or likelihood of conflict, no region is of greater consequence to American security or prosperity than the Asia Pacific, where we have fought three wars in the past fifty years. We also have a stake in reinforcing important trends toward political and market liberalization over the past decade in the Philippines, South Korea, Mongolia, Thailand, and Taiwan.

Given our key role in the region, the Clinton administration should focus a greater share of its diplomatic energies on three challenges: adapting our balancing role and alliances to new realities; striking a new strategic bargain with China; and building regional institutions that support fair and open trading, cooperation on security, and the rule of law.

Adapting our role as balancer of last resort

As is the case in Europe, our Asian allies and friends must assume greater responsibility for their own security. The U.S.-Japan security alliance remains the cornerstone of our forward-deployed military presence in the region. Laudably, the Clinton administration has taken steps to make this alliance more equal and reciprocal. Now, it must accelerate the process.

In high-level talks, the administration should obtain firm commitments from Tokyo that the United States can rely on Japan's support should we face a crisis in the Korean peninsula or Taiwan; that Japan will open its markets more rapidly; and that Japan will assume a larger global role commensurate with its status as the world's second largest economy.

While the administration has, for the moment, dissuaded North Korea from continuing its nuclear weapons program, it has not given consistent, high-level attention to the peninsula. New strains are evident in the U.S.-South Korea alliance. As we prepare for the likely endgame of Korean reunification, the administration should appoint a senior envoy, as it has for the Middle East, to better manage the potentially explosive transition ahead.

A new strategic bargain with China

The greatest Pacific challenge by far is China's bid for regional ascendancy. There will undoubtedly be a measure of tension in Sino-American relations as long as China is ruled by the current authoritarian regime. Regardless of Beijing's political coloration, however, China is likely to exhibit an assertive nationalism over the coming decades.

Since the 1989 Tiananmen Square massacre, Sino-American relations have been marked by a deepening cycle of recrimination. China is an ancient civilization in the midst of a massive social and economic transformation. Though encumbered by an aging band of autocrats, China's embrace of market-led growth has made it the world's third largest economy. As its modernization proceeds, China is gradually integrating itself into the international community. The question is, will China abide by international norms on trade, human rights, and nonproliferation of weapons of mass destruction, or will it play by its own rules?

The Clinton administration should pursue a new bargain with China based on Beijing's willingness to adhere to and help shape international rules; to accommodate vital U.S. interests; and to allow Taiwan more political autonomy. For its part, the U.S. should draw China into a web of international institutions with roles and responsibilities commensurate with its status as a great power. For example, China should be a full participant in the Missile Technology Control Regime and the Nuclear Suppliers Group. In addition, the administration should institute regular U.S.-China summits and propose new international councils in which China has a major role.

Trade and strategic issues should be at the core of this new bargain. With nearly $150 billion in annual exports, China cannot operate outside of globally agreed-to rules. This is a good example of the importance of coalition politics: Consensus with the EU and Japan is essential if we are to set high standards for China's entry into the WTO. On strategic issues, Chinese cooperation will be critical if we are to manage Korean unification without another war. Beijing's cooperation in South Asia and the Persian Gulf is essential, too. If China pursues destabilizing nuclear and missile exports to Pakistan, and if it helps Iran become a dominant military power in the gulf, then the prospects for confrontation will grow.

Fostering regional economic and political/security institutions

For the foreseeable future, the Asia Pacific region's stability will continue to rest on U.S. forces and alliances. However, we must redouble our current efforts to build collaborative regional institutions. For example, the United States should press ASEAN to develop institutional capacities to keep the peace regionally, mediate political and military conflicts, and respond to humanitarian emergencies. On the trade front, we must strengthen the Asia Pacific Economic Cooperation (APEC) forum as a force for liberalization in key sectors such as telecommunications, aviation, and finance. Finally, the administration should team up with Japan to jointly propose a nuclear cooperation regime in Northeast Asia modeled after the European Atomic Energy Community. This new body would advance peaceful uses of nuclear power and strengthen nonproliferation efforts.

Expanding Global Trade

The Clinton administration's commitment to free trade has done more for U.S. prosperity and the cause of democracy abroad than any of its other foreign policy initiatives. To his credit, Clinton fought successfully for NAFTA and the WTO despite fierce opposition from within his own party. This policy is paying off: During the President's first term, the United States once again became the world's largest exporter.

While continuing to press for open markets, the administration must also help working Americans who lose their jobs and perhaps careers to economic globalization. Trade expansion must go hand in hand with a new agenda, addressed in part elsewhere in this book, for empowering workers to master the new rules of the new economy, continuously upgrade their education and skills, take charge of their own economic security, and share in both the rewards and risks of global trade (see chapters 7 and 12).

America's next trade expansion strategy should include these three initiatives:

Strengthening the global trade system now institutionalized in the WTO

We must proceed to the next wave of trade issues, bringing new sectors such as services and informal barriers to trade under the discipline of the trade regime.

Expanding NAFTA to Chile

This should be the next step toward creation of a common market for the Americas. Congress should grant the President "fast track" authority to expand the trade pact to include Chile, a small economy which has met the higher standards for labor, the environment, and market reform that NAFTA demands. As we build steadily toward a hemispheric free trade zone, we should also explore a Transatlantic Free Trade Agreement.

Adapting the Bretton Woods' institutions to the new economy

The enormous volume of private capital flowing across borders has made nations more vulnerable to financial shocks; witness the tremors in global financial markets over the collapse of the Mexican peso in 1995. Private capital now accounts for about 90 percent of the financial flows to developing countries, eclipsing aid dollars.[7] Accordingly, international financial institutions created at the 1944 Bretton Woods conference and afterwards (the World Bank, IMF, and regional development banks) should refocus their mission on helping transition states adopt the market-oriented policies that will attract the private capital they need to grow.

Revamping Our Military for New Missions

Over the past six years, we have scaled down America's military forces by about 35 percent. Yet, their Cold War structure remains intact. The benchmark for defense planning remains the administration's 1993 Bottom Up Review, which was based on the dubious premise that America needs the capability to fight two major regional conflicts simultaneously.[8] It also assumed that U.S. military superiority over future regional opponents can be achieved without major investments in next-generation weapons. Thus, procurement is sacrificed to maintain the current force structure. Neither political party has seriously questioned this model; the administration and Republican defense budgets differ by less than 2 percent.[9] Yet, the issue is not spending more or less, but spending smarter.[10]

Rather than merely shrink the Cold War force, we should redesign it to exploit our technological advantages. The new model would trade Cold War mass for modernization and accelerate the adoption of the new information and communications technologies commonly referred to as "the revolution in military affairs." We also should renew the highly successful Military Base Closing Commission to align the military's infrastructure with the new force structure.

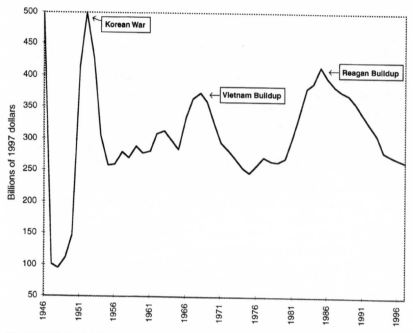

Fig. 13.1. Federal defense spending, fiscal years 1946–1997. Data from Center for Strategic Budgetary Assessments, "The Analysis of the FY 1997 Defense Budget Request, 1996."

The Clinton administration has a rare chance to effect a major paradigm shift in defense strategy. An amendment by Sen. Joseph I. Lieberman, Democrat of Connecticut, to last year's defense authorization bill offers such an opportunity. Based on a PPI Defense Working Group recommendation, the amendment, which was passed with broad bipartisan support, calls for the defense secretary to establish an independent National Defense Commission. It would develop an alternative to the force structure plan that the Defense Department will present to Congress in 1997. This commission can be a catalyst for achieving a bipartisan consensus on the creation of an Information Age defense—a smaller, more flexible force based on technological superiority in stealth, communications, and weaponry.

Controlling the Spread of Weapons of Mass Destruction

The demise of the Soviet Union prompted deep cuts in superpower nuclear stockpiles, and rallied support for the comprehensive test ban treaty and other steps to stem nuclear proliferation.[11] It also left us as the world's greatest conventional military power, sharply reducing our reliance on nuclear weapons to deter aggression. Nonetheless, even after the START II arms reduction accord is finally implemented, the United States and Russia will still have some 3,500 warheads each.

Four years ago, the late Defense Secretary Les Aspin mused that U.S. security concerns had been so transformed that, "If we now had the opportunity to ban all nuclear weapons, we would." Since then, however, the momentum toward deeper nuclear reduction has stalled. A growing number of former senior military commanders and Cold Warriors have begun to rethink the role of nuclear weapons in our defense strategy. Neither political party, however, has asked the basic questions: Are nuclear weapons still integral to our national security and, if so, how many do we need?

The alluring vision of a nuclear-free world is at best far off and ultimately may prove to be a mirage. But to strengthen our nonproliferation efforts, the United States should go beyond the START II cuts and engage all the declared nuclear weapons in a mutual build-down. The Clinton administration should offer to link the Russian Duma's ratification of START II to further reductions, down to 1,000 warheads or less if the other three nuclear powers in the UN Security Council (Britain, China, and France) agree to freeze their current arsenals and negotiate at least modest reductions. Our willingness to keep reducing our own nuclear arsenal will enhance America's credibility in dealing with the suspected, but nondeclared, nuclear powers (India, Pakistan, and Israel), as well as potential proliferators such as Iran, Iraq, and North Korea.

Revamping Our Foreign Policy Institutions

Seven years after the fall of the Berlin Wall, the United States has yet to conduct a tough-minded, blank-slate review of the institutions created to wage the Cold War. To effectively meet the challenges and carry out our new role as first among equals, we must redesign our foreign policy apparatus in the following ways:

Overhaul the diplomatic bureaucracy

The State Department now has twice as many assistant secretaries as it had in 1978, even though we are closing some thirty embassies and consulates. Meanwhile, the USIA—whose broadcasting, exchange programs, and information services are critical in an era when ideas and public diplomacy matter more than ever in world politics—has suffered severe budget cuts and has barely survived Republican attempts to kill it. The President, in consultation with Congress, should appoint a bipartisan commission to conduct a top-to-bottom reassessment of the foreign affairs and national security bureaucracies. The panel should be directed to offer a plan for the restructuring or elimination of agencies and bureaus as it deems appropriate.

Reinvent foreign aid

Contrary to popular myth, foreign aid spending ($12.3 billion in 1996) actually constitutes less than 1 percent of federal spending.[12] The real problem with foreign aid is that it is tied to an obsolete model of development and hobbled by congressional mandates and bureaucratic rigidity.

We must redirect our foreign aid policies to the new mission of nurturing emerging market democracies. In addition, we must abandon the old bureaucratic model of government-to-government aid and replace it with one that works through private, nonprofit nongovernmental organizations (NGOs) dedicated to building markets and civil institutions.

The Clinton administration should abolish the ossified Agency for International Development (AID) and replace it with a Freedom Fund that would

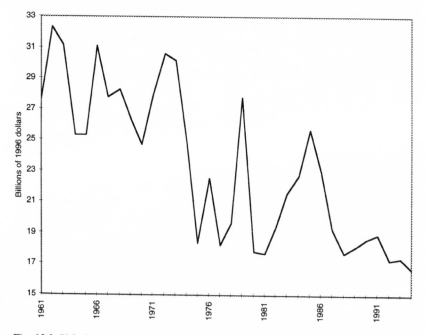

Fig. 13.2. U.S. foreign assistance, 1961–1994. Data from U.S. Agency for International Development, *U.S. Overseas Loans and Grants,* 1996.

steer grants to NGOs such as the National Endowment for Democracy, the Asia Foundation, Freedom House, and the African-American Institute. Over the years, these groups have been more efficient than AID at delivering help to the grassroots level. They are smaller, closer to the recipients, and a less inviting target for corruption than elephantine government-to-government projects. They also tend to be more innovative, accountable, and attuned to civic and voluntary action than the old bureaucratic structures.

This new approach of aiding democratic transitions should reflect America's top foreign policy priorities, such as consolidating Cold War gains by aiding Polish privatization, assisting the denuclearization of Russia and Ukraine, and aiding South Africa's new multiracial democracy.

Reforming and Refocusing the United Nations

After World War II, the United States pushed for the creation of the UN to provide a collective instrument for maintaining the peace, countering aggression, and fostering international cooperation. Despite its often disappointing performance, the UN remains an indispensable global forum and an expression of America's highest ideals.

As the UN celebrates its fiftieth birthday, it is time for the world's leading powers to take stock of its many functions and offshoots, and refocus it on new challenges. The Clinton administration, which has rightly called for streamlining the UN's bloated bureaucracy, should launch a more fundamental assessment of its structure and priorities.

Some UN endeavors—such as its efforts to assist refugees and the work of the World Health Organization—remain invaluable. But the UN's record on economic development and, more recently, peacemaking suggests the need for structural change.

Many UN economic agencies— the UN Conference on Trade and Development and the UN Industrial Development Organization, to name two—exist largely to provide sinecures for globetrotting bureaucrats and should be eliminated. Yet we do need a high-level forum for settling disputes over trade and investment in a volatile global marketplace. Therefore, the United States should press for creation of an Economic Security Council to act as an analogue to the UN Security Council. It should include Japan, Germany, India, Brazil, and other nations with a stake in improving global economic management and cooperation.

There is no diplomatic forum for consultation on global security matters in which all the major powers are represented. This reality has prompted calls to expand the UN Security Council to include Japan and Germany. As a practical matter, however, this would require altering the UN Charter, an extremely difficult task. An alternative would be to create a security version of the Group of Seven economic summit—a Group of Six comprised of the United States, the EU, Japan, China, Russia, and India.

The United States also should encourage a dramatic devolution of power from the UN to regional bodies. The Clinton administration's October 1996 proposal to help create a permanent African peacekeeping force is a step in the right direction: It will be less costly and often more effective for the United States to train and equip regional peacekeeping forces than to send our own forces abroad. Just as NATO has assumed responsibility for ending the conflict in Bosnia, we should view ASEAN, the Organization of African Unity, the OAS, and other regional bodies as building blocks for a decentralized collective security system, operating under the aegis of the UN and with the support of the major UN donors. If alleviating suffering is a legitimate concern of the whole international community, then the U.S. contribution should be in proportion to that of others. Both East Asia and the EU have GDPs roughly the size of America's. Decentralizing peacekeeping would provide a meaningful way to share responsibility for policing conflicts that otherwise are dumped into America's lap by default.

Conclusion

This chapter has proposed a new strategy for U.S. global leadership on the eve of the twenty-first century. The strategy of democratic realism starts with the premise that our actions abroad must reflect not only hard calculations of national interest, but also our democratic values. It calls for energetic U.S. engagement, backed by superior military forces, and informed by a clear hierarchy of strategic priorities in building a new international system on principles of economic and political freedom. Above all, it reaffirms our nation's historic obligation to use its unparalleled strengths—economic, military, and the broad appeal of our democratic values—to lead the world toward order, prosperity, and liberty.

Notes

1. See Roger Kaplan ed., *Freedom in the World—The Annual Survey of Political Rights & Civil Liberties 1995–1996* (Lanham, MD: University Press of America, 1996).

2. See Thomas L. Friedman, "Your Mission, Should You Accept It," *New York Times*, 27 Oct. 1996, sec. 4, 15.

3. Robert J. Dole, acceptance speech delivered at the Republican National Convention, San Diego, California, 15 Aug. 1996.

4. See Jonathan Clarke and James Clad, *After The Crusade: American Foreign Policy for the Post-Superpower Age*, (Lanham, MD: Madison Books, 1995), chapters 2–4.

5. For a thoughtful assessment of priorities along these lines see The Commission on America's National Interests, "America's National Interests" (Cambridge, MA: Center for Science and International Affairs, July 1996).

6. See Robert A. Manning and Gary L. Geipel eds., *Rethinking The TransAtlantic Partnership—Security and Economics in a New Era* (Indianapolis: Hudson Institute, Inc., and Washington, DC: Progressive Policy Institute, 1996) for a cross-section of the debate on the United States and the new Europe.

7. Stephen Fidler, "Private capital flows to Third World buoyant," *Financial Times*, 24 Jan. 1996, 6.

8. See John M. Shalikashvili, "A Word From the Chairman," *Joint Force Quarterly* (Summer 1996): 1.

9. For a critique of the Bottom-Up Review see Andrew F. Krepinevich, *The Bottom-Up Review: An Assessment* (Washington, DC: Defense Budget Project, February 1994). Also see Don M. Snider, Daniel Gouré, and Stephen A. Cambone, *Defense in the 1990's: Avoiding the Train Wreck* (Washington, DC: The Center For Strategic & International Studies, 1995).

10. For a discussion of new approaches to defense, see Peter A. Wilson, Robert A. Manning, and Col. Richard L. Klass (ret.), *Defense In the Information Age: A New Blueprint*, (Washington, DC: Progressive Policy Institute Report No. 26, December 1995).

11. For a discussion on post-Cold War nuclear strategy and non-proliferation see Robert A. Manning, *Back to the Future: Toward A Post-Nuclear Ethic—The New Logic of Non-Proliferation* (Washington, DC: Progressive Foundation, January 1994).

12. "Who's in Control? Many Don't Know or Care," *Washington Post*, 29 Jan. 1996, A1.

Afterword

Senator Joseph I. Lieberman

"The era of big government is over" may become the hallmark phrase of Bill Clinton's presidency. It neatly describes a central accomplishment of his administration: The President reversed the engines that power government bureaucracy, putting a halt to rising deficits and swelling federal employment rolls. More importantly, President Clinton broke with the traditional Democratic dictum that Washington holds the solution to every problem in America.

But if the big government era is history, what comes next?

Building the Bridge: 10 Big Ideas to Transform America is the answer. This remarkable book takes us off the comfortable road of partisanship and rigid ideology and sets us in a fresh new direction. It does not simply navigate a middle course between left and right. Rather, *Building the Bridge* lifts us to a new level. It defines a rational way of governing that adapts America's best traditions to the post-industrial, Information Age world in which we, and especially our children, will live.

To fulfill the authors' vision, we will have to:

- Abandon failed programs, but not the people they were created to help;

- Make government smaller and more effective;

- Empower people, not bureaucracies;

- Find new ways to help businesses grow and create jobs, and to educate and train workers for the careers of the future;

- Define our national interests in a context of democratic realism, enabling us to remake our armed forces and reshape our foreign policy to meet the threats and exploit the opportunities of the new millenium;

221

- Employ radical new strategies to rebuild crumbling cities, restore collapsing schools, and revitalize the legal and law enforcement communities to make our neighborhoods safer;

- Confront entitlement reform head on, so that rising costs do not destroy the government's ability to invest in the economy, health care, education, and the environment; and

- Recreate a sense of community and citizenship based on values we hold in common: faith in God, loyalty to family, respect for work, love of country, and mutual responsibility.

This agenda, the product of New Democrat thinking, is decidedly not a Democratic version of the Contract With America. That was a focus-group driven gimmick designed to win votes, not make progress. These are ideas to govern and live by, born of a belief that government has a limited but proper place in society, and must be responsible for organizing and investing public resources in a way that allows people to educate themselves, helps businesses grow and create jobs, and enables parents to raise their children in a healthy and safe environment.

To become the law of the land, however, any idea, no matter how good, must earn bipartisan support. Though designed by Democrats and aimed principally at Democrats, the ideas contained in this book are not sharply partisan. They did not arise from partisan trench warfare. Each one appeals to the "vital center" of American political life, of which President Clinton has spoken so eloquently since the election.

That phrase is adapted from Arthur Schlesinger's 1940s description of America's role in the post–World War II era, standing strong between the destructive poles of fascism and communism. Today, the vital center can move us beyond the barren battleground of left- and right-wing political discourse. That is exactly what Americans expect from us. In recent elections, they have bounced back and forth between the Republican and Democratic parties, all the while waiting for something better to come along. Ross Perot and Pat Buchanan thought they could fulfill the public's yearning, but their combination of protectionist and isolationist policies are outdated and ill-suited for the Information Age, and the voters rejected their message.

In contrast, President Clinton won election in 1992, and increased his margin of support in 1996, because he has articulated in word, and fulfilled in deed, the kind of changes most Americans sense we need.

With the election behind us, the window of bipartisan opportunity is open. Working together, Republicans and Democrats can achieve great things before the next election approaches, with its escalating political rhetoric and resultant legislative gridlock. The election results make clear that those who govern from the vital center will hold the balance of power in the Congress. Sensible legislation can flourish; extreme ideas of the left and right will certainly flounder.

The two parties can build the bridge to the twenty-first century together if they follow the blueprint outlined in this book. That is because it is based not so much on ideology, as on what works. It was designed not with the next election in mind, but the next generation. The ideas put forward here are not the end products of special interest accommodation. They were not designed to produce short-term spikes in public opinion polls. They are creative, common-sense ideas built for the long-haul of American history.

This is the stuff of which peaceful revolutions are made. And it is the stuff out of which twenty-first century America can succeed. *Building the Bridge* responds to the desire of America's people for nothing less than a transcendent reform of our national polity, and challenges America's leaders to work together as architects of a modern brand of governance that is suited for the third millenium—which is, after all, just four short years away.

Index

About the Contributors

Chuck Alston is executive director of the Democratic Leadership Council and editor in chief of *The New Democrat* magazine. A veteran political correspondent who covered Congress during the Reagan and Bush administrations, Mr. Alston was a syndicated columnist and an editor and reporter at *Congressional Quarterly* and the *Greensboro News and Record* (NC) prior to joining the DLC.

Al From is president and founder of the Democratic Leadership Council and chairman of the Progressive Foundation. A principal architect of the New Democratic philosophy, Mr. From played a prominent role in the 1992 election of President Bill Clinton and was appointed by Mr. Clinton to be his personal representative on the Democratic Platform Drafting Committee and deputy director for domestic policy for the Presidential Transition Team. Previously, Mr. From was executive director of the House Democratic Caucus, served in President Jimmy Carter's White House, and was staff director of the U.S. Senate Subcommittee on Intergovernmental Relations.

William A. Galston is a professor at the University of Maryland's School of Public Affairs and director of the University's Institute for Philosophy and Public Policy. He served from January 1993 through May 1995 as deputy assistant for domestic policy to President Bill Clinton, and is the author of six books and numerous articles in the areas of political philosophy, public policy, and American politics.

David B. Kendall is the senior analyst for health policy for the Progressive Policy Institute. He previously served on the staffs of former U.S. Representatives Michael A. Andrews (D-TX) and James R. Jones (D-OK), and has been an advisor to the Jackson Hole Group and President Bill Clinton's Task Force on National Health Care Reform.

Ed Kilgore is political director of the Democratic Leadership Council and former senior fellow of the Progressive Policy Institute, where he directed policy development on issues including crime, federal-state relations, welfare reform, and national service. Previously federal liaison for Georgia Governors Zell Miller, Joe Frank Harris, and George Busbee, Mr. Kilgore also served as communications director for U.S. Senator Sam Nunn (D-GA).

Debra S. Knopman is director of the Center for Innovation and the Environment at the Progressive Foundation. Dr. Knopman previously served as deputy assistant secretary for water and science at the U.S. Department of the Interior, chief of the Branch of Systems Analysis in the Water Resources Division of the U.S. Geological Survey, legislative assistant to Senator Daniel P. Moynihan (D-NY), and professional staff member on the U.S. Senate Committee for Environment and Public Works.

Robert A. Manning is senior fellow of the Progressive Policy Institute and Research Associate at the Sigur Center for East Asian Studies of George Washington University. He has served as advisor to the assistant secretary of State for East Asian and Pacific Affairs, advisor to the Office of the Secretary of Defense, and as a correspondent for *U.S. News & World Report* and the *Far Eastern Economic REVIEW.*

Will Marshall is president of the Progressive Policy Institute and the Progressive Foundation and was co-editor of PPI's 1992 bestseller, *Mandate for Change.* Previously policy director of the Democratic Leadership Council, Mr. Marshall was a speechwriter and spokesman for several elected officials and political campaigns. Before becoming involved in politics and public policy, he was a journalist in Virginia with the *Richmond Times-Dispatch.*

Tom Mirga is editor of *The New Democrat,* the magazine of the Democratic Leadership Council. Previously, he was news editor of *Education Week,* the newspaper of record for American precollegiate education.

David Osborne is co-author of the just-released *Banishing Bureaucracy: The Five Strategies for Reinventing Government,* as well as the *New York Times* bestseller, *Reinventing Government,* and *Laboratories of Democracy.* A fellow at both the Progressive Policy Institute and the National Academy of Public Administration, Mr. Osborne is a managing partner of the Public Strategies

Group, a consulting firm, and co-chair of the Alliance for Redesigning Government, a nonprofit learning network for reinventors.

Mark Penn is a partner in the public opinion firm Penn + Schoen, and was a top advisor to the 1996 Clinton-Gore presidential campaign. An expert in Latin American research, Mr. Penn received his initial training in research at Harvard's Department of Government and later at Corporate Planning at NBC. He has served as a consultant for many corporate clients and is developing the firm's new neural network programs which permit highly sophisticated market analysis.

Doug Ross is director of the Progressive Foundation's Scholars' Network and a former assistant secretary for employment and training at the U.S. Department of Labor. Previously, Mr. Ross was director of the Michigan Department of Commerce, visiting lecturer at the Institute for Public Policy Studies at the University of Michigan, Michigan state senator, and in the private sector, CEO of H. Leonard & Co., a food brokerage firm, and president of Michigan Future, Inc., a non-partisan venture to create and promote long-term development.

Robert J. Shapiro is vice president and a co-founder of the Progressive Policy Institute, where he directs economic studies. He also is co-chair of The Committee for Free Trade and Economic Growth, and a contributing editor for *International Economy* and *The New Republic*. Dr. Shapiro has served as principal economic advisor to President Clinton in his 1992 campaign, associate editor of *U.S. News & World Report*, legislative director and economic counsel to Senator Daniel P. Moynihan, and Fellow of Harvard University and the National Bureau of Economic Research.

Fred Siegel is a senior fellow of the Progressive Policy Institute where he specializes in urban policy and politics. Currently a professor of history and humanities at The Cooper Union in Manhattan, he previously taught at noted universities, including the Sorbonne, the State University of New York, Columbia University, and Queens College, and was editor of *Dissent Magazine* and the *City Journal*.

Kathleen Sylvester is vice president for domestic policy of the Progressive Policy Institute specializing in family policy, education, and reinventing government. A former journalist, Ms. Sylvester served as a consultant to Vice President Gore's National Performance Review. She is an associate of the Alliance for Redesigning Government, and a member of the board of visitors of the Georgetown University Graduate Public Policy Program.

Progressive Policy Institute

"One person with a belief is a social power equal to ninety-nine who have only interests."

—John Stuart Mill

The Progressive Policy Institute (PPI) is a center for policy innovation that develops alternatives to the conventional left-right debate. Founded in 1989, the Institute is fashioning a public philosophy for the twenty-first century by adapting America's progressive tradition of individual liberty, equal opportunity, and civic obligation to the challenges of the Information Age.

PPI advocates growth-oriented economic policies designed to stimulate broad upward mobility and foster a more inclusive, more democratic capitalism; social policies that move beyond maintaining the poor to liberating them from poverty and dependence; and a foreign policy of resolve in defending America's interests and promoting free institutions. The Institute also explores four issues that loom large on the public agenda of the 1990's: crime, health care, educational excellence, and environmental protection.

In addition to the original work of its own scholars, the Institute offers a platform to a new generation of progressive thinkers and writers around the country. Through its studies on public enterprise, PPI examines ideas for renewing the public sector by redesigning government along more entrepreneurial and less bureaucratic lines. Believing that effective governance also requires harnessing private energies and resources for public purposes, the Institute promotes creative ways to build America's civic infrastructure and to cultivate the civic virtues necessary for self-government to work.

The Progressive Policy Institute is a project of the Democratic Leadership Council. For further information about the Institute or to order publications please call or write:

518 C Street, NE
Washington, DC 20002
(202) 547–0001
Fax (202) 544–5002
E-Mail: info@dlcppi.org
WWW: http://www.dlcppi.org/